Global Business: Strategy in Context

Leslie P. Willcocks

SB Publishing
United Kingdom

Global Business: Strategy in Context

– an 'SB Publishing' book

Publisher:
SB Publishing
www.sbpublishing.org

Cover Design:
Steve Brookes
www.sbpublishing.org

Author:
Leslie P. Willcocks

This 1st edition published in 2021 by:
SB Publishing
60 Loxley Road
Stratford-upon-Avon
Warwickshire CV37 7DR
United Kingdom
Tel: +44(0)1789 267124
Email: info@sbpublishing.org

A CIP catalogue record for this book is available from the British Library

ISBN 978-0-995682-08-5

Printed and bound in Poland by Latitude Press Ltd.

Contents

Series Introduction   7

Chapter 1. Globalisation and Trade: Is It Really a Flat World?   13

1.1.   Introduction   13
1.2.   What is Globalisation?   14
1.3.   Trends Toward Globalisation   16
1.4.   The Globalisation Debates   20
1.5.   Does Distance Still Matter?   23
1.6.   What does Globalisation Mean for Firms?   25
1.7.   International Trade Theory: From Free Trade to Factor Endowments   27
1.8.   National Institutions and International Trade: Free or Protected?   32
1.9.   Government Intervention and Free Trade: The Debate   34
1.10. Conclusion   37

Chapter 2. Political, Economic and Legal Environments: Diversity or
              Growing Uniformity?   41

2.1.   Introduction   41
2.2.   An Institution-Based View of International Business   41
2.3.   Political Systems   43
2.4.   Economic Systems   47
2.5.   Legal Systems   48
2.6.   Country Development: Political, Economic, and Legal Issues   52
2.7.   Beyond the Nation State: Regional Economic Integration   53
2.8.   Regional Integration in Europe   55
2.9.   Regional Integration in the Americas   58
2.10. Regional Integration in Asia Pacific   62
2.11. The Multilateral Monetary and Trade Systems   63
2.12. Conclusion   72

Contents

Chapter 3. Cultural Social and Ethical Challenges: Towards CSR   75

3.1. Introduction   75

3.2. Cultures and International Business   76

3.3. Languages   81

3.4. Religion   82

3.5. Ethics   84

3.6. Corporate Social Responsibility Challenges   85

3.7. Institutions and CSR Strategies   88

3.8. What more can International Business do?   90

3.9. PESTEL Factors   94

3.10. Conclusion   99

Chapter 4. Strategy in Global Context: One Size Fits All?   103

4.1. Introduction   103

4.2. Strategy and Value Creation   104

4.3. Going International - Economies From Scale, Location, and Experience   109

4.4. Analysing the International Environment   111

4.5. Ghemawat's AAA Model for Strategy Development   117

4.6. Choosing a Strategy for International Business   121

4.7. Conclusion   126

Chapter 5. International Competitive Strategy: Debating Approaches   129

5.1. Introduction   129

5.2. Porter's Five Forces Framework   130

5.3. Generic Strategies   137

5.4. A Resource-Based Perspective on Competitiveness   141

5.5. Resource-based Competition: The VRIO Framework   144

5.6. Bringing Strategy and Environment Together: Which Strategy, When?   147

5.7. Debating Strategy and Competitiveness   152

5.8. Conclusion   158

Chapter 6. Market Entry and Evolution: Commitment Versus Risk   159

6.1.   Introduction   159

6.2.   The Decision to Enter Foreign Markets   159

6.3.   Foreign Direct Investment   165

6.4.   Governments and Foreign Direct Investment   169

6.5.   Major Modes of Entering Foreign Markets   171

6.6.   Assessing the Relevance of Strategic Alliances   178

6.7.   Going International: Growth Through Evolution   180

6.8.   Conclusion   181

Chapter 7. Global Business: Future Directions   185

7.1   Introduction   185

7.2   Globalisation Trends Revisted   185

7.3   Coming to Terms with the Crisis   189

7.4   Business Context: Disruption and New Scenarios   191

7.5   Global Business: Towards Systemic Risk   196

7.6   Global Business: Navigating the Future   196

7.7. Conclusion   199

The Author   201

Series Introduction

Author's Comments

Welcome to the new Global Business Foundations project. This series has grown out of an earlier text—*Global Business Management Foundations*. The book has been very popular, but the subject area is now so rich, and moves so fast, that the publisher suggested a series of books to keep pace with global developments. The rightness of this decision was confirmed by the 2020-2021 coronavirus pandemic and ensuing economic crises. This created the global realisation that, what I call (in this book) the 'new (ab)normal', is upon us, and may be for some time. The hard-won learning from 2020–2021 is that we need to respond differently, faster, but also more thoughtfully than before. We need to be better equipped, and better at anticipating uncertain futures. This series of books will be developed with these objectives always in mind.

The initial two books are *Global Business: Strategy In Context*, and *Global Business Management*. This, first, book is focused on the global business environment and devising international and competitive strategies for entering, and growing, in new markets. The second book will focus on the key operational aspects of making international business strategies work. The third book in the series will focus on global digital business. Further books are planned to keep pace with the ever-changing commercial world.

Global Business Strategy and Management: Overview

If business was the same everywhere, we could all get on with providing products or services and, through gaining competitive advantage, make profits. But despite the flattening effects of globalisation, international business demonstrates huge diversity, variability over time, and complexity. To understand business context, along with threats and opportunities, you need to consider the drivers and nature of globalisation, as well as the political, economic, social, technological, and legal differences that regions and countries exhibit. Then you need to work within the frameworks of multilateral organisations and regional economic blocs, and also take into account how the global financial system functions.

As a manager faced with this complexity, uncertainty and diversity, you then need to devise strategies that work internationally, in different parts of the globe; plan entry and marketing strategies for new markets; and decide with whom you need to establish alliances, and how your strategy is to evolve. You also, throughout, need to consider how globalisation helps to create systemic risk, and the implications of this for international strategy and business. These are all subjects we deal with in *Global Business: Strategy In Context*.

But then you need to worry away at the detail of managing and making sure operational performance delivers dynamic strategy in increasingly unpredictable, uncertain global and business environments. This is the content of our second book: *Global Business Management*. Specifically, we look at marketing and R&D, designing structure and organisation; devising sourcing and supply chain arrangements; establishing information systems that perform globally; and distinctive arrangements for managing international human resources. You also need to manage the financial complexities that internationalisation brings, and learn to run projects internationally, with diverse workforces and alliances.

As a student, or as a manager, you will find understanding and analysing international business and making managerial judgements full of fresh challenges. You will also find that the study of this subject area not only provides insights, but also gives you the analytical equipment and knowledge to actually perform in a business that operates globally. But, as a note of caution, all this will inform actions and guide experience, but not replace it. Learning optimises when knowledge is applied to experiences, resulting in better understanding, better knowledge, and improved performance.

This book is designed as an introduction to the subject, and is based on teaching undergraduate and masters degree courses in the Department of Management of the London School of Economics and Political Science. It also draws upon the author's thirty-five years' experience in working with companies, and running executive programmes around the globe. The specific objectives of this book are:

- To give you a research-based grounding in the context of international business, including the globalising trends; formal and informal institutions; political economic social, technological, legal issues; and the resultant diversity of international business.

- To prepare you to be able to discuss cultural, ethical and social issues for international business and suggest policies for corporate social responsibility.

- To provide an introduction to, and develop your ability to assess, international trade and investment; multilateral organisations; regional integration and the global financial system.

- To give insight into the contexts of international business, and enable you to work within these contexts to make judgements on strategising and managing operations in the global economy.

- To establish understanding of, and illustrate how, firms develop international business and marketing and R&D strategies; enter markets and alliances; and evolve on the global stage.

Our companion book—*Global Business Management*—takes the learning further into key, functional areas that underpin strategic positioning. Here we will look to fulfil five additional objectives:

- To establish understanding of and illustrate the major challenges and ways of running marketing and R&D functions in an international business.

- To give insight through frameworks, studies and examples, of how businesses manage organisation structure and architecture; sourcing and the supply chain; information systems; emerging technologies; and human resources, in different parts of the globe—globally, regionally and domestically.

- To give insight into how an international business can manage exchange rates in the context of the international monetary system.

- To understand the risks in international projects, and learn the action principles for effective project management.

- To establish future challenges, opportunities and directions for international businesses.

This present book is structured, organically, into two parts. The first part consists of Chapters 1, 2 and 3, and provides an introduction to the global business environment and covers trends towards globalisation, and the formal and informal institutions of countries. In particular we focus on international political, economic, legal, cultural and social diversity. The chapters also give you an overview of why international trade takes place; why firms invest abroad; and how the global financial system and cross-border institutions—like the IMF, World Bank and regional economic blocs—operate and impact upon business. This part provides the context of international business.

The second part consists of Chapters 4, 5, 6, and 7. These chapters give insight into how to analyse that context to arrive at competitive international strategies and enter markets. This part gives detail on how to arrive at strategies for international business. In the final chapter we look at future global trends, in the light of the 2020–2021 pandemic and economic crisis, and how businesses can deal with the challenges, while seizing the opportunities these developments are likely to present.

Anyone who studies this area will know that this is a fast-moving, dynamic subject, and this first text should be taken as the start pack—establishing the principles and foundations for studying international business environment and strategy. All readers are recommended to also consult regularly, in parallel, sources of news and articles on current affairs and world business, such as *The Financial Times, The Wall Street Journal*, and *The Economist*. There are many excellent, more regionally-based, journals and magazines, which also serve the purpose of picking up fresh patterns and practices. They also offer valuable, real-time case studies of international business and management being played out in specific contexts.

Acknowledgements

This book grew out of the many requests from students and practitioners for books based on the courses I have been running over several years. My LSE students have been a real tonic, in that they bring bright, new brains to subjects I think I know inside out, only to discover, from them, new information; new theories; new twists, and other ways of looking at the evidence. This indeed is a marvel of the collective intelligence and also of the cultural diversity we get at the university. Thanks must also go to the executives, for their wonderful, illustrative stories; the hard-won knowledge they bring to bear on issues; and their kindness and openness when it comes to research access—despite their intensely busy, globalised work patterns. Big thanks also to all staff and students across the world working with the University of London International programme for their very positive responses to the original text, and continuing suggestions for additions. I have addressed many of these in the first two books in the series, within the parameters of keeping the books readable, concise and interesting, and not being weighed down by over-referencing.

I would like to thank all at SB Publishing, especially Steve Brookes and Stephanie Lester, for their encouragement and support and for getting this book together and published in a remarkably short time. Over the years I have published quite a few books, and each time two things seem to be true. Firstly, the books seem to be getting published faster and faster. Secondly, as evidence for the reality behind the ideas in this book, the process involves more and more people from different countries across the world. Finally, I would like to thank my beloved wife Damaris, who makes all things possible.

"No man is an island, entire of itself. Each is a piece of the continent, a part of the main"

John Donne, Meditation xvii

"The current state of the world is one of semi-globalisation....distance still matters"

Pankaj Ghemawat, 2007

"Globalisation has made us more vulnerable. It creates a world without borders, and makes us painfully aware of the limitations of our present instruments, and of politics, to meet its challenges"

Anna Lindh, 2001

Chapter 1

Globalisation and Trade: Is It Really a Flat World?

1.1. Introduction

Globalisation can be defined as the shift towards a more integrated and interdependent world economy. In other words, the world is moving away from self-contained national economies, toward an interdependent, integrated global system. A major part of this is increased international trade and foreign direct investment. International trade occurs when a firm exports goods or services to consumers in another country. Foreign direct investment (FDI) occurs when a firm invests resources in business activities outside its home country. What does all this mean?

In his 2005 book, *The World is Flat,* Thomas Friedman gives the example of his Dell notebook. He found it had been designed in Austin, Texas, USA and Taiwan. Dell used 30 key components in the notebook, and these are sourced from over 20 countries around the world, with the factories owned by local firms but also in many cases foreign multinationals—defined here as firms that engage in foreign direct investments and operate in multiple foreign countries. And this is just the start of the notebook's global journey! Between 2003 and 2021, global sourcing became even more sophisticated and diverse, though there were signs of retreat from this in recent years (see 1.10). The global pandemic and related economic crisis also disrupted supply chains, and caused a sourcing rethink for most international businesses. Bringing supply closer to home, and diversifying sources were two further possibilities on the agenda.

What does all this mean for you and me? Well, consider my own, typical, day: I wake up in the UK in a bed made by Sweden's IKEA, then get dressed in a shirt made in India and American Levi's jeans that were produced in China. After putting on my Taiwanese-made trainers, and drinking an Italian-style cappuccino, I drive to work in my Japanese Honda that was manufactured in the UK. On the way to a client headquartered in the Netherlands, but with operations in the UK, I talked to my friend on an Apple iPhone designed in USA, about getting together later for Spanish-style tapas and Mexican Corona beer. As you can see, my day has already been filled with the effects of globalisation. But there are other effects. As examples only: Is my job safe? Are there new job prospects? Where is the next technological change going to come from? Is globalisation adversely affecting my environment? Is it causing a backlash and the rise of nationalistic politicians? In the light of the 2020–2021 global crisis, what downsides will result from the high level of interconnectivity?

From a business perspective, you can think of globalisation in terms of the globalisation of markets and the globalisation of production. The globalisation of markets refers to the merging of historically distinct and separate national markets into one huge global marketplace. As trade barriers between countries have fallen, companies like IKEA, Sony, Lenovo, Samsung, and Coca-Cola were able to sell their products to a global market where consumers are more and more alike. But the globalisation of markets does not mean that consumers are the same everywhere. Important differences between markets do exist. National markets are still very relevant—challenging companies to develop different marketing strategies and operating procedures. The second facet of globalisation—the globalisation of production—refers to the sourcing of goods and services from locations around the globe to take advantage of national differences in the cost and quality of factors of production like land, labour, and capital. Companies hope that, by sourcing and producing their products in the optimal location, they will be able to better compete against their rivals. Boeing, for example, outsourced about 65 percent of its '787' aircraft manufacture to foreign companies. Boeing believed that this strategy allowed it to use the best suppliers in the world, an advantage that would help to win market share over its rival, Airbus Industries. Even healthcare is globalised. For example, US and Canadian hospitals now routinely send X-rays via the Internet to be read in India; and some insurance companies even recommend having certain medical operations conducted in foreign countries.

This chapter introduces you to globalisation and international trade; the trends towards globalisation; and its main drivers. We explore the major debates for and against globalisation, and whether firms wishing to operate internationally can work on the basis of the assumption that the world is flat, or something else. We look at the implications of globalisation for firms wanting to extend themselves further globally. We explore theories of international trade and assess the role of governments and national institutions in supporting or acting as barriers to international trade.

1.2. What is Globalisation?

What is globalisation and what are the challenges it raises for business organisations worldwide? Some identify globalisation with the accelerated spread of communication and transportation technology. Others identify globalisation with the rising power of multinational enterprises (MNEs) and increased inequality in the world. Some experience it as increased competition for jobs, especially for low skilled workers; others emphasise how globalisation is a force eliminating differences amongst distinctive cultures and identities; still others argue this is exaggerated, and the world is still defined by national boundaries; and others see the world moving rapidly towards a homogenous character without national boundaries. Defining globalisation has big implications; how it is explained to the public influences how the idea is received. According to Peter Dicken this general 'wooliness' when describing globalisation, has led to *"heated and polarised argument across the entire political and ideological spectrum"* (Dicken, 2007).

However, there are some general characteristics upon which most can agree. Globalisation is recognised as a complex set of processes influencing the world economy. Globalisation involves increasing amounts of cross-border trade, with traditional distances between nations lessening, due to advances in transportation and telecommunications technology. Globalisation does involve the rise of MNEs and has seen the globalising of markets and production that has resulted in increased competition for jobs and between nations. Globalisation has also seen some erosion of differences amongst distinctive national cultures and identities, but, as we shall see below, and in Chapter 4 when we look at Ghemawat's CAGE framework, the extent may be exaggerated. Firms that treat all markets the same, and offer the same products/services everywhere, invariably learn the limits of this approach.

What is Globalisation?

- **Globality** is a social condition reflecting the world, moving away from self-contained, national economies toward an interdependent, integrated globally with a tighter **economic, political, cultural and environmental** system (interconnections and flows).

- **Globalisation** refers to the expansion and intensification of social processes/relations across world-time and world-space. It shifts the world from weakening nationality to **globality**.

Globalisation has also seen the development of international bodies to try to deal with all this increased interconnectedness. There are now international governing bodies such as the GATT (The General Agreement on Tariffs and Trade) and the WTO (World Trade Organisation), which hold the key to many economic decisions affecting the world, and have power over nations akin to a political body or national government (though this has been waning in recent years). These governing bodies symbolise the interconnectedness of the world just as the United Nations did after the end of World War Two. The International Monetary Fund (IMF) and the World Bank were created in 1944. The goal of the International Monetary Fund is to maintain order in the international monetary system, and, as we will see in chapter 2, the International Monetary Fund is a significant, if controversial, player in the global economy. The World Bank promotes economic development by making loans to cash-strapped nations wishing to make significant infrastructure improvements like building dams or roads. These international organisations influence, and sometimes decide the fate of, businesses and communities wishing to collaborate with, or limit their access to, other countries.

1.3. Trends Toward Globalisation

Globalisation is hardly new. People have been trading internationally for several thousands of years. However, the last 150 years have seen an intensification of globalisation, and what Jones (2004) depicts as two waves arising in each case from a combination of long-term trends and pendulum swings. Many, including Jones, see the first wave of globalisation as starting in 1880 and rising to a high in 1929 then declining and disintegrating from 1930 to 1980. A second wave started post World War II, and rose from 1950 to beyond 2010. Others see three waves, the first from 1870 to 1914; the second from 1945 to 1980; and the third from the 1980s to the present. We will focus on the current wave of globalisation (and, more recently, deglobalisation) that has evolved since World War II.

In the 1950s and 1960s, barriers to trade and capital movements were pervasive, even amongst developed countries. Meanwhile developing countries tended to nurture and protect domestic industries, while China and the USSR sought to develop self-sufficiently. In the 1970s and 1980s, globalisation as international trade remained largely a matter for developed economies in the Triad of North America, Western Europe, and Japan. However, globalisation accelerated dramatically in the 1990s. An emerging economy is one that has only recently established institutional frameworks that facilitate international trade and investment. Typically they have low or middle level incomes amongst their population, and above average economic growth compared to other nations. Emerging economies join in much more with global trade. This is particularly true of those largest in terms of population, namely Brazil, Russia, India, and China—the so-called BRIC countries. In the 1990s world output grew by 23 percent over the decade; global trade expanded by 80 percent; and the total flow of FDI increased fivefold. Gross Domestic Product (GDP) is the sum of value added by resident firms, households and governments operating in an economy.

In the first decade of the 21st century, world GDP, cross border trade and per capita GDP all soared to new, unprecedented levels, with half of the world's GDP growth coming from emerging economies (4.6 percent annual growth, 1997-2007). Developed economies averaged 2 percent annual growth in the same period. All this before the 2008-2009 global economic crisis, with global output, trade, and investment plummeting, and unemployment rising. From mid-2009 there was renewed confidence after massive government intervention in developing economies.

Economic recovery has, however, been slow in developed economies, while some emerging economies have rebounded faster. Overall the second wave theorised by Jones (2004), has become less steep from 2010-2012, as globalisation has slowed down—a process sometimes called 'slowbalisation'. Nevertheless, according to the World Trade Organisation (World Trade Statistical Review, 2019), world merchandise trade was US$19.67 trillion; commercial services US$5.63 trillion; while world trade and Gross Domestic Product (GDP) grew 26 percent between 2008 and 2018. China has been the world's largest exporter since 2009. In 2018 it exported over US$2 trillion worth of goods and services to the rest of the world. Throughout most of this period developing countries equalled or outperformed developed economies in trade and results. By 2020, the value of world trade was expected to be 160 times larger than it was in 1960. Interestingly, while world trade increased 3.3 times between 2000 and 2020, the world economy increased only 2.6 times. Fundamentally, we produce more than ever before, but we also have increased, even more, the rate at which we trade, internationally, in what we produce. Hence the enormous rise in international business. Of course the 2020–2021 crisis saw a big fall off in this trend, as many countries moved to what *The Economist* anticipated to become for several years 'the 90% economy' (*The Economist*, May 5th, 2020).

What has been driving globalisation? Two macro factors are important: first, the decline in trade and investment barriers since World War II and second, technological change—specifically dramatic improvements in communication, information processing, and transportation technologies. At the end of World War II, many advanced nations committed to removing barriers that prevented the free flow of goods, services, and capital between countries. They formalised the process through the General Agreement on Tariffs and Trade, or GATT. Since 1950, average tariffs have fallen significantly and in recent years have been as low as 4 percent. For manufactured goods, average global tariff rates in 2017 were 1.6 percent. Foreign direct investment (FDI) has also been rising as countries have, increasingly, opened their market to firms, though there has been a slow down in FDI in recent years (see 1.10). We have seen how the global economy has changed massively over the last 30 years. Hill and Hult (2019) suggest four trends have been particularly important in this change. Let's update the detail on these:

1. ***Changes in world output and world trade.*** In the 1960s, the USA dominated the world economy and world trade picture. US multinational companies were powerful, and because of the Cold War, a significant portion of the world was off limits to the Western companies. Today, this picture has changed. In 2008,

the USA accounted for only about 20 percent of world economic activity. Other developed countries saw their share of global economic activity decline over time as well. Developing nations saw just the opposite trend—their share of world output is rising, and by 2020, it is expected that they will account for more than 60 percent of world economic activity. Countries like China, Thailand, and Indonesia have emerged as global economic players. Most experts expect that similar trends will continue. Countries like the USA, the UK, Germany, and Japan—among the first to industrialise—will continue to see their standings in world exports and world output slip relatively, while developing nations like China, India, South Korea, and Thailand see their economies and role in global trade and investment increase. China has emerged to challenge the USA for its position as leading producer. By 2018, the USA accounted for 15.8 percent of world output, with China at 17.1 percent, and global leader; though the USA remained the largest economy overall. It is likely that India will become the third largest economy by 2030. Most forecasts suggest that today's so-called developing nations may account for more than 60 percent of world economic activity by 2025, with todays 'rich' nations declining from 55 percent in 2018 to 38 percent in 2025. This suggests that international businesses need to shift more attention to the developing counties of the world in the next five years.

2. *Foreign direct investment*. In the 1960s, the USA accounted for over 66 percent of worldwide foreign direct investment flows. The UK was a distant second with just 10 percent of worldwide investment flows. Today, investments by developing nations are on the rise, while the stock, or total cumulative value, of foreign investments by rich industrial countries, is falling. Developing nations, like China, have also become important destinations for foreign direct investment flows. The share of total stock of foreign direct investment by the world's six most important sources— USA, UK, Japan, Germany, France, Netherlands—and developing countries, changed significantly from 1980 to 2007. In particular, the USA's share had noticeably declined (from 38 to 18 percent), and the world's developing countries had shifted from under 1 percent to 15 percent. Increased growth in cross-border flows of foreign direct investment is very noticeable in the official figures, reaching an all-time high in 2007. The average yearly outflow of FDI increased from US$14 billion in 1970 to US$1.45 trillion in 2016; when the global stock of FDI was about US$27 trillion. One can also note the rising importance of developing nations as destinations for FDI. These two trends reflect the internationalisation of company operations. By 2017 more than 80,000 companies had more than 800,000 affiliates in foreign markets; employing over 75 million people; making US$36 trillion in

sales; and generating over 11 percent of global GDP. In 2016 China received a record US$ 249.8 billion in inflows. One interesting, overall result, globally, is that firms are finding their home markets under increased attack from foreign competitors.

3. *Types of companies*. The global economy has also shifted in terms of the type of companies that are involved. A multinational enterprise is any business that has productive activities in two or more countries. Since the 1960s, two important trends have emerged. Firstly, an increase in the number of non-US multinationals. Multinational firms from France, Germany, UK, and Japan have become more important, and there has been a notable decline in the role of US firms. Firms from developing countries, such as China and South Korea, have also emerged as important players. Think of South Korea's Samsung and Hong Kong's Hutchison Whampoa. By 2017, only 540 firms of the top 2000 global firms were US-based multinationals, a drop of some 236 firms in 15 years. This trend is expected to continue from 2020-2025. The second trend is the growth in the number of mini-multinationals. China's Lenovo, for example—acquired IBM's PC division in 2004 in an effort to become a global player in the PC industry, and moved its headquarters to the USA as part of its strategy. Another representative example: G.W. Barth makes cocoa bean roasting machinery. Based in Germany, with just 70 employees, nevertheless it has 70 percent of the global market for its roasting machines. Traditionally, global markets have been the venue for large firms, but today, thanks to advances in technology like the Internet, international sales can account for a significant share of revenues for small companies too.

4. *Change in world order.* The collapse of Russian communism brought about new opportunities in Eastern Europe, and China's economic development and enormous population has presented—and continues to present—huge opportunities for companies. Mexico and Latin America have also emerged both as new markets, and as source and production locations. India has been predicted to be a major global player in the near future. From an international business perspective, the growth of these markets creates new opportunities for foreign firms, but this growth is also an interesting, competitive threat. China and India, for example, are now home to a number of companies that either are, or could become, significant players in their global industries. At the same time, this world order is changing again as we move into the third decade of the 21st century. Several Eastern European states; Russia; and China, have been shifting towards more state involvement for some time, and in some cases, more authoritarian government. Over the years several Latin American countries (for example, Brazil, Chile and Mexico) have increased their attractiveness

as markets for exports, and as targets for FDI. Will this continue? Other parts of Latin America reflect a long history of economic mismanagement—Venezuela, for example, running into serious problems in recent years. Bolivia and Ecuador have seen shifts to more state involvement with FDI, less welcome. For international businesses, such newer developments change, once again, the risk profiles for those countries.

1.4. The Globalisation Debates

What does the global economy look like in the third decade of this century? The world has been moving toward a more global economic system but this interdependency creates new types of risk. For example, recall the global impacts of the financial crisis that swept through South East Asia in the late 1990s. Also the more recent financial crisis that began in the United States in 2008, and then affected economies across the globe. Note also the coronavirus pandemic which accelerated in a few months from one region in China to some 15,3000 confirmed cases and 5,735 deaths across over 120 countries by mid-March 2020. The spread continued during 2020 with massive adverse impacts on international business, global logistics, and share prices—a clear indicator of the downsides of global interdependence. Wars, natural disasters, climate change, and technological disasters (for example nuclear accidents) can also have serious knock-on effects. Proponents of globalisation, such as Bhagwati (2004), focus on the benefits of globalisation, but some people worry that the shift toward a more integrated and interdependent global economy is not necessarily a good thing. Critics worry, for example, that globalisation will cause job losses, damage the environment, and create cultural imperialism. Ian Goldin and Mike Mariathasan (2016), in their book *The Butterfly Defect*, discuss how globalisation creates systemic risks—adverse consequences from the 'butterfly effect' where, in an inter-connected world, small changes in condition in one system or part of the world can create major differences in a seemingly remote and unconnected system. They discuss financial sector risks; risks in supply chains and infrastructure; as well as pandemic, health, ecological, and social inequality risks. Supporters however, argue that globalisation means lower prices, more economic growth, and more jobs. Anti-globalisation protesters, who fear that globalisation is changing the world in a negative way, now turn up at almost every major meeting of global institutions like the WTO and IMF. Four major areas of debate recur:

1. *Jobs and income*. How do critics and supporters view globalisation and jobs and income? Critics of globalisation worry that jobs are being lost to low-wage nations. They argue that falling trade barriers are allowing companies to move manufacturing jobs to countries where wage rates are low. For example, clothing manufacturing has increasingly shifted away from the USA, where workers might earn $9 per hour,

to countries like Honduras where wages are less than 50 cents per hour. Critics believe that this leads to falling wages and living standards in the USA. In recent years the same arguments have been applied to services, which have been increasingly outsourced from Western Europe and the USA, to countries like India, Philippines and over 120 other locations. It has been argued, not always correctly, that this contributes to fewer jobs and lower living standards in the home nations. Such arguments do not take into account the gains and lower prices in the home market as a result of global sourcing practices. Supporters also claim that free trade will prompt countries to specialise in what they can produce most efficiently, and to import everything else. They argue that the whole economy will be better off as a result. In other words, if you can buy an imported shirt that was made for pennies in Honduras, you will have more money to spend on products the USA can produce efficiently, like computers and software. The debate is now extended and continues over the impact of automation on global sourcing and job numbers, skills and related incomes. Will jobs be repatriated from global locations? Will those jobs be automated, so leading to job loss wherever the work is located? (See Willcocks, 2021).

2. *Labour policies and the environment*. How do globalisation's supporters and critics view globalisation, labour policies and the environment? Protesters fear that free trade encourages firms from advanced nations, where there are costly environmental standards, to move manufacturing facilities offshore to less developed countries with lax environmental and labour regulations. However, advocates of globalisation claim that environmental regulation and stricter labour standards go hand-in-hand with economic progress, so foreign direct investment actually encourages countries to raise their standards. Some studies support this claim, with the exception of carbon dioxide emissions, which appear to rise along with income levels. Advocates of globalisation argue that by tying free trade agreements to the implementation of tougher environmental and labour laws, economic growth and globalisation can occur together, with a decrease in environmental pollution.

3. *Shifts in economic power*. A further concern raised by critics of globalisation is the worry that economic power is shifting away from national governments and towards supranational organisations like the WTO, the United Nations, and the European Union (EU). However, globalisation's supporters have argued that the power of these organisations is limited to that granted by their members. They also point out that the organisations are designed to promote the collective interests of members,

and they will not gain support for policies that do not achieve this goal. With a slowdown in globalisation in recent years, however, (see 1.10) some supranational organisations, like the IMF and WTO, have seen a waning of power and influence; and some regional economic blocs have seen turbulence—for example the United Kingdom deciding to leave the European Union by 2020; the renegotiation of trade agreements between Mexico, USA and Canada; and China looking to gain more influence in economic blocs and trade arrangements in Asia Pacific.

4. *Wealth distribution.* Critics of globalisation worry that the gap between rich and poor is growing and that the benefits of globalisation have not been shared equally. There is plenty of evidence for this (see 1.10). While supporters of globalisation concede the gap between rich and poor has become wider, they also contend that it has more to do with the policies countries have followed, than with globalisation. For example, many countries have chosen to pursue totalitarian regimes, or have failed to contain population growth; and many countries have pursued economic policies that have resulted in huge debt loads that are stagnating economic growth. Some 40 nations, with a combined population of over 700 million people, are designated as 'highly indebted poorer countries'. One also needs to point out the growing role of corruption and money laundering in redistributing wealth on a global scale.

Globalisation: Different Voices and Perspectives

Joseph Stieglitz	- *Globalisation and its Discontents* (1999); *Making Globalisation Work* (2003) > questions unregulated/liberal economic policies
Zygmunt Bauman	- *Globalisation* (1999); *Liquid Modernity* (2000) > questions the divisive outcomes of globalisation
Tom Friedman	- *The World Is Flat* (2003) > technology helps create a globalising world where differences disappear
Martin Wolf	- *Why Globalisation Works* (2005) > in favour of hyperglobalisation
Manuel Castells	- *The Rise of Network Society* (2008) > examines the complex role of Information and Communication Technologies
Wolfgang Streeck	- *How Will Capitalism End?* (2016) > capitalism in a critical condition: stagnation; inequality; low econ confidence
Stephen King	- *Grave New World: The End of Globalisation, The Return of History* (2017) > why globalisation is being rejected; the rise of nationalism
Pankaj Ghemawat	- *The New Global Road Map* (2018) > slowdown, turbulence, robust regularities
Richard Baldwin	- *The Globotics Upheaval* (2019) > impacts of automation

1.5. Does Distance Still Matter?

Still another debate has been over the degree of globalisation, its impacts and its implications for international business. Friedman (2005) believes globalisation is accelerating and is flattening the world so that every nation will eventually be part of the global marketplace and production process. Dicken (2007) calls this a 'hyper-globalist view'. Friedman takes a technological stance on globalisation, believing it to be shaped considerably by technological advances, cheap computer access, and the easy assimilation and transportation of knowledge over the World Wide Web. Before computer access was a worldwide phenomenon, geographical distance played a big impact on how firms conducted business. Without the ability to communicate easily and freely with other countries, a sweatshop in Hanoi, to take one example, would be rather tricky to co-ordinate from say France. Without the Internet, video conferencing—companies thousands of miles apart can communicating in real time—would not be possible. Moreover outsourcing would be harder, as there would be no reliable, efficient way of collaborating with other departments in the same office or in a different country.

Friedman argues that ten flatteners have shaped globalisation and have caused increased homogeneity in the world. These include: the fall of the Berlin Wall representing economic liberalisation; the development of internet protocols; workflow and open source software; the increased use of outsourcing and offshoring; the development of global supply chains; the increased use of specialised firms to carry out internal functions; the development of search engines; and, latterly, of wireless, digital, mobile, personal, and virtual technologies. From this perspective, technological capacity and connectedness define the parameters of globalisation, and this is only set to continue as the age of the personal technology relationship is gaining momentum; where people not content with established information-sharing bodies, take matters into their own hands with blogs, review sites, and establishing their own media channels. Everyone essentially becomes in control of their own personal networking and spread of influence.

However, Friedman may not provide the only valid argument for defining globalisation. Although to hyper-globalists, globalisation literally means the free co-operation and connection with nations all over the world, to people like Ghemawat (2001; 2017) and Dicken (2007), flattening is a gross overstatement and creates a general misconception about the extent of globalisation's reach. In his influential article, *Distance Still Matters*, Ghemawat (2001) argues that companies in their pursuit of the benefits from globalisation, consistently *"overestimate the attractiveness of foreign markets."* Ghemawat argues that the true amount of trade and investment between countries is influenced largely by geographical and cultural differences. He cites that countries 5,000 miles apart only perform 20 percent of the trade they would otherwise do if they were 1,000 miles apart. Furthermore, trade is ten times more likely to take place if a country was a former colony of another, which, Ghemawat argues, significantly lowers the cultural barriers to trade.

These figures, taken together, explain a key point in Ghemawat's argument—*"distance still matters and companies must explicitly and thoroughly account for it when they make decisions about global expansion."* Arguing against Friedman's flattening argument, Ghemawat elaborates that global communications and technologies have been argued to be *"shrinking the world, running it into a small and relatively homogenous place. But when it comes to business, that's not only an incorrect assumption but also a dangerous one."*

The cultural difference between countries is still wide and complex, and although outsourcing and foreign direct investment have recently grown considerably over the last two decades, it is evident, as we shall see in Chapter 3, that cultural differences still prove challenging. In support of Ghemawat's statement, Dicken (2007) argues that quantitative and aggregative evidence suggests that the world economy was *"more open and more integrated in the half century prior to the First World War, than it is today (2007)."* Ghemawat also supports this empirically-based analysis stating that cultural differences in religious beliefs, language, social norms, and behaviours have a huge impact in the risk involved in trading and the likelihood of succeeding. Therefore, according to these theorists, globalisation cannot be characterised as flattening the world. As Dicken puts it: *"there are undoubtedly globalising forces at work, but we do not have a fully globalised world."*

Dicken explains that part of the problem with defining globalisation is understanding that aggregative and quantitative analysis, though valid, are not the only story we should take on board when thinking about the world economy today. The economy today, he goes on to suggest, constitutes a deep and complex integration that cannot be captured in the statistics of trade and foreign direct investment (FDI). Instead globalisation is: *"a supercomplex series of multicentric, multiscalar, multitemporal, multiform and multicausal processes."* This explanation, in contrast to Friedman's linear model of technological progress, is more dynamic and circulatory in design. To summarise, it would seem that globalisation includes fluctuating levels of trade and FDI; economic growth of emerging markets; growing Transnational Corporations (TNCs); outsourcing and labour force migration; as well as technological innovations that have facilitated these movements.

Ghemawat complements this view by suggesting that companies often overestimate the ease with which their business can move abroad. The cultural, administrative, and geographical distance between nations presents a fundamental challenge to firms facing the globalisation of the world economy today. Ghemawat uses the example of Rupert Murdoch's venture in Asia with Star Television network, which assumed that the Asian audiences would be enthusiastic about English language programmes and films. Furthermore, Murdoch's underestimating of the administrative differences between Asia and the USA led him into political calamity as he claimed, live on television, that freedom to watch what one wanted was a threat to Asian *"totalitarian regimes everywhere"*. This led to the blocking of Star TV from Chinese television, which is a huge market for Murdoch. Coca-Cola also had problems in the Peruvian market when they attempted to replace Inca Kola, the national beverage, with their own US-branded Cola. The Peruvian people held mass demonstrations against Coca-Cola until their Inca Cola was returned to the shelves. Being sensitive to national differences is not just a consideration; in international business it may well be an imperative for survival—something we explore in detail in later chapters.

Ghemawat followed up his views with a more recent, empirically-based book called *The Laws of Globalisation and Business Applications* (Cambridge University Press, 2017). Here he finds plenty of evidence (up to 2017) to confirm his earlier analysis. This resulted in Ghemawat postulating two laws that contradict Friedman's 'flattening' thesis:

1. *The law of semi-globalisation* holds that international interactions, while non-negligible, are significantly less intense then domestic interactions.

2. *The law of distance* suggests that international interactions are dampened by distance in terms of cultural, administrative, and geographic distance; and are often affected by economic distance as well. Ghemawat adds that this law also holds in cyberspace. We will examine this CAGE model further in Chapter 4.

1.6. What does Globalisation Mean for Firms?

Let's take stock of the point we have reached. All this means that managing an international business, or any firm that engages in international trade or investment, will be different from managing a domestic business. In particular, firms operating internationally will find that countries and cultures differ – a subject we will explore in much more detail in Chapters 2 and 3. It will emerge from those chapters that the range of problems faced by managers is greater and more complex, not least because government intervention in markets creates limitations for companies, as does the way the global trading system operates and the existence of international institutions (see below and Chapter 2). At the same time firms can work with the forces for globalisation and improve their global performance. Such forces include:

- *Low barriers to trade and investment*. These mean that firms can see the world as their market, rather than a single country. Low trade and investment barriers also mean that firms can locate production facilities in the optimal location, wherever in the world that might be. Production and sales now take place in multiple markets creating interdependency between countries for goods and services (see above).

- *Technological change*. Major advances in communication, information processing, and transportation technology have made what had been possibilities into tangible realities. The cost of global communication has fallen, for example, because advances in the Internet, telecommunications and information processing, help firms coordinate and control global organisations at a fraction of what it might have cost even a decade ago. Just looking at the Internet, global e-commerce sales surpassed US$ 2 trillion for the first time in 2017, and have been on a rising trend since. The Internet is a global equaliser, lessening the constraints of sale, location and, obviously, time zones. The microprocessor that facilitates high-power, low-cost computing, is perhaps the most important of these developments. Major multinationals, like Boeing, Bosch, Apple and Microsoft, outsource much of their production and activities to other countries. Let's look at just one example. Dell took advantage of these innovations to control its globally dispersed production system. When a customer submits an order via the company's website, that order is immediately transmitted to the suppliers of the various components, wherever they are located in the world. Suppliers have real time access to Dell's order flows, and can then adjust their production accordingly. Dell uses inexpensive airfreight to transport its products to meet demand as needed. The company maintains a customer service operation in India, where English-speaking personnel handle calls from the USA. Indeed, the Internet has made it possible for even small companies to play a role in the global economy. Yet, less than twenty five years ago, this technology did not even exist. Growth in Internet usage has gone from fewer than one million users in 1990, to more than two billion users in 2012, and to 4.39 billion in 2019.

- *Transportation improvements.* Improvements in transportation such as commercial aircraft, containerisation and the development of super freighters have also facilitated the growth of globalisation. The time it takes people and products to get from one place to another has shrunk, as has the cost. As just one example, Ecuador has been able to capitalise on falling transportation costs to become a global supplier of roses. Containerisation has been very influential. It reduces, greatly, the costs of shipping goods long distances. This is important because, even in 2020, 90 percent of the world's traded goods were still shipped by sea.

There is evidence that there are huge global shifts in the ways in which we do business, and overall, the strongest companies are international, but are also, as we shall see in Chapter 7, strategically sensitive to localising their products or service when operating in different markets. For example, Google search engine found this to be a winning combination in its expansion into China. Here, despite an initial backlash, Google pursued a local strategy for its Chinese market using a Chinese name for its search engine. It also customised its web page to fit the tastes of Chinese internet users who tend to spend longer on a given page, and read the left hand side of the screen first. However, global linkages and interdependencies, and working in foreign markets, also mean global risks. As a symbol of the risks of globalisation for a firm, Google also ran into subsequent problems with the Chinese government on a number of issues.

1.7. International Trade Theory: From Free Trade to Factor Endowments

Free trade refers to a situation where a government does not attempt to influence through quotas or duties what its citizens can buy from another country or what they can produce and sell to another country. Economists have debated the merits of free trade for centuries. You probably do not need trade theories to explain some patterns of trade. It is easy to see, for instance, why Saudi Arabia exports oil and Brazil exports coffee. But other patterns are harder to explain—why Switzerland exports watches and pharmaceuticals, or why Japan exports consumer electronics. Why is India a major outsourcing destination for IT services, but has no sizeable domestic market in this area? Why does Ford assemble cars made for the American market in Mexico, while BMW and Nissan manufacture cars for Americans in the USA? You can probably think of your own trading puzzles!

We need to understand such patterns of trade and the factors that influence them. So let us look at the several theories of trade, and also at the important role of national governments in influencing modern patterns of international trade. A little historical background is useful here, since three quite old theories still influence modern day thinking—for better or worse. The first of these is mercantilism. The main idea behind the mercantilist philosophy, which was around in the mid-16th century, was that the accumulation of gold and silver were essential to the wealth and power of a nation. It was in the best interests of a country to try to maximise its holdings of gold and silver by encouraging exports and discouraging imports. To achieve this, imports were limited through tariffs and quotas, while exports were maximised through government subsidies. A key flaw in this philosophy, however, was that it was a zero-sum game. A country could only achieve its goal of maximising a trade surplus at the expense of another nation. If one country successfully exported more than it imported, and consequently increased its holdings of gold and silver, another country would fail to achieve a trade surplus and would become relatively weaker. The more modern version of mercantilism is protectionism, where a country actively shields its domestic firms from imports while promoting exports, for example China in 2008-2013 keeping the exchange rate of the renminbi low. From 2016 the USA also sought to become more protectionist in both posture and practice. Thus the two most powerful economies in the world had, by 2021, developed much more focused less liberal trade policies.

A second influential set of ideas came from Adam Smith who argued, in his *Inquiry Into the Nature and Causes of The Wealth of Nations* (1776), that trade without government intervention could be beneficial to countries if each country produced and exported those products in which it was most efficient, or in his words, had an absolute advantage. Smith argued that if countries specialised in the production of goods in which they had an absolute advantage, firstly each country could produce more, and secondly they could then trade these goods for the goods produced by other countries. The result would be a win-win game rather than the zero-sum gain under protectionism. Note that such absolute advantage is a rare occurrence. What happens if one nation has an absolute advantage in the production of all products? Or a nation cannot establish an absolute advantage in any product or service?

Ricardo developed the theory of trade further by arguing for comparative advantage. It actually still makes sense for a country to specialise in the production of those goods that it produces most efficiently and to buy goods that it produces relatively less efficiently from other countries. This is true, even if it means buying goods, in which it has an absolute advantage, from other countries, i.e. goods it could produce more efficiently itself. The key issue here is **opportunity cost**. Peng and Meyer (2019) usefully point out how practical this idea of comparative advantage is by the example of a student. Assume she studies a degree to become a business manager. Firstly, while studying, she does not make sweaters, food or software but buys these from others in order to focus on getting the best degree possible. Assume, however, that she has to drive a taxi to make some money to pay for studies, and becomes an excellent taxi driver. Once she gets her degree, her salary might be, say, $100,000 with high prospects, while the best she can earn as a taxi driver might be $50,000. Therefore she hires taxis, even though she may have an absolute advantage in that skill, because the opportunity cost of driving taxis and being a business manager, instead of focusing on just the latter, are very big indeed. Both she and taxi drivers gain from this application of the theory of comparative advantage.

A key idea in all this is productivity. Smith looked at absolute productivity differences between countries, while Ricardo looked at relative productivity differences. Ohlin (1933) extended Ricardo's work by suggesting that a country's comparative advantage is a result of differences in **national factor endowments**. The Heckscher-Ohlin theory argues that countries will export goods that make intensive use of factors of production, like land, labour, and capital, which are locally abundant. At the same time, countries will import goods that make intensive use of factors that are locally scarce. For example, a country like China, with abundant low-cost labour, historically produces and exports products that are labour intensive—like textiles—while the UK, which lacks abundant low cost labour, imports textiles from China. (Note that by 2021 China was looking to become much more capital and technology intensive). Another example (and many can be cited) is Brazil, which, with its abundant resources of land, water, and weather, has become an agricultural powerhouse. One example here is its production of half the world's exports in sugar-based ethanol, which has been mandated as an additive to gasoline used in cars since the 1970s.

OK, enough history. These trade theories paint a static picture of the world, but as we know things move all too quickly these days. In the 1960s Vernon and Hirsch produced the first dynamic theory to account for changes in the patterns of trade over time. They asked the question: *"Why are some products that used to be made at home, now imported from other countries, especially less developed ones?"* For example, the UK used to be a major producer of textile products, but is no longer. Vernon (1966) suggested that as products mature, both the sales location and the optimal production location would change. As these change, so will the flow and direction of trade. Products move through different stages of their life cycle, and as they do, where they are produced and sold change too.

Vernon considered that the product life cycle consisted of three stages: **new**, **maturing**, and **standardised**. Moreover, there were three types of nations: **lead innovation nations** (in the 1960s he saw this as the USA); **other developed nations**; and **developing nations**. Vernon observed, at the time, that most of the world's new products were developed by American firms and sold initially in the USA. He attributed this to the wealth and size of the US market. While demand was growing in the USA, there would be only limited demand by high- income consumers in other advanced countries. Therefore, there would be little incentive for firms in foreign countries to produce the product, so other developed markets would be served by exports from the USA. But, as demand for the new product grew in other advanced countries, foreign producers would begin to produce the product. US producers, in an effort to capitalise on foreign demand, would also begin to produce in the foreign markets. Exports from the USA slowed down as they were replaced by foreign production. As the US market and the foreign markets matured, the product became more standardised, and price became more important to consumers. Some foreign producers, with lower wage costs, exported to the USA market during this stage. Later, production shifted to developing countries where wages were even lower, and the USA became an importer of the product.

While the product life cycle theory was useful for explaining trade patterns for products like photocopiers, that were developed in the 1960s and 1970s, today, given the effects of globalisation and the integration of the world economy, the theory does not hold up well. Today, you can think of many products that were designed and introduced outside the USA, like video game consoles that were initially introduced in Japan, or Europe's wireless phones. In addition, many products are introduced simultaneously in the USA, Japan, and Europe. Production of these new products is often globally dispersed from the start.

In an effort to resolve some of the shortcomings of other theories, researchers in the 1970s began to look for other explanations of trade. This new vein of thought, called strategic trade theory, argued that, because of the unit cost reductions that are associated with a large scale of output (economies of scale), some industries can support only a very few firms. Moreover, in some industries, to achieve economies of scale, firms need to have a major share of the world's market. The costs of developing new aircraft, for example, are so high, that firms have to hold a significant share of the world market in order to gain economies of scale. There are reasons why there are only two makers of large commercial aircraft in the world! **First mover advantage** is an important concept here. Firms that achieve first mover advantages will develop economies of scale, and create barriers to entry for other firms. Airbus, for example, should enjoy the first mover advantages associated with its A380 5550-seater super jumbo plane. Consider the dilemma. Airbus had to sell at least 250 super jumbos just to break even on the project. The market over the following twenty years is expected to be just 400 to 600 planes, so Airbus has first mover advantages based on scale economies. Could Boeing compete? Should it?

This theory suggests that government should support certain strategic industries that can gain first mover, hard-to-replicate advantages. Typically these have high up-front entry costs, in terms of research and building capabilities, and are highly capital-intensive, thus creating high entry barriers. In our Airbus example above, the project received substantial subsidies from European governments. However, in other cases a government might lack the information or knowledge to identify a strategic industry, and where first mover advantage could be gained. Strategic trade theory supports comparative advantage theory because it actually identifies a source of comparative advantage. Governments might use this information to implement strategic trade policies that nurture and protect firms where first mover advantages and economies of scale are important.

Bringing it to country level, have you ever wondered why some countries have certain industries that seem to be superior to those of other countries? Why is Japan so strong in the global auto industry? It wasn't always. Why does Switzerland dominate the pharmaceutical industry? In 1990, Michael Porter identified four factors that he argued promoted or impeded the creation of competitive advantage in an industry. Together, he called these factors the **diamond of competitive advantage**.

1. The first factor, called *factor endowments*, refers to a country's position in the factors of production that can lead to a competitive advantage—things like the skilled labour or infrastructure that were important to achieving a competitive advantage in a particular industry. For example, the forests and timber that are abundantly available can explain the paper industry in Scandinavia. High-tech industries gather around university cities, e.g. Cambridge, UK, Munich, Germany, because scientists and graduates are readily available there.

2. **Demand conditions**, the second factor, refer to the nature of home demand for the industry's products/services. For example, sophisticated and demanding Japanese customers for iPods, console games, and mobile phones have pressured Japanese consumer electronics firms to be highly competitive.

3. The third factor, ***related and supporting industries***, refers to the presence or absence of supplier and related industries that are internationally competitive and contribute to other industries. According to Porter, successful industries will be grouped in clusters within countries. If a country has world-class manufacturers of semi-conductor processing equipment, it will tend to have a competitive semi-conductor industry.

4. The fourth factor—***firm strategy, structure, and rivalry***—refers to the conditions in the nation that govern how companies are created, organised, and managed, as well as the nature of domestic rivalry. When the domestic rivalry is strong, there is greater pressure to innovate, improve quality, reduce costs, and invest in advanced product features.

Was Porter successful at increasing our understanding of trade patterns? Porter argued that a nation's success in an industry is a function of the combined impact of the four points on his diamond. He also suggested that government could play a role. For example, government imposed subsidies could affect factor endowments, or by imposing local product standards, a government could change demand conditions. Antitrust laws, and so on, could influence rivalry among firms. If his arguments are correct, his model ought to predict the patterns of trade we see in the real world, but so far his theory is not well tested. Several critics have pointed out how national culture as a shaping factor is missing from his Diamond. He also puts too much emphasis on domestic conditions creating industry advantage. India's IT industry, for example, has arisen largely as a response to the export market, rather than India's domestic market. Rugman and D.cruz (1993) pointed out that for small, open trading economies where firms earn the majority of their revenues outside their home country, the Diamond of their target markets is more relevant than their own home Diamond. Thus for Canada the North American Double Diamond is more relevant than a Canadian one: the US-Canada free trade agreement meant that both US and Canadian firms could go to both countries for resources and highly skilled labour to make up their factor conditions. Firms on both sides would have to benchmark and compete against each other to gain market share. (Of course later, with the USA/Mexico/Canada trade agreements, this became a triple diamond). Even supply and related industries are converging due to cross border supply chains. Reich (1990) took the argument further by pointing out that almost all factor conditions—such as capital, technology and raw materials—are internationally mobile nowadays except the nation's workforce. Industries are no longer the competitive base for a nation; it is the skilled workforce underpinning the success of industries. But, of course, given the level of labour mobility globally since he was writing, even that may be less true.

1.8. National Institutions and International Trade: Free or Protected?

Free trade refers to a situation where a government does not restrict what its citizens can buy from another country or what they can sell to another country. Many nations today claim to support free trade, but, in reality, most countries are only nominally committed to free trade. They tend to intervene in international trade to protect the interests of politically important groups, and national interests. The global recession of 2008–2009 led to an increase in protectionist policies in many countries. This has accelerated from 2016, and again with the 2020–2021 crisis. Countries and governments can intervene in markets in several ways. Let us look at these now:

- *Tariff barriers*. A tariff is a tax levied on imports that effectively raises the cost of imported products relative to domestic products. There are two kinds of tariffs. Specific tariffs are levied as a fixed charge for each unit of a good that is imported, and ad valorem tariffs are levied as a proportion of the value of the imported good. Tariffs are beneficial to governments because they increase revenues. They are also beneficial to domestic producers because tariffs provide protection against foreign competitors by increasing the cost of imported foreign goods, though of course, this means higher prices for consumers. There is general agreement that tariffs are unambiguously pro-producer and anti-consumer. It is also argued that tariffs reduce the overall efficiency of the world economy because they encourage domestic producers to manufacture goods that could be produced more efficiently elsewhere. Tariffs are often imposed because of special interest groups' ability to influence political decisions. An often cited example are farming interests and their influences in Europe, USA, and Japan, but you can point to many other sectors across the world protected by tariff policies. By 2020, the USA and China were using tariffs against each other as part of a major falling out over trade practices.

- *Subsidies* are government payments to domestic producers. Governments can give subsidies in various ways including cash grants, low interest loans, and tax breaks. They can help domestic producers compete against low cost foreign imports, and they can help them gain export markets. One of the biggest recipients of subsidies in most countries is agriculture. Do subsidies help producers be more competitive, or do they tend to protect inefficient producers and promote excess production? One study showed that if developed countries eliminated their agricultural subsidies, we would see an increase in global trade in agricultural products, and a savings of over US$160 billion. Another report suggested that removing all tariffs and subsidies to agriculture would raise world income by US$182 billion. Consumers typically absorb the costs of subsidies. Subsidies are widely used beyond agriculture, and are the subject of regular disputes among nations. For example, Boeing and Airbus have received substantial subsidies from governments over 40 years. The USA regularly complained about China subsidising auto part exports up to 2012, when it was subject to a US government complaint. Even in the 2000-2010 period countries were spending more than US$300 billion on subsidies a year, with over 70 percent being spent by 21 developed nations. Given the move to more protectionist policies in the last few years, this figure was probably much higher by 2021, but spread across many more nations.

- An ***import quota*** is a direct restriction on the quantity of some good that may be imported into a country. In the USA for example, there is a quota on cheese imports. A tariff rate quota, which is common in agriculture, is a mix of a quota and a tariff where a lower tariff is applied to imports within the quota than to those over the quota. A quota rent is the extra profit that producers make when supply is artificially limited by an import quota.

- ***Voluntary export restraints*** are quotas on trade imposed by the exporting country, usually at the request of the importing country's government. In 1981, Japan established voluntary export restraints for the auto industry. Japan believed that by setting its own limits it could avoid potentially higher limits that could be set by the USA. As a result of the 1981 voluntary export restraints for example, Japanese producers earned an extra US$1 billion from the higher prices charged to consumers because of the trade barriers. Import quotas and voluntary export restraints benefit domestic producers by limiting import competition, but they do raise prices of imported goods.

- ***Export tariffs and prohibitions***. Countries sometimes put a tariff on an exportable good, in order to ensure there is a sufficient supply domestically. For example, historically, China has placed such tariffs on some steel products and grain, because it needed these to support its building boom, and feed its people. Such tariffs are rare because they inhibit exports, but sometimes they are used to attack an economic competitor who is short of vital goods/services. A more likely approach is not to use tariffs but impose a partial or total export ban. For example, in 1975 the US government banned crude oil exports to ensure sufficient domestic supplies. OPEC was restricting supplies to drive up prices and confront Western countries for their support of Israel during Middle East conflicts.

- *Local content requirements* are another form of trade barrier where the government demands that some specific fraction of a good be produced domestically. Like other types of trade restrictions, local content requirements benefit producers, but probably not consumers!

- *Administrative trade policies* are bureaucratic rules designed to make it difficult for imports to enter a country. The Japanese are known for this type of trade barrier, which frustrates companies trying to break into the market. Since 2008 Indonesia and Malaysia have limited imports to certain ports. India has, in the past, banned Chinese toys, citing safety concerns. As with other trade barriers, these policies can hurt consumers if they deny access to foreign products that may be superior to those available at home.

- *Antidumping policies.* Dumping is selling goods in a foreign market below their cost of production, or selling goods in a foreign market at below their fair market value. Dumping is viewed as a method by which firms unload excess production in foreign markets. Some dumping is considered to be predatory behaviour, where producers use profits from their home markets to subsidise prices in foreign markets with a goal of driving indigenous competitors out of the market, and then later raising prices and earning substantial profits. To stop this type of behaviour, countries implement antidumping policies, or countervailing duties, designed to punish foreign firms that are dumping and protect domestic producers from this type of unfair competition.

1.9. Government Intervention and Free Trade: The Debate

Many argue that, economically over the long term, free trade is best. For example, it is argued that free trade can increase a country's stock of resources. Thus, since the 1990s, US and West European companies have been investing in Eastern Europe increasing the amount of capital that's available to use there. Free trade can also increase the efficiency of resource utilisation. Thus if firms can sell to a bigger market, they can gain from the economies associated with large-scale production. Studies show that countries that adopt a more open stance toward international trade tend to have higher growth rates than those that close their economies to trade. There may be times when restrictions on trade are counterproductive, e.g. when they involve retaliation and trade wars, or efforts to further domestic policies. For example, strategic trade policies that are designed to establish domestic firms in dominant positions in the global market will probably result in retaliation. So when the European Union provided US$15 billion in subsidies to Airbus, the USA took steps to protect Boeing. In the end, the subsidies probably cancelled each other out, and consumers and taxpayers footed the bill. Those who argue against such subsidy cite many such examples. A favourite one involves policies adopted by the European Union to protect consumers from imported agricultural products. It is often pointed out this may well do nothing more than protect inefficient farmers and politicians who relied on the farm vote, and actually cause consumers to pay more for food.

But still others argue that a country needs to protect its own domestic industries and also its new, emerging industries. One of the problems with the latter argument, though, is determining when an industry has grown up enough to stop government support. In fact, many people believe that protecting these industries is really no different from sponsoring the development of inefficient industries. Others argue that, regardless of the economic arguments, protectionism can advance a country's political, social and environmental agenda. The main political arguments for government intervention can be summarised:

- National security concerns are often evoked to protect defence-related industries in, for example, France, USA and the UK.

- Governments also claim that trade barriers are sometimes necessary to protect consumers. For example, the European Union has limited imports of hormone-treated beef for many years, and this has been a source of a huge conflict between the European Union and the USA.

- Sometimes governments intervene in markets to retaliate against moves made by other governments. China has been under fire in recent years for failing to take proper steps against product and intellectual property piracy. Many nations have threatened to implement trade barriers against Chinese products if the practice isn't stopped. China initially responded with threats of increasing its own barriers to trade, although it subsequently backed off.

- Governments also argue that intervention in the market is necessary to support their foreign policy objectives. A country might, for example, extend favourable trade terms to another country with which it is trying to build a relationship, or implement policies designed to punish countries. For example, the US maintains trade embargoes against Cuba, Iran and North Korea, and has had, in the last few years, an ongoing 'trade war' with China over a range of economic and foreign policy issues.

- Protecting industries and jobs is the most frequently cited reason for governments trying to reduce foreign competition, especially when the competition is perceived as unfair, for example subsidised (see above). As an example, one study claimed that

Chinese subsidies and currency manipulation between 2001 and 2015 contributed in a major way to the growth in the USA-China trade deficit in that period, leading to some 3.4 million American jobs being lost. Such claims give background to the increased economic tensions between the two countries in the last few years.

- Protecting human rights is another argument used by governments that intervene in the market. The basic idea is that the best way to change human rights practices in a country is to encourage it to trade. This will raise income levels, which generally means that human rights practices improve. Another way is to make the adoption of better employment and human rights practices part of the conditions of trade.

- Environmental and social responsibility arguments are sometimes used to start trade interventions against certain countries, e.g. the USA banning shrimp imports from India, Malaysia, Thailand and Pakistan, arguing that their fishing techniques also trapped sea turtles—a protected species in USA waters.

- Protecting infant industries and supporting strategic trade policies are common economic arguments for state intervention. They have been used extensively by developing nations in recent years, not least to justify protectionism. This, of course, may be counter-productive if it does not result in an infant industry becoming efficient and able to compete against international competitors. This happened, for example, to the Brazilian car industry. Note also that capital markets have developed financing of infant industries, and the relevant firms may now be much less reliant on government funding. This can be seen, for example, in Taiwan and South Korea, and their steel, shipping, textiles and semi-conductor industries. Governments also argue for the need to protect strategic industries and trading. The argument here is that such industries and their firms can contribute significantly to national income, and need to be given first mover advantage in their own country. An example is the liquid crystal industry in Japan in the early 1980s; another is government R&D grant support for Boeing in the 1950s and 1960s. Another argument might be to give a firm or industry support to compete against another foreign firm that already has first mover advantage. This happened with Airbus, which was probably backed by a US$18 billion subsidy from four European governments, and became a major world competitor to Boeing.

1.10. Conclusion

This chapter has explored the major characteristics of globalisation and provided a basic understanding of the global economy and its broad trends. We have sought to explain the major trends in globalisation, and the major players in the globalisation process. At the same time the chapter entered into the major globalisation debates and assessed under what conditions and for whom globalisation can be considered an advantage or disadvantage. It also articulated the implications of globalisation for firms operating internationally. We also looked at the evolution of theories of trade, and entered into the debate about whether free trade or protectionism or a balanced mix of each worked best internationally and for which interested parties. We also saw how globalisation and the global economy have slowed in recent years, and the major new trends that have emerged, not least 'slowbalisation', the retreat from several aspects of globalisation, but also the new emerging trends and what has been driving them. All this helps to set some of the global context for businesses seeking to operate internationally.

By 2020, even before the pandemic crisis, there had been long signs of some retrenchment by countries and companies. The move away from globalisation saw many countries become more protectionist. Meanwhile global companies have tended to shrink back to their domestic or regional bases. In 2016 multinational cross-border investment fell by 10-15 percent. The share of trade accounted for by cross-border supply chains has stagnated since 2007. Meanwhile multinationals' profits have been falling. Global integration had offered huge potential for economies of scale. But in fact the profits of the top 700 multinationals firms based in developed economies dropped by 25 percent between 2012 and 2017, with worldwide return on equity (ROE) being 8 percent in 2017. Multinationals in emerging countries have fared little better. By 2017 their return on equity was 8 percent. Multinationals are no longer achieving superior performance, and international sales and profits are inferior to domestic returns. Why is this? In brief, the advantages of economies of scale and arbitrage (see Chapter 4 and Ghemawat's AAA model) have worn away. And protectionist policies by countries and economic unions have been tightening. While technology companies have been a bright spot, for many industrial; manufacturing; financial; media and telecoms; and natural-resources firms, global reach has become a burden, not an advantage. This trend does not look like changing over the next three years. An interesting question is how far the 2020 coronovirus pandemic will increase the shift to deglobalisation and protectionism, or whether such systemic risks will prompt more global coordination and cooperation.

In our final chapter we will add to this picture and will discuss in more detail the major new trends that have emerged, not least 'slowbalisation', the retreat from several aspects of globalisation. We will also look at the new trends emerging from the 2020 crisis, and what has been driving them.

All this helps to set the global context for businesses seeking to operate internationally.

Hopefully this chapter raises questions for you, not least as a taxpayer, an employee, and as a global citizen and stakeholder. This means you have embarked on the fascinating journey of understanding the global context in which we all live, and in which organisations and businesses operate, though in contexts they can also influence. The next two chapters are about that context, but in much more detail. To start this, in the next chapter, we look at the national, regional, and multilateral institutions that importantly shape the conduct of international business.

References

Bhagwati, J. (2004), *In Defence of Gloalisation*. Oxford University Press, Oxford, UK

Dicken, P. (2007), *Global Shift*, Sage Publications, London, UK

Economist, The, (2020), 'The 90% Economy', *The Economist*, May 2nd, page 7

Friedman, T. (2005), *The World Is Flat*, Farrar, Strauss and Giroux, New York, USA

Ghemawat, P. (2001), 'Distance Still Matters: The Hard Reality of Global Expansion', *Harvard Business Review*, December

Ghemawat, P. (2017), *The Laws of Globalisation and Business Applications*, Cambridge University Press, Cambridge, UK

Goldin, I. and Mariathasan, M. (2016), *The Butterfly Defect,* Princeton University Press, Princeton, USA

Hill, C. and Hult, T. (2019), *International Business*, McGraw Hill, New York, USA

Jones, A (2010), *Globalisation: Key Thinkers*, Polity Press, Cambridge, UK

Ohlin, B. (1933), *International and Interregional Trade*, Harvard University Press, Cambridge, UK

Peng, M. and Mayer, K. (2019), *International Business*, (3rd ed.) Cengage, London, UK

Porter, M. (1990), *The Competitive Advantage of Nations,* Free Press, New York, USA

Reich (1990), 'Who Is Us?', *Harvard Business Review*, January-February

Rugman, A.M. and D'Cruz, J.R. (1993), 'The Double Diamond Model of International Competitiveness The Canadian Experience', *Management International Review*, 33, 17-39

Smith, A. (1776), *An Inquiry Into the Nature and Causes of The Wealth Of Nations*, W. Strathan, London, UK

Vernon, R. (1966), 'International investment and international trade in the product cycle', *Quarterly Journal of Economics*, Vol. 80, 190-20

Willcocks, L. (2021), *Global Business Management*, SB Publishing, Stratford-upon-Avon, UK

World Trade Organisation (2019), *World Trade Statistical Review 2019*, WTO, Geneva

'Laws and institutions, like clocks, must occasionally be cleaned, wound up and set to true time'

H.W. Beecher, 1813-1887

'Countries differ greatly in the extent to which they are different from one another'

P. Ghemawat, 2007

Chapter 2

Political, Economic and Legal Environments: Diversity or Growing Uniformity?

2.1. Introduction

Of course you know that political, economic, and legal systems of countries differ; but you may not know what these differences are, the degree of difference (are countries actually becoming similar?) and how and why these differences are important to companies that do business in foreign markets. In practice, firms operating abroad should have a thorough understanding of the formal institutions of each country they are in, or are thinking of entering. In this chapter, we are going to explore these institutions and related systems—known collectively as the 'political economy' of a country—and what they mean for businesses operating internationally. In doing so, we are going to introduce something called 'an institution-based perspective'. The key functions of institutions are to reduce uncertainty, reduce transaction costs, and constrain opportunism. As we shall see, political, economic, and legal institutions establish the formal 'rules of the game' for operating in a particular country. We will look at the equally and sometimes more important informal rules in the next chapter.

In this chapter we also look at international institutions that are important contextual features of international business. Here we consider the roles of organised regional blocs, using examples in Europe, Americas, and Asia Pacific, and the institutions of the international monetary and trading system.

2.2. An Institution-Based View of International Business

Peng, Wang and Jiang (2008) and Peng and Meyer (2019) argue that, essentially, a country's institutions establish the formal and informal rules of the game for operating in that country.

Firms operating internationally need to know these, because the 'rules' differ between countries, and because they shape greatly what can be achieved, and what is not possible. Institutions can be formal or informal. In this chapter we focus on the formal institutional framework—laws, regulations, and rules—of a country, that controls individual and firm behaviour. As we shall see, different governments have regulatory power to coerce compliance to varying degrees. In the next chapter we will look at informal rules—norms, values, ethics shaped by culture, religion, and other social forces.

What do institutions do? Essentially their key role is to reduce uncertainty; and limiting the range of acceptable actions does this. Institutions have developed over time because the potential, adverse consequences of uncertainty can be devastating. For example, if you were trying to do business in the Middle East in 2021—say in Egypt; United Arab Emirates; Israel; Qatar; or Lebanon—imagine the immense difficulties of just understanding the business *context*, let alone deciding what to do. Uncertainty increases transaction costs, a term made highly popular by Oliver Williamson, a Nobel Economic prizewinner (Williamson, 1985). Transaction costs are the costs associated with carrying out an economic transaction or, in short, the costs of doing business—for example search; negotiation; getting to contract; monitoring supplier performance. Transaction costs will increase if others behave opportunistically, defined rather nicely by Williamson as 'self-interest seeking with guile'. Institutional frameworks can reduce the potential for such opportunistic behaviour. This is important for international business, because if transaction costs become prohibitively high in a country, people may choose not to undertake trade in that country at all.

Institutions are evolving all the time and international business managers need to keep up with these changes. For example, in the last 20 years, China, Poland, Russia, and Vietnam have been sometimes moving from central planning to market competition—though each in different ways and at different speeds—and sometimes these processes have been reversed. These are often called 'transition economies'. Institutional transition can be defined as fundamental and comprehensive changes to the formal and informal rules of the game that affect organisations as players.

In summary, Peng and Meyer (2019) argue convincingly that, for international business, institutions matter. They suggest that at the heart of an institution-based view there are two core propositions. Firstly, managers and firms rationally pursue their interests and make choices within the formal and informal constraints of a given institutional framework. Secondly, although formal and informal institutions combine to govern firm behaviour, in situations where formal constraints fail or are unclear, informal constraints will play a larger role in reducing uncertainty and providing constancy to managers and firms. More on informal constraints in Chapter 3, but try this out now if you want: Take an organisation you are familiar with—a workplace, a university, a hospital maybe. There are formal ways of getting things done, for example assigning a task to someone with a deadline. What are these formal ways? What happens if they do not work? The chances are that it will be a mixture of formal and informal institutions that prevail to get the task assigned and the person to agree, and perform.

2.3. Political Systems

A political system represents the rules of the game on how a country is governed politically. It is helpful to think of political systems as having two dimensions: firstly, the degree to which they emphasise collectivism as opposed to individualism, and secondly, the degree to which they are totalitarian or democratic.

Collectivism versus individualism

Collectivism refers to a system that stresses the primacy of collective goals over individual goals. In other words, in a collectivist society, the needs of a society as a whole are generally viewed as being more important than individual freedoms. In modern times collectivism has been equated with socialism, and state ownership of the basic means of production, distribution, and exchange. During the late 1970s, communism, with strong command economies, was a dominant force in the world. Think of the former Soviet Union for example, and its Eastern European neighbours, like Poland, Czechoslovakia, and Hungary. Think also of China, Cambodia, and Vietnam, and of Angola and Mozambique, Cuba, and Nicaragua. By 2000, the world was a very different place. The Soviet Union for example, had been replaced by 15 republics that were structured as democracies. China, though it still limited political freedom, was moving away from its strict communist ideology, though in recent years it has moved towards blending communism with confucianism, while centralising more state power. Today, only a few fringe states like Cuba and North Korea still practise a strong brand of communism. Social democracy, which incorporates belief in a mixed economy of central planning, state, and private enterprises has also been retreating, though at different speeds depending on the country. For example, countries like the UK, France, and Germany have placed less emphasis on state-ownership of the means of production and have seen moves towards privatisation—selling state-owned enterprises to the private sector.

Individualism suggests that individuals should have freedom over their economic and political pursuits. People and economists such as Adam Smith, Milton Friedman and Friedrich von Hayek have championed this philosophy. Individualism is based on two key concepts: firstly, that individual freedom and self-expression are guaranteed, and secondly, that people are allowed to pursue their own self-interests (within the rule of law) in order to achieve the best overall good for society. For international companies there is a debate about how important individualism and the

43

related idea of free market economics are for creating a favourable business environment, and about who gains from applying these concepts in international trading environments.

Clearly collectivism and individualism conflict as creeds, and this has often fuelled tensions between different countries for example, most notably, between the USA, Western Europe and the Soviet Union during the so-called Cold War, and may help to explain something of the trade tensions between USA and China in recent years.

Totalitarianism

You can think of **totalitarianism** and **democracy** as being at opposite ends of a political dimension. At one end you have totalitarianism, where one person or political party exercises absolute control over all spheres of life, and opposing political parties are forbidden; and at the other end there is democracy—a political system in which government is by the people, and is exercised either directly or through elected individuals. While we generally think of democracy as going hand-in-hand with individualism, and totalitarianism being associated with collectivism, grey areas do exist. For example, China is still under totalitarian rule, but has adopted free market policies that tend to be associated with individualism (though in recent years commentators have pointed to some return to greater communist party control). In recent years Russia has become increasingly totalitarian, while still holding to some democratic forms, e.g. elections. The world has seen four major forms of totalitarianism:

- *Communist totalitarianism.* This system advocates achieving socialism through totalitarian dictatorship. While this form of totalitarianism has been declining worldwide, countries like Vietnam, Cuba, and North Korea still follow the philosophy.

- *Theocratic totalitarian* is a system whereby political power is monopolised by a party, group, or individual that governs according to religious principles. You can think of countries like Saudi Arabia or Iran when you think of this type of system. Both countries are greatly influenced by the principles of Islam, and both countries restrict political and religious freedom.

- *Tribal totalitarian.* This system is where a political party that represents the interests of a particular tribe, monopolises power. This type of system has occurred, for example, in some African nations like Zimbabwe, Uganda and Tanzania. In Kenya there are some 40 tribes, but the Kikuya tribe has been persistently best represented politically in government.

- *Right wing totalitarian* is a system that may allow individual economic freedom, but individual political freedom is restricted to avoid forms of socialism. A nation's military often backs this declining type of system; although you might recall its presence in Germany and Italy during the 1930s and 1940s. Military dictatorships were frequent in Latin America, e.g. Brazil (1964-1985) and Chile under General Pinochet. They could also be found at various times in Asian countries like Taiwan, Indonesia, Philippines and South Korea, though these have since become more democratic.

Democracy

A pure democracy is based in the belief that people should be directly involved in decision making. The most common form of democracy today, however, is representative democracy, where elected representatives vote on behalf of constituents. Some of the embraced characteristics of democracies include freedom of expression, free media, regular elections, a fair court system, and free access to state information. The political system is governed by institutions. The rules are usually laid down in a constitution, determining things like how elections are organised, how votes are translated into representation in a parliament, and how much power elected officials and representatives have. There are notable variations in representation methods, including:

- *Proportional representation versus first-by-the-post*. Countries such as Germany and Denmark have systems whereby all votes are added up and seats allocated to political parties in proportion to the number of votes they gained. Countries like India, USA, and UK have a first-past-the-post system where each constituency elects one representative based on who in the election wins the most votes.

- *Direct versus indirect elections of government*. Some countries have direct elections for certain posts, e.g. citizens of France and the USA directly elect their presidents with executive power to appoint ministers. In most countries citizens elect representatives who then, on the citizens' behalf, elect and monitor government and ministers.

- *Representative versus direct democracy.* In most countries citizens elect representatives to act on their behalf.

- *Centralisation of power.* There are variations between countries in the degree of power held by central, regional and local governments. For example, in federated countries like Australia and the USA, states wield quite a lot of power. In the UK central government has devolved quite a lot of functions to Scottish, Welsh, and Northern Irish assemblies.

Political systems matter for international business because they:

- Set the rules, and whose interests are served by the rules.

- Determine whether and how businesses can influence legislative processes through lobbying (mostly legal) or corruption (usually illegal).

- Influence how frequently, and in what ways the rules of the game for business change. This can be a major source of political risk, i.e. risk associated with political changes that may negatively affect domestic and foreign firms.

It is important to point out that many countries have features of both democratic and more totalitarian tendencies. In such counties some democratic institutions exist but in weak form, while totalitarian traits may deny or limit such institutions as free speech, independent media, multiple political parties, civil liberties, and the rule of law. This can be clearly seen in Russia, for example, where, by 2021, there were still elections and opposition parties, but independent media and civil liberties operated within political, legal and economic power concentrated at the centre of government. Robert Mugabe and his ZANU-PF party in Zimbabwe subverted democratic institutions and established a monopoly political power there from 1980 to his death in late 2019.

Political Systems

Democracy - political system in which citizens elect representatives to govern the country on their behalf.

Supports global business by preserving individuals right to freedom of expression and organisation.

Totalitarianism (or dictatorship) - system in which one person or party exercises absolute political control.

- Communist totalitarianism
- Right-wing totalitarianism
- Theocratic totalitarianism
- Tribal totalitarianism

In general, totalitarianism is not as good for business as democracy. Totalitarian nations often entail higher political risk due to wars, riots, protests, chaos and breakdowns, which can negatively impact firms.

2.4. Economic Systems

Keep in mind that a nation's political system and its economic system are connected. Indeed there is a whole area of study called political economy which focuses on production and trade—their relations with law, custom and government, and with the distribution of national income and wealth. As mentioned above, in countries where individual goals are given primacy over collective goals, free market systems are likely to exist; but in countries where collective goals are dominant, markets are likely to be restricted and state-owned enterprises are common. All have implications for firms operating internationally. An economic system refers to the rules of the game on how a country is governed economically. Broadly there are three types of economic system:

- *Market economy.* Here goods and services are privately owned and production quantities are determined by supply and demand. In a market economy, governments encourage free and fair competition and discourage monopolies. Note that, amongst countries, there have been very few *pure* market economies! In 2001, Hong Kong had the highest degree of economic freedom, but by 2021 there had been some noticeable government intervention its legal system and economy. The 2008/2009 financial crisis, and its aftermath, saw increased government intervention in many countries across the world, and more recent moves towards protectionism (see Chapter 1). The 2020–2021 crisis saw market economy ideas in flux as countries and supra-national institutions wrestled with how to reignite economic growth.

- *Command economy.* Here the government plans the goods and services that a country produces; the quantity in which they are produced; and the price at which they are sold. Businesses are state-owned and the government allocates resources for the good of society as a whole. Examples are the former Soviet Union, and, in 2020, North Korea. Socialist-inclined governments have sometimes moved their countries towards more government planning and state ownership—for example India and France—but in both cases these approaches have fallen into disfavour with more centrist or right wing governments coming into power.

- *Mixed economy.* Here elements of both a market economy and a command economy are present. Governments often take control of industries that are considered vital to national interests. During the 2008/2009 financial crisis, for example, the US government took an 80 percent share in AIG to stop the company from collapsing and damaging the broader financial system. Examples of mixed economies include France, UK, and Sweden in the 1980s, though subsequently all three counties have reduced state ownership and undertaken more privatisation. India, Brazil and Italy have also sought, over the years, to reduce their large state-owned sectors, though they still retained a number of such state-owned enterprises into 2021.

Most countries entered the third decade of the 21st century more or less as market economies—they organised themselves by market forces, but also had varying degrees of non-market coordination. The varieties-of-capitalism view (Hall and Soskice, 2001) embodies this reality, and suggests that, due to history, culture, resources, and other factors, countries can vary enormously on how they combine market and non-market mechanisms to coordinate economic activity. Moreover these economies will be constantly changing in the modern dynamic global environment. The view suggests two main types of economy:

- ***Coordinated market***. This operates through a system of coordinating by market signals together with a variety of other means, for example Italy, Netherlands, and Japan. Such economies may well have more employment protection, and less ability to raise capital through the stock market. In Germany, for example, employees have representatives on corporate boards (unlike in UK) and government is much more directly involved in vocational training. In Asia, many countries have embraced liberal market principles but also have a strong state providing direction and investment supporting the economic development path, e.g. South Korea, Singapore.

- ***Liberal market***. This operates through a system of coordination primarily through market signals. Hall and Soskice (2001) suggest UK, USA, Canada, and Australia were examples in 2000, though it is important not to understate the extent of government involvement in economic development even in these states. For example the 2008/2009 crisis prompted the UK and US governments to nationalise some banks and tighten banking regulations. The 2020–2021 crisis also saw greater government intervention in economies to attempt to restore stability and stimulate economic growth.

Indeed, the 2020–2021 pandemic and economic crisis led to a lot more government intervention in economies worldwide. Throughout 2020 commentators speculated as to how temporary the measures taken would be, and the degree to which some aspects of government control would become more permanent. Most commentators expected quite a lot of country variation.

2.5. Legal Systems

A legal system represents the formal rules that regulate behaviour, along with the processes by which the laws of a country are enforced and through which redress for grievances is obtained.

Why is it important for international managers to be familiar with different legal systems?

It is because a country's laws regulate business practice, define the manner in which business transactions are to be executed, and set down the rights and obligations of those involved in business transactions. The legal system impacts the attractiveness of a country as a business investment or a potential target market (see also Chapters 4 and 6). A country's legal system is strongly influenced by its political system. So, countries that are collectivistic, totalitarian states restrict private enterprise, while individualistic market economies support private enterprise and consumer rights. There are three broad types of legal system, though many legal systems are influenced by multiple legal traditions:

- **Common law** is based on tradition, precedent, and custom. So, judges look at how previous cases have been treated to decide how to treat current cases. Then, as new precedents are made, laws can be amended if necessary. Thus an important part of common law is case law, which is a rule of law created by precedents of cases in court. Common law is English in origin but has stretched to many English-influenced countries—in Africa, Asia, South Africa, also Canada and the USA—and is based on statutes, customs and court decisions. Judges are arbiters, and juries are decision-makers. The implications for business are greater freedom to design contracts and codes of practice. Detailed contracts are needed to fill in for gaps in the legal framework; more legal disputes involving much use of lawyers; and greater legal burden, may favour the more powerful companies.

- **Civil law** is based on a detailed set of laws organised into codes. This type of system, which is practised in more than 80 countries including Germany, Japan, and Russia, is less adversarial than common law because under civil law, judges only have the power to apply the existing law, not interpret the law. Here law is codified in books of law, and judges lead the proceedings including questioning and deciding. For businesses the implications tend to be relatively short contracts and codes of practice, and more consumer and employee protection available under the law. Businesses often complain about the bureaucracy of civil law, but civil law also often gives greater legal certainty. Examples include the French code civil, Germanic civil law and Nordic civil law.

- **Religious, or theocratic law** is based on religious teachings. Today, Islamic law is the most widely practised theocratic law system in the world. Example countries include Iran, Libya, Saudi Arabia, and Morocco. In practice, Islamic jurors and scholars have been struggling to apply the foundations of Islamic law to the modern world, including to commercial activities, and many Muslim countries today are actually practising Islamic law combined with common law or civil law. As one example, the Koran actually outlaws the payment or receipt of interest, and in some Islamic states this has been embodied in formal law. Sharia-compliant banking was about US$2 trillion in size in 2015, and operated in some 105 countries, but mostly in Turkey; Qatar; Kuwait; Iran; UAE; Saudi Arabia; and Malaysia.

Why is it important for international companies to be familiar with the legal system of the countries in which they operate? One key reason is because each system approaches the enforcement of contracts in a different way. So, suppose you come from a common law state, and you have signed an agreement with a company operating under a civil law system. Which law should apply? In order to deal with this type of scenario, as of 2016 about 83 countries had signed the United Nations Convention on Contracts for the International Sale of Goods, or CIGS, which established a uniform set of rules governing certain aspects of the making and performance of everyday contracts between sellers and buyers who have their places of business in different nations. One problem has been that important trading nations, like India and the United Kingdom, did not sign the convention.

Issues for international businesses

Legal systems are also important for dealing with several other important issues for international businesses:

- **Property rights.** Property rights are the legal rights over the use to which a resource is put and over the use of any income that may be derived from that resource. As you have probably already guessed, the laws on property rights differ across countries. In some countries, even though there are laws protecting property, the laws are not consistently enforced. Property rights can be violated through private actions and through public actions. Individuals perform private violations, like theft, piracy, or blackmail. Keep in mind that this type of violation can take place in any country, but in countries with weak legal systems, like Russia, it is a much bigger problem. When public officials, like politicians and bureaucrats, violate property rights, they might use legal mechanisms such as levying excessive taxes—as in Venezuela in the 2000s—requiring special expensive licences, or even simply taking assets into state control.

- **Intellectual property issues.** Intellectual property rights are rights associated with the ownership of intellectual property—which can include anything from computer software or a chemical formula for a new drug to a screenplay or a music score. Intellectual property can be protected in three ways:

a. A patent gives the inventor of a new product or process exclusive rights to manufacture, use, or sell the invention.

b. A copyright is the exclusive right of authors, composers, playwrights, artists, and publishers to publish and dispose of their work as they see fit.

c. A trademark is a design or name, which may be officially registered, that allows merchants or manufacturers to designate or differentiate their products.

Protection of intellectual property rights varies by country. China and Thailand have been among the world's biggest violators of intellectual property rights. Pirated products like Rolex watches, Levi's jeans, and computer software are widely available in both countries. In Latin America, about 68 percent of all software is pirated, and in China some studies estimate that the figure is 86 percent. Nearly 200 countries have signed the Paris Convention for the Protection of Industrial Property to protect intellectual property rights and are part of the World Property Organisation, but enforcement of property regulations is still lax in many countries. What can you do if your intellectual property is stolen? You can lobby your government to take action. You can also file your own lawsuit. For example, Starbucks was successful against a Chinese firm that opened stores that were virtually replicas of the traditional Starbucks store.

- *Product safety and product liability.* Product safety laws set certain standards to which a product must adhere and product liability involves holding a firm and its officers responsible when a product causes injury, death, or damage. These vary greatly across countries and this often leads to an ethical dilemma for companies. What should a company do if the standards in a foreign market are lower than the standards at home? Should they comply with home standards even if this puts them at a competitive disadvantage?

- *Corporate governance.* This involves the rules by which shareholders and other interested parties control corporate decision-makers. Variations across countries are closely related to differences in economic and legal systems. Generally, common law systems have evolved in ways that provide strong protection for financial investors i.e. shareholders. In civil law countries, for example Germany and Denmark, the law tends to offer less protection for shareholders and more rights to other stakeholders in the firm, for example, non-managerial employees who tend to be represented on corporate supervisory boards.

2.6. Country Development: Political, Economic, and Legal Issues

The political, economic, and legal environments of a country can have a significant impact on its economic development, and on its attractiveness as a potential investment location or target market. Economic development levels can be measured using gross national income per person, or GNI. But GNI measures can be misleading because they do not take into account cost of living differences. So, we adjust these numbers by purchasing power. Using purchasing power parity or PPP, we can adjust the numbers to reflect how far your money actually goes in a particular country. What does this mean for companies? Well, looking at a PPP adjusted GNI for India in 2007, we would conclude that the average Indian could only consume about 6 percent of the goods and services consumed by the average American. Should US firms have discounted India as a potential market then? No, because if we look a little deeper we would find that the country had an emerging middle class of about 100 million people, which represents a tremendous opportunity for foreign companies. Are there other ways to measure economic development? Nobel-prize winning economist Amartya Sen argues that rather than simply focusing on material output measures, like GNI per capita, we should consider the capabilities and opportunities people enjoy when measuring economic development. Sen (1999) believes that economic progress includes things like removing impediments to freedom—such as tyranny, poverty, and the neglect of public facilities—and a democratisation of political communities so that citizens have a voice in decisions. So Sen argues, for example, that providing basic health care and education is essential for economic growth. The UN has incorporated Sen's ideas in its Human Development Index, or HDI, which measures the quality of life in different countries. HDI is based on life expectancy at birth, educational attainment, and whether average incomes in a country are sufficient to meet the basic needs of life in that country.

Why do some countries succeed in economic development while others fail? Some argue that investment and technological progress explain capital accumulation, higher productivity and thus increasing economic success. Many policy makers and scholars contend that innovation and entrepreneurship are the engines of long-run economic growth, and that furthermore innovation and entrepreneurship require some form of market economy. In other words, new products and business processes can increase the productivity of labour and capital. Think of some of the innovations by Microsoft, Apple, Samsung or Dell—all of which were formed by entrepreneurs— and how they have changed not only the way of doing business, but also how many people live today. Similarly, innovation and entrepreneurship probably require strong property rights. If the innovations by Microsoft were not given protection, there would have been little incentive for the company to continue to develop new software and other products.

Others argue that human capital is the key to prosperity, so developing countries must invest in higher education. Others relate success to market friendly macro-economic policies by government, including low inflation; stable exchange rates; low trade barriers; and low government budget deficits. Peng and Meyer (2019) line up with the argument of North (2005) and see political, economic, and legal institutions as the basic determinants of a national economic performance because these influence incentives, and the costs of doing business:

- Institutions ensure that firms are able to make gains from trade.

- Lack of strong formal market-supporting institutions force firms to trade on a much more informal basis, incurring political, legal and economic risks in conditions of instability, and an over-dependency on informal relationships.

- Emerging formal market-supporting institutions support foreign firms moving into complicated long-distance trade with a country because they can see reasons for specialisation and growth in size, and making long-term commitments to international trade there.

- If property rights are protected, this will fuel innovation; entrepreneurship; more economic growth; and increased inward investment.

2.7. Beyond the Nation State: Regional Economic Integration

The idea behind regional economic integration is that, without trade barriers, member countries will be better off. However, there is some concern that as more countries become involved in regional agreements, the trading blocs will begin to compete against each other. We can observe across the world five levels of economic integration:

1. A *free trade area* removes all barriers to the trade of goods and services among member countries, but members determine their own policies toward nonmembers. The European Free Trade Area (EFTA) between Norway, Iceland, Liechtenstein, and Switzerland, is the most enduring free trade area. Another well-known free trade area is the North American Free Trade Area or NAFTA, though this was subject to major change during 2019–2020 (see below).

2. A *customs union* eliminates trade barriers between members, and adopts a common policy toward non-members. The EU began as a customs union, but, as we will discuss later, it has moved beyond this level of integration. The Andean Pact between Bolivia, Columbia, Ecuador, and Peru has been an example of a customs union.

3. A *common market* has no barriers to trading between members; has a common

policy toward non-members; and allows free movement of the factors of production. This is a significant step up from a customs union, and requires members to cooperate on fiscal, monetary, and employment policies. The EU was a common market for many years before moving to the next level of integration. Eventually, MERCOSUR, an agreement between Brazil, Argentina, Paraguay, and Uruguay, had hopes of becoming a common market.

4. The next level of economic integration is the ***economic union*** which involves the free flow of the factors of production between members; the adoption of a common external trade policy; a common currency; harmonisation of tax rates; and a common monetary and fiscal policy. So, again, this is a significant increase in integration from the previous level. The EU is currently an imperfect example of an economic union. For example, not all members have adopted the common currency (though the UK, with its pound sterling, formally left the EU in January 2020) and there are still differences in tax rates across the countries.

5. In a ***political union***, independent states are combined into a single union where the economic, social, and foreign policy of members is coordinated. An example is the USA. The EU has also headed toward this level, but some members have wanted limits placed on these ambitions.

Countries integrate for both economic and political reasons. We know, from our discussion of trade theory in Chapter 1, that free trade can be beneficial to countries. We will see that, for various reasons, trade barriers still exist despite the efforts of the World Trade Organisation (WTO). Regional economic integration offers countries a way to achieve the gains from free trade, at least on a limited basis, more quickly than would be possible under the processes offered by the WTO. The political case for integration has two main points. Firstly, by linking countries together; making them more dependent on each other; and forming a structure where they regularly have to interact, the chances of violent conflict and war decrease. Secondly, economic integration gives the bloc of countries greater power and makes them much stronger politically when dealing with other countries than if they were to act independently.

If integration is beneficial, why does it not occur more often? Two key issues limit integration. Firstly, while a nation as a whole benefits from integration, some groups may actually lose. Critics of NAFTA, for example, were concerned about the potential for job loss in the USA if companies shifted production to take advantage of Mexico's low cost labour. From 2016, the US administration has been more aggressive on these and other trade issues relative to Canada and Mexico. By 2020 it had renegotiated the treaties between the three countries. Secondly, countries that integrate their economies lose some degree of national sovereignty. Integration requires that countries give up some control over monetary policy, fiscal policy, and trade policy. For example, most of the countries belonging to the EU have given up their currencies and adopted the euro instead. Some economists point out that integration only makes sense when the amount of trade it creates is greater than the amount that it is diverting. Trade creation occurs when low cost producers within a free trade area replace high cost domestic producers, while trade diversion occurs when higher cost suppliers within a free trade area replace lower cost external suppliers.

2.8. Regional Integration in Europe

As we said, faced with the inevitable limitations of global institutions, many countries have chosen to organise themselves into regional blocs to pursue joint economic and sometimes political objectives. In this section we will look at some of the major economic blocs as examples only, remembering that there are many such blocs, though none as large as the ones described here.

In Europe, there is the European Union (EU), which is the world's most integrated group of countries with 27 members (the United Kingdom formally left in early 2020). The EU Single Market is based on freedom of movement of goods, capital, people, and services. This is implemented though harmonisation of regulation in some sectors, and mutual recognition of national regulation in others. The EU aims to facilitate free movement of people within the union, particularly to enable people to take up a job in another country. The euro has become a common currency in 16 countries that have transferred their monetary policy to the European Central Bank. EU competition policy aims to ensure that a competitive environment is maintained in cases of mergers and acquisitions, cartels, collusion and state aid. Formal political structures of the EU resemble a government, yet national governments wield power through the Council. The decision-making processes in the EU are based on democratic principles, yet they are often far removed from the individual citizens in member countries. Enlargement creates not only benefits but also costs for existing EU members, who thus may be less enthusiastic to admit further members. While a member, the UK had an ambiguous relationship with the EU, grounded in its history and its political culture. For example, like several other European countries, it refused to have the euro as its currency.

Today, The European Union consists of many countries. The original agreement between Belgium, France, West Germany, Italy, Luxembourg, and the Netherlands was expanded in 1973 to include Great Britain, Ireland, and Denmark. In 1981, Greece joined, then Spain and Portugal in 1986, and Austria, Finland, and Sweden in 1986. Ten more countries joined in 2004, and three more in 2007. The European Community was founded in 1957 by the Treaty of Rome. This became the European Union in 1993, after the Maastricht Treaty was ratified, extended political cooperation, and committed members to adopt a single currency by 1999. This created the single largest currency zone in the world after the US dollar. Euro notes and coins started circulating in 2002. However, three members, Britain, Denmark, and Sweden opted out of the eurozone. Five institutions govern the EU:

- *The European Council* resolves major policy issues and sets policy directions.

- *The European Commission* is responsible for implementing EU law and monitoring member states to ensure they are in compliance.

- *The Council of the European Union* is the ultimate controlling authority.

- *The European Parliament* debates legislation proposed by the commission and forwarded to it by the council.

- *The Court of Justice* acts as the supreme appeals court for EU law.

For our purposes, the most relevant aspect of the EU is the institutional framework it provides for business. Four aspects of EU policy shape greatly how international business can be done:

- *The 'single market'.* The EU has created an institutional framework that establishes many of the rules by which businesses compete. It has removed most internal trade barriers between member countries. Internal customs and passport controls have been abolished. A prime focus has been on establishing the four freedoms—free movement of people, goods, services, and capital amongst member countries. A common external tariff is applied to all imported goods across the customs union. The EU has attempted to harmonise— create common rules, standards and regulations on the free movement of goods—and has made considerable headway, but this has been a difficult and complex political process, with national or local regulations sometimes being allowed to stand if deemed more effective than EU stipulation. The single market for services has been even more difficult to implement. Service sectors like banking and telecommunications have complex regulatory regimes. Services always have some local component and common standards may be difficult to apply across different cultures, and customers with differing expectations. Moreover, and a bigger point for goods and services, harmonisation represents liberalisation and threatens protectionism in local markets.

- *The free movement of people.* People from EU member states are free to work in other EU countries, but there can be barriers. The EU has moved to guarantee mutual recognition of professional experience, qualifications, and training across EU countries. It has also encouraged the movement of EU students and the advancement of higher education across EU countries. The Schengen Agreement laid the basis for passport-free travel across member states, but also tightened regulations and policing for non-EU state citizens arriving at EU borders—the so-called Schengen area.

- *European competition policy.* The European commission regulates for competition issues such as over-dominant players, or illegal collusion, but only in cases involving multiple countries. National authorities are the regulators where only a national market is affected. The EU commission also looks to regulate mergers and acquisitions, including foreign mergers, if they seem to represent a substantial impediment to effective competition within the EU. Note that the EU also regulates governments, for example, when 'state aid' or subsidies are being offered to subsidise companies or protect local jobs, or make attractive a particular location to a multinational looking to make a foreign direct investment. Competition policy has numerous exceptions however, not least during the 2008/2009 financial crisis, when governments bailed out their home country banks.

- *The euro as a common currency.* Having one currency, rather than several, is easier for companies and individuals. The same currency is used across the bloc, so companies will save the cost and risks of converting currencies. Having a single currency will also make it easier to compare prices across Europe. Adopting a single currency will make it easier to do the same thing in Europe, and force companies to lower prices. The lower prices should then encourage producers to look for ways to reduce their production costs in order to maintain their profit margins. So, by adopting a common currency, we should see greater efficiency. Another benefit of the euro is that it should boost the development of a highly liquid pan-European capital market. Finally, the capital market will provide a greater range of investment options to individuals and institutions. While there are many benefits of adopting the euro, there are also some disadvantages. A major cost involved in adopting a common currency is that individual countries lose control over monetary policy. The three countries that opted out of the eurozone did so because they did not want to give up this autonomy. A second disadvantage of the euro is that the EU is not an optimal currency area; or an area where similarities in the underlying structure of economic activities make it feasible to adopt a single currency and use a single exchange rate as an instrument of macro-economic policy. In other words, because of differences in member economies—take Portugal and Finland for example—they might react differently to external shocks. So, a change in the euro exchange rate that helps Finland might actually hurt Portugal. Some critics have argued that instead of establishing the euro and then moving toward political union, the EU should have achieved political union status first.

In January 2020, the United Kingdom became the first member state to leave the EU. Following a 2016 referendum, the UK signified its intention to leave and negotiated a withdrawal agreement.

The UK was to be in a transitional phase until at least 31 December 2020, during which it remained subject to EU law and part of the EU single market and customs union. Before this, only three territories of member states had left the EU or its forerunners.

The EU is a significant, emerging superpower—even without the UK. Containing, in 2020, some 5.8 percent of the world population. In 2017, the EU (including the United Kingdom) had generated a nominal gross domestic product (GDP) of around US$20 trillion, constituting approximately 25 percent of global nominal GDP. Additionally, all EU countries have a very high Human Development Index, according to the United Nations Development Programme. Through the Common Foreign and Security Policy, the EU has developed a role in external relations and defence. The union maintains permanent diplomatic missions throughout the world and represents itself at the United Nations, the World Trade Organisation, the G7 and the G20.

2.9. Regional Integration in the Americas

We will now look at just three trade blocs in the Americas, and assess their levels of success:

The North American Free Trade Agreement (NAFTA)

This became law in 1994. Under NAFTA, tariffs on 99 percent of the goods traded between Mexico, Canada, and the USA were abolished, and so were most of the restrictions on the cross-border flow of services. The agreement also protected intellectual property, removed most restrictions on Foreign Direct Investment between the three countries, and allowed each country to maintain its own environmental standards. In addition, two commissions were established to intervene when environmental standard or legislation involving health and safety, minimum wages, or child labour are violated.

What are the benefits of NAFTA? NAFTA's supporters argued that it would provide economic gains to all members. Mexico should benefit from more jobs, as companies from Canada and the USA shift production south to take advantage of lower cost labour. The jobs would help Mexico grow economically, with the country looking to get preferential treatment for 80 percent of its exports. In the USA and Canada, consumers would benefit from the lower-priced products that come from Mexico, and companies would benefit not only from low cost labour, but also from having access to a large and more prosperous market.

How did NAFTA's critics see the agreement? NAFTA's critics worried that the loss of jobs and wage levels that were to occur as a result of NAFTA would be detrimental to the USA and Canada.

They also raised concerns that pollution would increase as companies shifted production to take advantage of Mexico's more lax environmental regulations. In addition, some critics raised concerns that Mexico would lose its sovereignty, as the country became dominated by US firms that were not really committed to helping the economy grow, but rather just saw it as a cheap assembly location.

After the first decade of NAFTA, most people agreed that both the critics and the supporters of the agreement were probably guilty of exaggeration. By most statistical measures NAFTA had been a success, with trade between the countries and FDI into Mexico growing very fast indeed. For example, studies showed that the concern over jobs turned out to be a non-issue. Jobs in Mexico boomed while job losses in USA were very small. Some US firms persevered because most components in Mexican assembly plants used US-made parts, unlike Asian-based assembly plants. One positive that came from the agreement was increased political stability in Mexico. This, of course, may also be beneficial to the USA and Canada. Some Mexican critics pointed out that job gains have stagnated as USA and Canadian multinationals shifted more work to China rather than Mexico. The future may well see some enlargement with several other Latin American countries, including Chile indicating that it would like to join.

But NAFTA's more recent history has been more problematic, partly because of the more aggressive negotiating stance adopted by the US administration elected in 2016. After US President Donald Trump took office in January 2017, he sought to replace NAFTA with a new agreement, beginning negotiations with Canada and Mexico. In July 2017, the US administration provided a detailed list of changes that it would like to see to NAFTA. The top priority was a reduction in the United States' trade deficit. The administration also called for the elimination of provisions that allowed Canada and Mexico to appeal duties imposed by the United States and limited the ability of the United States to impose import restrictions on Canada and Mexico. The list also alleged subsidised state-owned enterprises and currency manipulation. From June to late August 2018, Canada was sidelined as the United States and Mexico held bilateral talks. On 27th August 2018, Mexico and the United States announced they had reached a bilateral understanding on a revamped NAFTA trade deal that included provisions that would boost automobile production in the US According to an article in *The Economist*, on 30th August 2018, the deal *put the Mexican car industry into a straightjacket.'* For example, Mexico agreed to increase the rules of origin threshold, which would mean that 75 percent, as opposed to the previous 62.5 percent, of a vehicle's components must be made in North America to avoid tariffs. The deal also included a 10-year data protection period against generic drug production on an expanded list of products that benefits pharmaceutical companies—particularly US makers producing high-cost biologic drugs. There was also a 'sunset clause'—a 16-year expiration date with regular 6-year evaluations, to possibly renew the agreement for additional 16-year terms; and an increased de minimis threshold in which Mexico raised the de minimis value to $100 from $50 regarding online duty- and tax-free purchases. (The de minimis threshold refers to the value of imported goods below which no duty or tax is collected, and the customs declaration is very simple.)

Negotiations with Canada followed. According to an August 2018 article in the *Ottawa Citizen*, key issues under debate included supply management; pharmaceuticals; cultural exemption; the sunset clause; and de minimis thresholds. In September 2018, the United States, Mexico, and Canada reached an agreement to replace NAFTA with the United States–Mexico–Canada Agreement (USMCA). NAFTA remained in force, pending the ratification of the USMCA. In January 2020, the revised agreement was signed into law in the USA.

A range of trade experts have said that changing trade relations would have a range of unintended consequences for the US, including reduced access to the US's biggest export markets; a reduction in economic growth; and increased prices for gasoline, cars, fruits, and vegetables. The worst affected sectors would be textiles, agriculture and automobiles. According to Chad P. Bown, senior fellow at the Peterson Institute for International Economics, *"a renegotiated NAFTA that would re-establish trade barriers is unlikely to help workers who lost their jobs—regardless of the cause—take advantage of new employment opportunities."* Others have suggested that repealing NAFTA will not lead to increased car production in the USA.

Was NAFTA so bad for the USA? The new agreement certainly saw a move towards trade barriers and protectionism by the USA. In a 2015 report, the Congressional Research Service summarised multiple studies as follows: *"In reality, NAFTA did not cause the huge job losses feared by the critics or the large economic gains predicted by supporters. The net overall effect of NAFTA on the US economy appears to have been relatively modest, primarily because trade with Canada and Mexico accounts for a small percentage of US GDP. However, there were worker and firm adjustment costs as the three countries adjusted to more open trade and investment among their economies."*

Andean Community and Mercosur

It is useful to look at regional blocs that are less successful. The Andean Pact between Bolivia, Chile, Ecuador, Columbia, and Peru was formed in 1969, and modelled on the EU. However, by the mid-1980s, it was clear that the Pact had more or less failed to achieve any of its goals. In the late 1980s though, many Latin American countries began to adopt free market policies, and in 1990 the Andean Pact was re-launched, and operated as a customs union. In 2003, the Andean Community signed an agreement with MERCOSUR to work toward a free trade area. You will recall that Mercosur is South American trade bloc. It established by the Treaty of Asunción in 1991 and Protocol of Ouro Preto in 1994. Full members are Argentina, Brazil, Paraguay and Uruguay.

Mercosur began in 1988 as a free trade agreement between Brazil and Argentina. It was expanded to include Paraguay and Uruguay in 1990, and has been making progress toward free trade between the countries. However, some critics have argued that, rather than creating trade, Mercosur, by establishing high tariffs to outside countries, is actually diverting trade in some industries, and that companies in these industries would be unable to compete in global markets. In recent years, the future of this group has been unstable, not least because of politics. Venezuela pulled out of the Andean Community in protest against Colombia and Peru signing trade deals with the USA. Uruguay demanded the right to sign a separate trade deal with the USA despite being a Mercosur member. The central problem has been that members of both trade blocs actually trade very little with each other but mainly with the USA. Other economic blocs have been proposed but seem hard to organise and sustain in the difficult political disunity of the continent.

With the cooperation agreement with Mercosur, the Andean Community gained four new associate members: Argentina, Brazil, Paraguay, and Uruguay. These four Mercosur members were granted associate membership by the Andean Council of Foreign Ministers. They met in an enlarged session with the Commission (of the Andean Community) on 7 July 2005. This move reciprocated the actions of Mercosur, which granted associate membership to all the Andean Community nations by virtue of the Economic Complementarity Agreements (Free Trade Agreements) signed between the CAN and individual Mercosur members.

Mercosur's purpose is to promote free trade and the fluid movement of goods, people, and currency. As you can see, since its foundation, Mercosur's functions have been updated and amended many times; it currently confines itself to a customs union, in which there is free intra-zone trade and a common trade policy between member countries. The official languages are Spanish, Portuguese, and Guarani.

The bloc comprises a population of more than 270 million people, and the combined Gross Domestic Product of the full-member nations is in excess of US$3.0 trillion a year (US$3.393 trillion in 2018) making Mercosur the fifth-largest economy in the World. It is the fourth-largest trading bloc after the European Union.

The working of Mercosur has not met with universal approval within interested countries. Chile has, to a certain extent, preferred to pursue bilateral agreements with trading partners, and there have been calls from Uruguayan politicians to follow this example.

Mercosur signed free trade agreements with Israel in December 2007; with Egypt in August 2010; the State of Palestine in December 2011; and Lebanon on 18th December 2014.

In 2016, Brazilian presidents, Dilma Rousseff, and later Michel Temer, along with Argentine

President Macri began to place pressure to negotiate a free trade agreement between Mercosur and the European Union and other Latin American nations. In June 2019, the European Union–Mercosur Free Trade Agreement was confirmed. The bilateral trade deal opens 100 percent of EU trade and 90 percent of Mercosur trade. The deal, however, has taken a long time to be ratified.

2.10. Regional Integration in Asia Pacific

One of the most important efforts in Asia Pacific is the Association of South East Asian Nations, or ASEAN. ASEAN was formed in 1967 with five founding nations, later increased to 10, including Brunei; Cambodia; Indonesia; Laos; Malaysia; Myanmar; The Philippines; Singapore; Thailand; and Vietnam. There are two observer nations: Papua New Guinea and Timor Leste. ASEAN's goals are to promote free trade between members and achieve cooperation on industrial policy, but so far, it has made only slow progress. However, a new agreement between the six original members came into effect in 2003 to create a free trade area, with the creation of the ASEAN Economic Community by 2015.

Across all nations of ASEAN, there is a population of over 622 million people. The region has one of the largest economies in the world, and it is believed that by 2050, it will have the 4th-largest economy in the world. It also has one of the largest labour forces in the world, falling behind only India and China. The total region stretches across over 1.7 million square miles. The organisation focuses on boosting economic and trade growth, with all member states having a free trade agreement. Travel within the region is also easier for member states. All member states have signed a treaty against the development of nuclear weapons. Most have also signed on to a counter-terrorism pact. Technical and research cooperation is also promoted across the member states. Initiatives include overseeing the protection of the environment and wildlife through the Centre for Biodiversity.

ASEAN has suffered because members' main trading partners—USA, Japan, China, and Europe—are outside the ASEAN bloc. On average intra-ASEAN trade has represented only 27.6 percent of ASEAN country exports. Size of intra-ASEAN trade also varies from country to country so benefits of membership are unevenly distributed. Furthermore, ASEAN experiences internal political tensions, and much more economic, religious, and cultural diversity than, say, the EU.

However ASEAN does act as a group in negotiating agreements with other countries, or groups like the EU for which it is an important trading partner. It has signed free trade agreements with Korea, Japan, Australia, and New Zealand; and the ASEAN China Free Trade Agreement—effective

2010—fundamentally converting a major rival into a potential partner in raising exports and GDP for all parties.

As a region, ASEAN has undeniably grown in importance. Southeast Asia is quickly establishing itself as an Industry 4.0 hub. Geopolitically, it has become a valuable site of contention with major powers such as the USA and China looking to establish their influence over the region. In 2018, in response to US President Donald Trump's more insular policies, ASEAN proposed a trade agreement of its own: The Regional Comprehensive Economic Partnership (RCEP). The RCEP could be one of the biggest trade deals in history as it would encompass 25 percent of global gross domestic product (GDP); 45 percent of the total population; 30 percent of global income; and 30 percent global trade. Other countries involved in this trade agreement are India; China; Japan; South Korea; Australia; and New Zealand. But passing the agreement has been a challenge on its own. In 2018, ASEAN and the countries involved missed its fourth deadline to sign the deal, despite having negotiations for more than a year. It was reported in November 2019, however, that Southeast Asian countries were committed to signing the mega Asia Pacific trade pact in 2020. ASEAN Secretary-General Lim Jock Hoi had also said that ASEAN leaders, together with their counterparts from the five RCEP participating countries had agreed to push forward and sign the trade pact in 2020.

2.11. The Multilateral Monetary and Trade Systems

We have looked at formal institutions operating at country and regional level, but firms operating internationally also have to bear in mind the influence and impact on the business environment of two international institutions—the International Monetary Fund (IMF) and the World Trade Organisation (WTO). Both have their supporters and detractors.

The International Monetary Fund

The IMF is a multilateral organisation promoting international monetary cooperation and providing temporary financial assistance to countries with balance of payments problems. It has three primary activities on behalf of its 189 member countries:

1. Monitoring the global economy.

2. Providing technical assistance to developing countries.

3. Lending to countries in financial difficulties.

Any country can apply to join, as long as it meets a few requirements. These include providing information about its economy and paying in a sum of money called a quota subscription. The richer the country, the higher its quota.

The IMF's lending activity focuses on helping countries with severe balance of payment problems. The IMF acts as a lender of last resort, with loan repayments typically expected within one to five years. As one example, IMF bailouts in 2008/2009 were to Hungary (US$15.7 billion); Iceland (US$2.1 billion); Ukraine (US$16.4 billion); Romania (US$17.1 billion); Latvia(US$2.4 billion); Georgia (US$0.75 billion); Armenia(US$0.54 billion); Belarus (US$2.6 billion); Pakistan(US$7.6 billion); and Serbia (US$0.53 billion). There have been quite a few more since! These loans are mainly funded by quota subscriptions. In 2018, Argentina received the largest loan in the IMF's history at US$57billion. The IMF can lend its members a total amount of US$1trillion.

IMF loans come with strings attached. **IMF conditionality** typically imposes conditions that require 'belt-tightening' by pushing governments to embark on reforms that they probably would not have undertaken otherwise. To attack inflation and government deficits, the IMF typically looks for cuts in government expenditure, amongst other things, in agreement with that government. In principle the conditions imposed are designed to also ensure the country can repay its IMF loans. In the 1990s and early 2000s the IMF often went into action in emerging economies including Mexico; Russia; Indonesia; South Korea; Turkey; and Brazil. The financial crisis of 2008 and subsequent events, for example the financial crises in Greece, Spain, Ireland, and Portugal in 2010-2012, led to renewed debates around the pros and cons of IMF conditionality. Criticisms include:

- The IMF's lack of accountability. It has very few officials, who are not elected and do not always have deep knowledge of the country being bailed out.

- The IMF's 'one-size-fits-all' economic strategy may be inappropriate. Some economists argue that balancing the budget may not be the best policy; that deficit spending has been a successful policy for pulling countries out of crisis; that cutting spending in more vulnerable developing countries undergoing a major economic crisis to balance the budget may make matters much worse, not better. On the other hand, some critics have argued that the IMF has sometimes not been tough enough, allowing countries to run up deficits not sustainable in the medium and long term.

- Bear in mind, of course, that it is difficult to say whether IMF policies are better or worse than the alternatives, because it is difficult to know what would have happened if a country had not adopted IMF recommendations.

- A major limitation identified in the 2008-2013 crisis is that the IMF has no power over countries that do not need its loans despite having large budget or current deficits. Notable cases are the USA and the EU.

The IMF continued operations throughout 2020–2021. Trade tensions, weak economic growth, a slowdown in manufacturing and companies' debts, and the impact of the coronavirus pandemic, were big topics throughout 2020. Through the fund and other activities, such as the gathering of statistics and analysis; surveillance of its members' economies; and the demand for particular policies, the IMF continued to work to improve the economies of its member countries. The organisation's objectives stated in the Articles of Agreement are: to promote international monetary co-operation; international trade; high employment; exchange-rate stability; sustainable economic growth; and making resources available to member countries in financial difficulty. IMF funds come from two major sources: quotas and loans. Quotas, which are pooled funds of member nations, generate most IMF funds. The size of a member's quota depends on its economic and financial importance in the world. Nations with larger economic importance have larger quotas. The quotas are increased periodically as a means of boosting the IMF's resources in the form of special drawing rights.

What are the achievements of the IMF? The IMF is often described as a 'lender of last resort'. In times of crisis, countries look to it for financial assistance. Economists like Harvard University's Benjamin Friedman have said it's difficult to measure the organisation's success because we can't know if its policies are ***"worse than whatever the alternative would have been"***. However, some praised the Fund's role in supporting Mexico after it declared it would be unable to repay its debts in the early 1980s. More recently, Brazil obtained IMF loans in 2002 to avoid defaulting on its debts. The government was able to turn the economy around relatively quickly, and pay off its entire debt two years ahead of schedule.

What are the main criticisms? The conditions the IMF imposes on countries to which it lends money have sometimes been described as 'harsh'. In the past, these have included lower government borrowing, cutting corporate taxes and opening up their economies to foreign investment. It was in Greece that the eurozone financial crisis started back in 2009, and Greece was the hardest-hit economy. After it received bailout loans from the IMF, Greece had to make some changes. Critics said the austerity—intended to get government borrowing needs down—was excessive and did damage to the economy and society. The unemployment rate in Greece still remained high at 17 percent in 2020, down from a peak of over 27 percent in 2013.

The World Trade Organisation

In the late 1940s the world community developed several institutions to facilitate international trade and political integration. These included the United Nations, the International Monetary Fund and World Bank, together with the General Agreement on Tariffs and Trade (GATT), and its successor, the World Trade Organisation (WTO).

GATT was created in 1948 to reduce the levels of tariffs amongst participating countries. By the 1980s it had been successful but had left out trade in services and intellectual property protection. For trade regulation there were a lot of loopholes requiring reform. Moreover GATT's success in removing tariff barriers led to countries developing non-tariff barriers, and GATT did not have effective dispute resolution mechanisms for these. In 1995 participating countries extended GATT by creating the WTO.

The WTO is the main multilateral organisation making rules for international trade, and resolving trade-related conflicts between nations. It has both political and economic functions. Peng and Meyer (2019) suggest that in recent years it has focused on:

- Handling disputes constructively. Its role here has increased in recent years.

- Making life easier for all participants. This involves setting out a common set of rules for international trading partners. For example, the WTO's ***principle of non-discrimination*** means that a country cannot discriminate against some trading partners and not others.

- If you lower tariffs for one WTO member country you must do so for all WTO members (regional trade groups are an exception here—see below).

- Raising incomes, generating jobs, and stimulating economic growth. The essential role here is cutting trade barriers, with the WTO estimating that if it helped cut trade barriers by a third, this would raise worldwide income by about US$600 billion. There is a debate however, about the environmental impacts of more trade, and how it is conducted and who benefits.

The WTO has six main areas:

1. The umbrella agreement establishing the WTO.

2. The old GATT agreement covering international trade of goods.

3. A new agreement covering the trade in services—General Agreement on Trade in Services.

4. An agreement covering intellectual property rights—Trade-Related Aspects of Intellectual Property Rights.

5. Trade dispute settlement mechanisms.

6. Trade policy review for looking at an individual country's trade policies.

Clearly, the WTO does a lot more than was previously done under GATT, though developing countries often complain that agricultural policies of developed countries were not included under the WTO remit. In recent years it undertook two major initiatives:

- *Trade dispute settlement.* The WTO has a procedure to resolve conflicts between governments over trade-related matters. You can see these at work in the cases you will look at in the Activity below. The procedure is designed to avoid the weaknesses of the old GATT system, which saw long delays, blocking by accused countries, and lack of enforcement. The WTO first facilitates negotiations between the parties, but if consultation fails, it establishes a group of experts to hear the evidence, write a report and adjudicate. All this happens within 12 months (or 15 months if there is an appeal). A limitation is that the WTO does not have its own enforcement capability. It makes a recommendation, not an order. It is up to the offending country to change its practices or not, though the WTO can authorise the winning countries to impose trade sanctions and tariff barriers to encourage compliance.

- *The Doha Development Agenda.* Also called the Doha Round, initiated in Qatar in 2001. This was the first time the WTO participating countries established the aim of promoting economic development for developing countries. The four ambitions were to (1) reduce agricultural subsidies in developed countries; (2) cut tariffs, especially in industries of interest to developing countries, e.g. textiles; (3) free up trade in services; and (4) strengthen intellectual property protection. You might guess which group of countries supported which aim! However, by 2003 numerous countries had failed to deliver on their promises of 2001. The development agenda continued to be problematic into the 2020s.

Agriculture has been a particular problem with developing countries demanding that Japan, the EU, and USA reduce farm subsidies, but this was rejected. Meanwhile, partly in retaliation, developing countries, led by India, refused to tighten protection on intellectual property and make concessions on service trade. By the 2006 round in Geneva there was still little movement on global agreements, though, outside the WTO altogether, regional and bilateral (between country) agreements were accelerating, and have been since then. One example of such an agreement is the Australia-New Zealand Closer Economic Relations Trade Agreement (ANZCERTA or CER). The USA has signed 17 bilateral free trade and investment agreements with countries as diverse as Australia, Singapore, Peru, Oman, and Jordan, while three more are in the process of ratification. Advocates of bilateral FTAs see them as a convenient substitute for global free trade. Critics argue they: permit countries with large markets to use their bargaining power more effectively; lead to a hub and spoke system of international trade that further strengthens the countries at the hubs; and create fragmented rules for businesses operating in multiple countries, and increase trade diversion.

Here are some criticisms of the WTO:

- *Free Trade benefits developed countries more than developing countries.* It is argued, developing countries need some trade protection to be able to develop new industries; this is important to be able to diversify the economy. It is known as the 'infant industry argument'. Many developed economiesused a degree of tariff protection in their development phase. Economist Ha Joon Chang argues WTO trade rules are like *"pulling away the ladder they used themselves to climb up"* (see his book: *'Kicking Away The Ladder ...'* (Anthem Press, 2003)).

- *Most favoured nation principle.* This is a core tenet of WTO rules—countries should trade without discrimination. It means a local firm is not allowed to favour local contractors. But it is argued that this gives an unfair advantage to multinational companies, can have costs for local firms, and hurt the right of developing economies to favour their own emerging industries.

- *Failure to reduce tariffs on agriculture.* Free trade is not equally sought across different industries. Both the US and EU retain high tariffs on agriculture, which hurts farmers in developing economies who face tariff protection.

- *Diversification*. Arguably developing countries that specialise in primary products (e.g. agricultural products) need to diversify into other sectors. To diversify they may need some tariff protection, at least in the short term. Many of the existing industrialised nations used tariff protection when they were developing. Therefore, the WTO has been criticised for being unfair and ignoring the needs of developing countries.

- *Environment.* Free trade has often ignored environmental consideration; e.g. free trade has enabled imports to be made from countries with the least environmental protection. Many criticise the WTO's philosophy that the most important economic objective is the maximisation of GDP. In an era of global warming and potential environmental disaster, increasing GDP may be the least important objective. Arguably the WTO should do more to promote environmental considerations.

- ***Free trade ignores cultural and social factors.*** Debatably, a reasonable argument for restricting free trade is that it enables countries to maintain cultural diversity. Some criticise the WTO for enabling the domination of multinational companies, which reduce cultural diversity and tend to swamp local industries and firms.

- ***The WTO is criticised for being undemocratic.*** It is suggested that its structure enables richer countries to win what they desire; arguably they benefit the most.

- ***Slow progress.*** Trade rounds have been notoriously slow and difficult to reach an agreement.

- ***WTO has become overshadowed*** by TIPP agreements, which fall outside the spread of WTO rules.

There are responses to these criticisms, for example:

- Failure of countries to agree tariff reduction in agriculture is not the fault of the WTO, but of countries themselves.

- Free trade and growth of exports have been an important factor in raising living standards, especially in Southeast Asia, which has benefitted from the remarkable growth of world trade.

- The growth of world trade has helped reduce absolute poverty.

- In recent years, the WTO has made more efforts to consider the situation of developing economies. Recent rounds have put pressure on developed countries to accelerate removing restrictions on imports from the least-developing countries.

- The WTO has over 160 members representing 98 percent of world trade. Over 20 countries are seeking to join the WTO.

- WTO has been given credit for helping to avoid trade disputes.

During 2019, and early 2020, the WTO faced challenges on multiple fronts. The organisation's Dispute Settlement Body (DSB) faced several systemic tests. The first of these was the viability of the Appellate Body (AB). Due to the retirement of previous AB members, and the continued refusal of the United States to appoint new ones before its concerns over the AB are addressed by the WTO membership, there were only three sitting members on the AB. Unless WTO members agreed to appoint new members, this number would fall to one by December 2019—at which point the AB would no longer be able to function. At the end of 2018, the EU, China, India and nine other WTO members proposed modifications to the Dispute Settlement Understanding (DSU) that would, in their view, provide solutions to all of the issues on which the United States has criticised the functioning of the AB for the previous 12 months; the United States, however, rejected all elements of the proposal. Some observers believed that the United States may have already decided to put the AB out of business at the end of 2019, and that it had no intention, before then, of engaging with other members to try to correct the AB practices about which it had complained.

There were multiple unsettled disputes between countries not being resolved at the WTO during 2019. As just one example, WTO ruling in China's favour on some issues, and against the USA, has led some to believe the USA would threaten to leave the WTO. Finally, despite the proposals by some members to reform the WTO in 2018 (e.g. with respect to agricultural and industrial subsidies, state-owned enterprises, etc.), members appeared to be far away from finding common ground on which to start a serious discussion—let alone an eventual negotiation—on elements of WTO reform. Director-General Roberto Azevêdo continued to hold consultations on the subject in 2019, but it appeared doubtful that members would be able to forge agreement around a single agenda in the near future.

Other multilateral organisations

While the WTO and IMF are the most important multilateral organisations, there are others—not least the United Nations, whose mission is to secure world peace. Peng and Meyer (2018) usefully organise all these in terms of three agendas driving global collaboration and negotiation. Inevitably they will all be extended as a result of the 2020–2021 pandemic and economic crises. The major initiatives are:

- *The economic development agenda*. As two examples, the World Bank supports major projects that otherwise would not get off the ground, particularly in developing economies. The European Bank for Reconstruction and Development serves transition economies, mainly in Central and Eastern Europe. There are also regional development banks such as the Asian development Bank based in Manila; The Inter-American Development Bank based in Washington; and the African Development Bank based in Abidjan (Ivory Coast). Worried by traditional WTO control by USA and Europe, emerging 'BRIC' economies formed a 'New Development Bank', while China led a new development bank—the Asia Infrastructure Investment Bank—focused on infrastructure investment in Asia Pacific. Two years after its formation, 80 countries had joined its governance structure, and the bank had approved 24 projects in 11 countries.

- *The climate change agenda*. A major global concern is the environmental impact of human activity. The chief focus has been on the detrimental global warming effects of greenhouse gas emissions. The 1997 Kyoto protocol got developed countries pledging to cut GHG emission levels by 6 percent from 1990 to 2012. Unfortunately, the USA, the leading emitter at the time, refused to sign the protocol. Nor did the protocol include India and China, which developed very fast, with China becoming by 2009 the leading source of GHG. The 2009 Copenhagen meeting of countries agreed that more action had to be taken, but sparked disagreements about exactly who had to do what by when. The result was a weak non-binding Copenhagen Accord. This remains a difficult issue on which to make global progress. In December 2015, in the Paris Agreement, many countries made substantive commitments towards creating a sustainable low carbon future. These included keeping the rise in global temperature to below 2C above pre-industrial levels, and investing US$100 billion to support this aim. By 2018, 195 countries had signed the agreement, but the USA announced its intention to withdraw. By 2021 little further progress had been made on this agenda, partly hampered by the pandemic and ensuing economic crisis.

- *The financial sector regulation agenda*. Bank crashes can harm not just the home country but can have adverse consequences internationally. A country like UK, for example, is responsible for regulating its own banks, including foreign subsidiaries, and can constrain foreign banks operating in the UK. The Basel Committee for Bank Supervision disseminates minimum regulatory standards, revised in 2004, and known as Basel II; revised again in 2011 as Basel III. This established minimum requirements for liquidity, and procedures for risk metrics. In the aftermath of the 2008 financial crisis these have been criticised as inadequate. Some argue that national regulation of international banks is not enough. However, there is, as yet, no agreement as to how global bank supervision could be carried out. There are also real dilemmas in banking regulations that need to focus on basic capital requirements for a bank, and on how to assess the riskiness of a bank's investment portfolio. A bank wants to lower its financial reserves, while lending to high interest customers. Meanwhile policy objectives for the financial system would include financial stability combined with lending to encourage entrepreneurs and innovators. As a result, risk-rating agencies, like Fitch and Moody's, play an important role in assigning ratings to different assets and these ratings can then indirectly affect how much equity a bank needs to hold. This can have undesirable impacts, for example causing investors to make similar decisions about a bank, thus creating a systemic impact and risk. Ratings by Moody's and Fitch of sovereign bonds issued by governments can also have impacts on a government's ability to raise capital in the financial markets, and also influence a government's spending plans.

2.12. Conclusion

In this chapter we introduced the institution-based perspective on international business; pointed out that there are both formal and informal institutions in countries, and that these may differ across countries. The key functions of institutions are to reduce uncertainty, reduce transaction costs, and constrain opportunism. In practice, firms operating abroad should have a thorough understanding of the formal institutions of each country they are in, or are thinking of entering.

We detailed the main types and characteristics of political, economic, and legal systems found in the world; the debates surrounding these different systems; and pointed out the implications of these in terms of establishing the rules of the game for and challenges in conducting business internationally. We then moved on to look at a five-type model of formal institutions at the regional level. The chapter then detailed the major examples of trading blocs, the first being the political institutions of the EU, and how and why the institutional framework created by the EU is pivotal for business. We then described the advantages and disadvantages of regional and bilateral economic integration in the Americas and Asia Pacific. Finally, at cross-regional level, we assessed the multilateral institutions of the global monetary and trade systems, and their current challenges.

From 2016, we saw a number of emerging trends gaining a higher profile. The United Kingdom had voted, in 2016, to leave the European Union. Whatever the outcome, this threw a lot of uncertainty into both the United Kingdom's economic position, and also that of the European member states. In January 2020 the UK formally left the EU. But the challenges for the UK and EU would not work themselves through until 2023 at the earliest.

Meanwhile Donald Trump's election as US president in 2016, saw the USA fall out with several economic blocs—not least in South America and Europe, but also aggressive trade stances with China. By 2018 the pattern of political, economic and social disruption looked set to continue across the course of the first term of the presidency. Meanwhile China continued to invest in many countries on many fronts (through the so-called 'Belt and Road' Initiative), while stretching its national logistics routes across many parts of Central Asia and into Europe. Its 'Made In China 2025' plan also set out to use subsidies and protectionism to create world leaders in ten industries, covering nearly 40 percent of its manufacturing. Conflicts in the Middle East, Northern Europe, Africa, and several other parts of the globe looked set to continue to make international trade unpredictable, while populism and swings to right wing politics in many countries also unsettled trading environments. Chinese and Russian expansionism continued to add to the dynamism and unpredictability of the international business environment. All this has threatened the stability of institutions in many countries, resulting in the need for much more thorough and regular analysis of environmental and institutional factors on the part of international businesses. When the coronavirus pandemic hit in early 2020, this only made institutional resilience even more urgent, and likewise the need for international businesses to scan their environments ever more rigorously. How this resilience can be achieved will be one important storyline going forward from 2021.

Clearly these national, regional, and global institutions are highly important shapers of how business can be conducted internationally. However, they are not the only—and often not the most important—rules of the game with which international business needs to contend. In the next chapter we follow the institution-based perspective through into the area of informal institutions embracing culture; social norms; religion; language; and ethics. We then consider how business organisations respond to formal and informal institutional frameworks by exploring their approaches to corporate social responsibility.

References

Chang, H. (2003), *Kicking Away The Ladder*, Anthem Press, London, UK

Hall, P. and Soskice, D. (eds). (2001), *Varieties of Capitalism*, Oxford University Press, Oxford, UK

North, D. (2005), *Understanding The Process of Economic Change*, Princeton University Press, Princeton, USA

Peng, M. and Meyer, K. (2019), *International Business*, Cengage Learning, London, UK

Peng, M. Wang, D. and Jiang, Y. (2008), 'An Institution-Based View of International Business Strategy', *Journal Of International Business*, 19, 920-936.

Sen, A. (1999), *Development As Freedom*, Anchor Publishing, London, UK

Williamson, O. (1985), *The Econmic Institutions of Capitalism*, Free Press, New York, USA

'A nation's culture resides in the hearts and souls of its people'

M. Gandhi

'Present global culture is a kind of arrogant newcomer. It arrives on the planetary stage following four and a half billion years of other acts, and... declares itself in possession of eternal truths. But in a world that is changing as fast as ours, this is a prescription for disaster'

C. Sagan

Chapter 3

Cultural Social and Ethical Challenges: Towards Corporate Social Responsibility

3.1. Introduction

If you ever visit a foreign country, you will notice a lot of differences in how people dress, the food they eat, or their choice of transportation. Perhaps a particular religion influences how society works, or a different language is spoken. In time you will notice that the people also have different gestures and manners, and different rituals, codes of behaviour, and ways of working. All of these things are manifestations of culture. And just as you would adapt for differences from home, when doing business in foreign countries, firms need to adapt as well.

In this chapter we look at the informal institutions firms need to take into account when operating internationally. **Informal institutions** are rules that are not formalised, but exist as norms, values and ethics. In situations where **formal institutions** are unclear or fail, informal institutions tend to play a bigger role in reducing uncertainty. In particular we will focus on the differences between countries in culture; religion; language; ethics, and approaches to corporate social responsibility. Culture is a system of values and norms that are shared among a group of people and that, when taken together, constitute a design for living. Values are abstract ideas about what a group believes is good, right, and desirable; and norms are the social rules and guidelines that prescribe appropriate behaviour in particular situations. Long-standing cultural differences still influence how business is being done. Also, bear in mind that culture is dynamic—always changing. It is also important to consider how culture might affect the cost of doing business in a particular location.

We also discover, in this chapter, that managers and firms ignorant of foreign languages and religious traditions may end up making mistakes that harm their business. We also explore different approaches to ethics in international business, and how variations in ethics across countries can create ethical dilemmas, as can a range of differences about dealing with such issues as the environment, labour, human rights, and corruption. What relevance does the recent development of corporate social responsibility (CSR) have to such ethical dilemmas?

We explore firms' different CSR strategies, and whether CSR is vital to, or a diversion from, what international firms need to be focusing on.

3.2. Cultures and International Business

Informal institutions come from socially transmitted information and are part of the heritage that we call culture. They tell individuals in a society what behaviours are considered right and proper, and what would be unacceptable. Typically, cultures have no clearly defined origin, but have evolved over time. Those within a society tend to perceive their own culture as *'natural, rational, and morally right'*. This self-centred mentality is known as **ethnocentrism**. Culture can be seen as the collective programming of the mind that develops over time, which distinguishes the members of one group or category of people from another. Though we talk, for example about French culture, or Chinese culture, culture is not necessarily divided by national boundaries. Some countries like Switzerland even have multiple, distinct cultures. Similarly, some cultures transcend national boundaries. For example, you might think of how the values promoted by Islam influence many countries.

Culture has been described as *'the way things are done round here'*, and also as the shared norms, values and assumptions of a group, organisation, or society that translate into distinctive behaviours. Values are a fundamental building block of culture. They provide the context within which a society's norms are established and justified. Values can include things like a society's attitudes toward individual freedom; loyalty; collective responsibility; and marriage. The social rules that govern people's actions toward one another are called **norms**, which you can think of as the routine conventions of everyday life, like dress codes, social manners, and accepted codes of conduct. These may get translated into the actual laws of a country.

How is a culture shaped into being? The values and norms of a culture evolve over time and are a function of a number of factors at work in a society, including religion; political and economic philosophies; education; language; and social structure. Social structure refers to the basic social organisation of a society. There are two important elements to consider here: firstly, the degree to which the basic unit of social organisation is the individual rather than the group—usually we think of the individual being dominant in Western societies, and the group being more important in other societies; secondly, the degree to which the society is stratified into classes or castes.

How can we understand differences in culture? It is usual to distinguish between three approaches:

1. ***The context approach.*** Context is the underlying background upon which interaction takes place. Edward Hall proposed high-low context dimensions to culture. In low-context cultures (such as in North American and Western European countries), communication is usually taken at face value without much reliance on unspoken context. In other words, yes *means* yes. In contrast, in high context cultures (such as Arab and Asian countries) communication relies a lot on the underlying unspoken context, which is as important as the words used. For example, 'yes' does not necessarily mean, *"yes, I agree"*, it might mean, *"yes, I hear you"*. Clearly, failure to understand context and differences in interaction style can lead to misunderstandings in international business. On this theory, Chinese, Korean, Japanese and Arab cultures are high context, while German, Canadian and Swiss, for example are low context. This looks a bit simplistic! Critics point out that the context approach may exaggerate the lack of context in so-called 'low context' approaches, and that all cultures, national, business or otherwise, as products of history and tradition, have important unspoken aspects, which are as important as the words used. Also the context approach only looks at one dimension, unlike the dimensions approach detailed below.

2. ***The cluster approach.*** A cluster here is a group of countries that share similar cultures. There are three main theories of clusters. Ronen and Shenkar (1985) identified 14 clusters, while the GLOBE—Global Leadership and Organisational Behaviour Effectiveness—study, (House et al., 2004) sees ten, of which five are similar to the Ronen and Shenkar study. The GLOBE study also used in its survey, nine dimensions of culture, thus also falling into the 'dimensions' approach described below. Huntingdon (1996) proposed eight 'civilisations'—Slavic Orthodox, Islamic, Western, Hindu, African, Latin American Confucian, and Japancse. Which civilisation do you belong to? All these studies have methodologies that have been coolly received by some scholars. However, the clusters are a useful way of looking at things, because we need to understand that in international business people will feel more comfortable doing business with countries and businesses from the same cluster. However, the approach tells us little about differences between countries within a cluster, for example between Italy and Spain, or Argentina and Brazil.

3. ***The dimensions approach.*** The most extensive studies exploring this have been done by an IBM psychologist called Geert Hofstede. He and colleagues identified five dimensions of culture:

a. *Power distance* focused on how a society deals with the fact that people are unequal in physical and intellectual capabilities. A culture would rank high on this dimension if it allowed these inequalities to grow over time into inequalities in wealth and power, while cultures that ranked low on power distance played down the inequalities.

b. *Individualism versus collectivism* focused on the relationship between the individual and her fellows. In individualistic societies, individual achievement and freedom are valued, and in collectivist societies the ties between individuals are stronger.

c. *Masculinity versus femininity* looked at the relationship between gender and work roles. In cultures that were identified as masculine, there was a sharp distinction between sex roles, and traditional masculine values influenced cultural ideals, while in a more feminine culture, there was little differentiation between men and women in the same job.

d. *Uncertainty avoidance* measured the extent to which different cultures socialised their members into accepting ambiguous situations and tolerating uncertainty. So, in a culture that ranked high on uncertainty avoidance, people placed a premium on job security, retirement benefits, and so on; while in a low uncertainty culture, people were more willing to take risks, and were less resistant to change.

e. *Long-term orientation*. This was a later addition from a further study. In a long-time-oriented culture, the basic notion about the world is that it is in flux, and preparing for the future is always needed. In a short-time-oriented culture, the world is essentially as it was created, so that the past provides a moral compass, and adhering to it is morally good (Hofstede, 1997).

f. Hofstede and Minkov (2010) expanded his study to include a sixth dimension to capture attitudes toward time; persistence; ordering by status; protection of face; respect for tradition; and reciprocation of gifts and favours. This dimension refers to the degree of freedom that societal norms give to citizens in fulfilling their human desires. Indulgence is defined as *'a society that allows relatively free gratification of basic and natural human desires related to enjoying life and having fun'*. Its counterpart is defined as *'a society that controls gratification of needs and regulates it by means of strict social norms'*. (see also geerthofstede.com and the 6-D model of national culture).

Note that Hofstede's studies record only *relative* culture differences between countries. For example Austria, Israel, and Denmark scored low on power distance, so power is distributed more equally in those countries than in Malaysia and Guatemala, who scored the highest on power distance. Likewise the USA is highest on individualism, while South American countries tend to be much lower. On long-term orientation Asia Pacific countries tend to score higher than West European countries and the USA.

It is important to note though, that while Hofstede's original study gave us many important insights into cultural differences, his study was flawed in that he made the assumption that there is a one-to-one relationship between culture and the nation-state—the research was culturally bound since it was conducted only by Europeans and Americans—and the study may have been biased since it took place within a single company, IBM. The original study was also a 1967–1973 set of surveys. Even IBM's culture will have changed between then and 2021, let alone cultures throughout the world. It is important for you to understand the strengths and limitations of Hofstede's work. It provides a good starting point for a cultural analysis that needs to be more fine-grained if it is to influence actual management practice. Each organisation may well have its own distinctive culture of 'how things are done around here' and it is important to understand, for example, the culture of Toyota, compared with that of Ford when operating as an international car component supplier.

A further 'dimensions' approach to culture is offered by Trompenaars (1993) who built on the work of Hofstede to arrive at seven dimensions of culture in the workplace:

1. ***Universalism versus particularism***. In universalist cultures rules and regulations are applied in all situations, regardless of circumstance—Switzerland, Canada, and USA are given by him as examples. The most particularist countries were Korea, Russia and China.

2. ***Individualism versus collectivism.*** As per Hofstede above.

3. ***Neutral versus emotional***. How often emotions are displayed and whether emotions and subjectivity are thought to be good bases for decision-making. Italy and France come out as the most emotional countries, while in his study the least emotional, in the workplace at least, are Japanese, Germans, Chinese, Swiss, and Indonesians.

4. ***Specific versus diffuse.*** Do workplace hierarchical relationships stay specific to the workplace, or do they extend into the wider social context (diffuse)? Australia and Netherlands came out as the most specific, while China, Japan, India, and Singapore as the most diffuse.

5. ***Achievement versus ascription.*** Are status, power, and authority achieved through merit or does the culture ascribe these by class, gender, age, and education? The former is found more in Norway, Sweden, UK, and USA for example; the latter more in Egypt, Turkey, and Argentina—again only as examples.

6. ***Sequential versus synchronic attitudes towards time.*** Sequential refers to time seen as a sequence of events, and relates to punctuality and meeting deadlines. Synchronic refers to several events/tasks juggled at the same time with less concern about precision or being on time. Latin American, Arabic, and south Mediterranean cultures come out as more typically synchronic, while north European cultures tend to be sequential.

7. ***Attitude towards environment.*** Does the culture emphasise subjugation and control of the natural environment, or working with nature in harmony with the environment? Trompenaars' work provides a useful framework for investigating how culture plays out in particular countries and workplaces, and for discovering cultural differences and then how to deal with these. It also has the merit of using initial research involving 1,500 employees in 50 different countries, and in addition focused not just on culture at the country level, but also in *actual* business workplaces, thus being directly useful to practising managers. However, there may have been quite a lot of changes since the original study, though Trompenaars and colleagues have produced more up-to-date research that continues to monitor cultural diversity.

What are the implications of all of this for managers? It is vital for international firms to develop cross-cultural literacy. To be successful, you have to be able to conform and adapt to the value system and norms of the host country. One way you can gain knowledge of the local culture is to hire local citizens. Developing a cadre of cosmopolitan managers who have been exposed to different cultures can also be helpful. It is important to avoid being ethnocentric, or believe that your ethnic group or culture is superior to that of others.

A second reason for companies to be aware of cultural differences is the link between culture and competitive advantage. The value systems and norms of a country influence the cost of doing business, which of course then affects the competitive advantage of the firm. A society's class structure affects the relationship between management and labour—look at Japan's strong worker loyalty system, and lifetime employment guarantees, which affect the success of Japanese companies. Similarly, a more individualistic culture promotes entrepreneurial activities as compared to a culture that emphasises collective behaviour. These differences provide companies with insight as to which countries are most likely to produce competitors, and which countries will be the best for investing or selling. For example, if you are comparing two countries with similar wage costs, you will recognise that the country with the better education system, less social stratification, and group identification is probably the better site for production facilities.

What should the corporate response be to the issue of cross-cultural management, as it has been called? Certainly firms need to develop an awareness of cultural diversity in their workforce, but also need to encourage adaptation in personal behaviour and organisational practices to suit the ever-changing mix of cultures within the firm, subsidiaries, and markets they serve. Clearly this has training and development implications for firms operating internationally. The better firms will also leverage the cultural diversity within the organisation and combine the best aspects of different ways of doing things. Collinson, Narula and Rugman (2017) summarise a number of research studies and suggest that cultural diversity can be managed by:

- **Recognising diversity**—map the national culture and ethnic groups within the firm and use this to identify which elements of consistency and standardisation can be promoted.

- **Building diversity issues** into such areas as recruitment; HRM planning; strategy; location decisions and alliances. This helps avoid clashes and inefficiency.

- **Identifying** where and to what degree **local divisions** should be encouraged to take the lead in expressing and managing diversity.Encouraging cross-border discussion and interaction as well as focused training. Give international experience to fast-track managers (see also Willcocks, 2021).

- Getting a **cultural balance** in particular areas of strategic and tactical decision-making. For example, changing brands for particular markets. Ensure a numerically balanced pool of managers to give diverse inputs into decision-making.

- **Lead from the top** with behaviours that signal the valuing of cultural diversity. Match the geographic diversity of the firm's business with a culturally mixed group of senior managers and board directors.

3.3. Languages

Let us look at how language defines culture. Language is how we communicate with each other—both in the spoken form and in the unspoken form—and it is also how we perceive the world.

Some countries have more than one language and distinct culture. Canada for example, has both an English speaking and a French speaking area—both with their own cultures. Belgium is divided into Flemish and French speakers, and four different languages are spoken in Switzerland. Chinese is the mother tongue of the largest number of native speakers (20 percent), though English is the most widely spoken language in the world.

Of the world's population, 6 percent are English native speakers; 5 percent speak Hindi; 5 percent are native Spanish speakers; 4 percent speak Arabic; and 4 percent Russian. Other languages make up 56 percent of the world's native speaking population. There are approximately 6000 languages in the world. This makes for a great deal of diversity, and plenty of room for mistranslation and misunderstanding! Language is a system of shared meanings that enable people to communicate effectively, but meanings are often complex and contextually rich and embedded, thus it can be difficult to translate meaning from one language into another.

Many multinationals have adopted English as their official corporate language, to enable knowledge sharing and communication across borders—not least with customers, suppliers, and fellow employees. But note that, even though English is the 'lingua franca' (i.e. the default global business language), sharing English as a language in a business meeting can still create problems. People from different cultures may understand the same words differently. For example, famously it is said that the USA and the UK are two nations divided by a common language.

What about unspoken language? Why is it important? Well, think for a moment about how you stand when you are talking with another person. You probably stand about an arm's length away. But in Latin America people tend to stand much closer together. Now picture yourself at a business meeting with someone from Brazil. He might try to stand at his customary distance causing you take a step backward because he has invaded your personal space. You may be annoyed at him for standing so close to you, and he may interpret your response as aloofness.

Your meeting is already off to a bad start. Similarly, consider the circle you might make with your thumb and forefinger. In the United States, you have signalled a positive response, but if you make the same gesture in Greece, you have just insulted someone! We could provide multiple examples of such international misunderstandings. Because facial expressions, hand gestures, and other types of unspoken language can mean different things in different cultures, it is important to do your homework before meeting with someone from another culture.

How to handle language differences? In organisational settings, translation and interpretation by professional linguists is highly useful. Translating documents, and having interpreters at meetings are typical practices. Companies can adopt a corporate language (in Europe and USA this is typically English); encourage non-native speakers to learn the local language; bring multi-lingual people into key bridging positions—especially those involving much international communication; and provide language training for staff and suppliers and customers. As one example, most international airlines ensure that staff members on board a flight can speak a mix of languages, reflecting the language capabilities of the bulk of likely customers.

3.4. Religion

Religion is another important determinant of culture, especially in countries where a single religion is dominant. Religion is the system of shared beliefs and rituals that are concerned with the realm of the sacred. Religions with the greatest following today are: Christianity (1.7 billion); Islam (1 billion); Hinduism (750 million); and Buddhism (350 million). You might include Confucianism with these. Not strictly a religion, Confucianism influences behaviour and shapes culture in many parts of Asia. Closely related to religion are ethical systems, or sets of moral principles or values that guide and shape behaviour. You might think of Christian ethics or Islamic ethics.

Most followers of Christianity live in Europe, the Americas, or other countries settled by the Europeans. Christians are divided into Roman Catholics; those who belong to the Orthodox Church; and Protestants. Muslims are found in more than 35 countries, particularly in the Middle East. Islam is an all-embracing way of life—prayers take place five times a day; women dress in a certain manner; and pork and alcohol are forbidden. How does Islam affect business? The Koran—the sacred book for Islam, like the Bible is for Christianity—supports free enterprises and legitimate profits, and the right to protect private property, but advocates using profits in a righteous socially-beneficial manner. The central tenets of Hinduism, which is mainly based in India, are spiritual growth and development. Many Hindus believe that the way to achieve nirvana is through material and physical self-denial.

Hinduism, at least in its pure form, creates interesting challenges for companies. For example, because the religion emphasises spiritual rather than individual achievement, the drive for entrepreneurial behaviour that is so common among Protestants, for example, may not be present. So, it may well be that a devout Hindu may not see promotion or additional responsibilities as being desirable. Buddhism's followers are located mainly in Central and Southeast Asia, China, Korea, and Japan. Buddhism stresses spiritual achievement and the afterlife over involvement in this world. As with Hinduism, there is a lack of emphasis on entrepreneurial behaviour.

Confucianism is practised mainly in China and teaches the importance of attaining personal salvation through right action. Moral and ethical conduct is important, as is loyalty. What do the principles of Confucianism mean for business? The key principles of the ideology—loyalty, reciprocal obligations, and honesty—could translate into lowering the costs of doing business.

Knowledge of religions is crucial even for non-religious managers. Religious beliefs and activities affect business through religious festivals, daily and weekly routines that vary across religions (e.g. prayer times, sacred days, fasts) and activities and objects with symbolic values—positive or negative—that lead to rules as to what the believer can and cannot do. For example, in India cows are holy in Hindu religion and may not be disturbed or eaten. Some objects or practices are taboo or banned—Muslims are not supposed to eat pork. Recall the international furore over the Danish newspaper publishing cartoons involving the Muslim prophet Mohammed.

Religious differences, more than any other differences, tend to raise emotions, and thus are challenging to handle for businesses. Showing respect for other religions and associated values will help you by avoiding conflict and creating a basis for doing business. An individual's religion may also help shape his/her attitude toward work and entrepreneurship.

3.5. Ethics

Ethics refer to the principles of right and wrong, standards and norms of conduct governing individual and firm behaviour; they relate to an individual's personal beliefs about whether a decision, behaviour or action is right or wrong. Ethics are not only an important part of informal institutions but are also deeply reflected in formal laws and regulations. Business ethics are the accepted principles of right or wrong governing the conduct of business people. For example, many advocate that businesses must, these days, do much more than conform to existing law. A business needs to think beyond profit and loss; fulfil more than just the legal requirements (see *Corporate Social Responsibility* below); engage in transactional integrity and trustworthy behaviour as a basis for ongoing relationships; and take a multi-stakeholder view as to who should benefit from corporate activity. An ethical strategy would be a course of action that does not violate these principles.

Unethical behaviour can have many root causes including:

- Personal ethics of managers and government officials.

- Organisational cultures that emphasise narrow economic, rather than ethical, goals.

- Societal culture.

- Decision-making processes—especially ones that exclude an ethical dimension

- Leadership—one can think of examples over the years at Enron, Daimler, Hewlett Packard, where employees took their cues from the leaderships, resulting in unethical behaviours being discovered, and resultant public scandals.

- Unrealistic performance goals for example from a parent company to a subsidiary, where goals can only be attained by cutting corners and behaving in an unethical manner.

Managing ethics overseas is challenging because what is ethical in one country may be unethical elsewhere. How to deal with ethical dilemmas that arise when operating internationally? **The Friedman Doctrine** argues that the only responsibility of business is to increase profits. Milton Friedman (1970) claimed that as long as the firm stayed within the letter of the law, ethics did not enter the equation. So, in other words, he would argue that it is not the responsibility of a company to take on social expenditures beyond what the law mandates, and what is required to run a business efficiently. What Hill (2019) calls the **naïve immoralist** approach, argues that if a manager of a multinational company sees that firms from other countries are not following ethical norms in a host country, that manager should ignore the norms as well. Peng and Meyer (2019) suggest three approaches. **Ethical relativism** follows the cliché, *'When in Rome, do as the Romans do'*. **Ethical imperialism** refers to the absolute belief that *'There is only one set of ethics and we have it'*. Firms often run into problems adopting either of these two approaches. Therefore Donaldson (1996) suggests a **'middle of the road'** approach in international business by observing three principles when overseas:

1. Respect for human dignity and human rights

2. Respect for local traditions

3. Respect for institutional context

In practice these principles may clash in specific circumstances, leaving the business manager to behave as diplomatically as he/she can in the prevailing situation. For example, where do you draw the line on gifts; appointing family members to jobs; or hiring children under the working age in your own country, but not in the country where they are working for you? Then there is corruption, defined as the abuse of public power for private benefit, usually in the form of bribery (in cash or in kind). What is acceptable in which cultures and what is not acceptable, and is therefore corruption?

Ethics provides a useful bridge between culture, language, religion, and is the subject of a major way forward—corporate social responsibility—which we will now look at.

3.6. Corporate Social Responsibility Challenges

People involved in business run into ethical situations daily. In international business, they are often magnified because of differences in things like legal, political and economic systems, and culture, language and religion. How can firms deal with the ethical dilemmas that arise when operating internationally? A major approach is corporate social responsibility (CSR), defined as: *'the consideration of, and response to issues beyond the narrow economic, technical, and legal requirements of the firm in order to accomplish social benefits along with the traditional economic gains the firm seeks.'*

As we shall see, globalisation has created many concerns in its wake (see also Chapter 1). Moreover, a stakeholder view of the firm sees a business as responsible not just to its shareholders for its performance, but also to a much wider constituency. There are primary stakeholder groups on whom the firm directly relies for its continuous survival and prosperity—managers, employees, customers, shareholders, and governments. There are also secondary stakeholder groups who do not engage in transactions with the firm, but influence or are affected by the firm, though not essential for its survival. If you take an **instrumental view** you will take notice of all stakeholders because this may indirectly improve the firm's financial performance. If you take a **normative view**, your firm will be self-motivated to fulfil social obligations because it is the right thing to do. As a result of rising global concerns and the stakeholder view, firms increasingly develop CSR **'triple bottom line' strategies** that take into account their economic, social, and environmental performance. This is sometimes labelled as the three "P's of **Profit**, **People** and **Planet**. International businesses are faced with at least four major CSR concerns:

1. *Environment* is currently a high profile topic, especially the irreversible damage that human-made pollution is causing. A key concern is **sustainability**, defined as: *'the ability to meet the needs of the present without compromising the ability of future generations to meet their needs.'* Because many countries are establishing strong environmental regulations to try to limit further damage, companies have to adopt new, often costly, measures to abide by the laws. For example, new regulations may be forcing your company to take expensive steps to stay within the law. You know that these regulations have not been imposed in some other countries, known as **'pollution havens'**, particularly those that are less developed and/or trying to attract inward investment—a so-called **'race to the bottom'**. Should you shift your production to another country where the laws do not exist, or are only loosely enforced? Your first response might be that the ethical approach is to stay home and adopt the costly compliance measures. But, you might worry that competitors that do not take this approach will have an advantage. This brings up a phenomenon called the **tragedy of the commons**.

   The tragedy of the commons occurs when a resource held in common by everyone, like the ocean or the atmosphere, is overused by individuals, and degraded. What are the social consequences of this? If everyone else is pumping pollutants into the ocean, should you do otherwise? Thus an MNE (multinational enterprise) could choose to lower standards when operating abroad, seeing it as an opportunity to lower costs by producing where regulations impose least costs, and using the threat of relocation to prevent the foreign government from raising legal requirements. On the other hand there may be some advantages in raising standards when operating abroad. This may be to satisfy closer monitoring by stakeholders; to achieve scale advantages from common practices and standards throughout the organisation; to lower the risk of catastrophic disruptions; and perhaps achieve first mover advantage in new technologies and practices that are environmentally friendly. One should not also underestimate the public relations advantages of raising standards.

2. ***Employment practices.*** These frequently present ethical dilemmas. Suppose work conditions in a host country are inferior to those in the home country. Which standards should you apply—the home country standards or the host country standards? Nike found itself in the midst of a huge controversy in the mid-1990s when it was reported that the working conditions at some of its sub-contractors were poor. While neither the subcontractor, nor Nike was actually breaking the law, there was strong reason to suspect that workers were being exploited. For example, in one factory in Vietnam, women were paid just 20 cents an hour—well below the living wage of $3 per day—to work with toxic materials six days a week. Nike was forced by public pressure to establish a code of conduct for all of its subcontractors, and implement a monitoring system to ensure that the code was followed. The pressure to lower conditions in foreign operations is particularly strong with **'footloose plants'** that are labour intensive and can easily relocate when local regulations get tighter. Another problem area is where an MNE buys products or components from foreign firms. Is Adidas, Nike, or Starbucks responsible for labour and work conditions of another, foreign firm? MNEs like Adidas sometimes introduce standards of engagement on their suppliers. These are written policies and standards for corporate conduct and ethics. But what happens if suppliers fail to meet standards or provide misleading evidence? MNEs can be more pro-active, e.g. by joint problem solving and diffusing best practices.

3. ***Human rights.*** You may not think much about your human rights—things like freedom of association, freedom of speech, freedom of assembly, and so on are often taken for granted in many countries. But these freedoms are not respected in all countries. Think about the apartheid system that denied basic political rights to black people in South Africa, for example, or the situation in the Darfur region of western Sudan where the Sudanese government has been accused of genocide by several other countries. Should companies do business in countries with repressive regimes? Some people argue that the presence of multinational companies actually helps bring change to these countries; for instance, it is some people's belief that change is occurring in China because investments by multinationals are helping to raise living standards. Others, however, argue that some countries like Myanmar, which has one of the worst human rights records in the world, are so brutally repressive that no investment can be justified.

4. ***Corruption.*** Is it necessary to be ethical when dealing with corrupt government or individuals? This is something firms have to consider. At what point does 'gift giving' become bribery for example? From a government perspective, bribery is invariably not allowed. The Organisation for Cooperation and Development (OECD) passed an anti-bribery measure in 1997 that obligates member states to make bribery of foreign public officials a criminal offence. Despite laws like these, bribery continues to be a common practice for some firms. In fact, some economists believe that in certain cases speed payments—payments made to speed up approval for business investments—can be justified if they enhance public welfare by creating jobs, and so on. Others argue however, that corruption can become ingrained as a way of doing business, and hard to stop if part of a country's way of getting things done.

3.7. Institutions and CSR Strategies

What are the moral obligations of firms operating internationally? The formal and informal institutions operating in a country greatly influence types of CSR strategies firms can adopt, and the levels of success experienced. In liberal market economies, like the USA and the UK, firms have a high discretion over their activities. So far as they undertake CSR this will be *explicit* corporate activity undertaken voluntarily as policies, programmes, and strategies, with the extent of these actions dependent on the expectations of different stakeholders of the firm. In more coordinated market economies, for example in Germany and Scandinavia, much more *implicit* CSR takes place with CSR being part of the fabric of the legal, political, and social and cultural institutions, and indeed may not only be morally demanded but legally demanded, e.g. in Germany paying health care benefits for all those employed for more than 20 days a month. Note however that, amongst developed countries in particular, there has been some convergence towards more CSR regulation.

Do companies have a responsibility to take into account the social consequences of their actions when they make business decisions? Should companies always choose the path that has both good economic and good social consequences? You might answer yes, firms have a social responsibility simply because it is the right way to operate. Many people believe that companies need to give something back to the societies that have made their success possible. Others, however, do not share this view. Peng and Meyer (2019) suggest firms adopt different responses to ethical challenges:

- ***Reactive strategy***—deny responsibility and do less than required. An example of a reactive strategy is when Ford marketed the Pinto in the early 1970s, knowing that its gas tank was designed badly and could explode under certain conditions. Ford did not recall the Pinto or make improvements, seeing high costs involved. After frequent accidents it only recalled the vehicle in 1978 under intense government and media pressure.

- A *defensive strategy* involves regulatory compliance while rejecting informal pressure from the media and interest groups to do more. An example is Nike in the early 1990s, accused of running 'sweatshops', while the incidents continued to take place in contractors' factories in Vietnam and Indonesia. As legislators considered changes to the law, Nike acknowledged an ethical responsibility beyond the legal boundaries of the firm, though at the time seeming to see CSR as a cost and nuisance.

- An *accommodative strategy* accepts responsibility to apply norms and standards commonly held but not enshrined in law. Typically here top managers see CSR as a worthwhile policy and social obligation. Nike, Adidas and the sportswear industry have in recent years been much more accommodative on CSR, and by 2000 Ford had also become more willing. When Ford Explorer vehicles equipped with Firestone tyres had a large number of fatal rollover accidents, it recalled all vehicles, launched a high profile media campaign and terminated its relationship with Firestone.

Sometimes, it can very difficult for companies to decide how to behave in specific situations. Managers will be influenced by their personal ethics, and their cultural perspective, but these may or may not be appropriate in a given situation. However, there are several things that managers can do to be sure that ethical issues are considered when decisions are made:

- Firms can hire and promote people with well-grounded personal ethics. While it may seem obvious that you should hire people with a strong sense of business ethics, it can be hard to know whether a person fits this category. So businesses often require references, or give prospective employees tests as a way of finding out more.

- It is also important for individuals to find out about the ethics of a prospective employer. You might ask, for example, whether a firm has a formal code of ethics, or how senior managers are viewed, and so on.

- Firms can build an organisational culture that places a high value on ethical behaviour. To develop this, they need to articulate values that place a strong emphasis on ethical behaviour. Some firms do this by establishing a formal code of ethics. Once a code has been developed, leaders need to emphasise it and act on it. Companies can encourage employees to adopt the code by offering incentives and rewards to employees who behave in an ethical manner.

- Firms can make sure that leaders articulate the rhetoric of ethical behaviour and act in a manner that is consistent with that rhetoric.

- Managers can develop moral courage. Companies can strengthen the moral courage of employees by committing themselves to not retaliate against employees who exercise moral courage, say no to superiors, or otherwise complain about unethical actions.

- Firms can put decision-making processes in place that require people to consider the ethical dimension of business decisions.

3.8. What more can International Businesses do?

3.8.1. Stakeholder Analysis

We pointed out above that a business has many stakeholders. A **stakeholder** is defined as *'any group or individual who can affect, or is affected by a project or organisation.'* At the very least a business's stakeholders include government; suppliers; customers; environmental groups; employees; communities social groups; as well as shareholders. This has led to the development of **stakeholder analysis** as a way of understanding who those stakeholders are, their interests, and their levels of influence. Typically when an organisation looks at its stakeholders, it will analyse the power, legitimacy and urgency of the claims of each cluster of stakeholders. This will inform decisions about how much, and which type, of attention stakeholders receive from management. The strengths of stakeholder analysis include:

- **Normative value:** it accepts that stakeholders have legitimate stakes in corporate activity and that stakeholders have intrinsic value.

- **Descriptive value:** it provides a language and concepts to describe corporations, the way they work and their impacts on the wider environment.

- **Instrumental value:** it is a managerial tool designed to achieve business goals: for example, increased profitability, growth, sustainability. The stakeholder model also allows for the testing of the connections between managing stakeholders and what it will take to realise business targets.

The limitations of stakeholder analysis include:

- In principle, stakeholder approaches are neutral, but applying an approach ethically is still contingent on the managers' behaviour.

- It can be too easy to overlook and/or misrepresent silent voices, interests at-a-distance, or non-human interests (e.g. features of environment).

- The use of stakeholder theory does not necessarily imply ethical behaviour.

3.8.2. Making the Sustainability Journey

Sustainability has become a critical component of corporate social responsibility approaches in recent years, especially in the face of climate change challenges. The idea here is that businesses must support wider sustainable development beyond their own profit goals. A 1987 report by the World Commission on Environment and Development defined **sustainable development** as *'development that meets the needs of the present without compromising the ability of future generations to meet their own needs'*.

In many publications (see https://sustainabilityadvantage.com), Bob Willard has suggested a five stage sustainability journey for business enterprises. The stages are:

1. Pre-compliance

2. Compliance

3. Beyond compliance

4. Integrated strategy

5. Purpose/passion

According to this framework, companies evolve from an unsustainable model of business (Stages 1, 2 and 3), to a sustainable business framework (Stages 4 or 5). Executive thinking also evolves from positioning 'green', 'environmental', and 'sustainable' initiatives as expensive and bureaucratic threats in the early stages, to seeing them as catalysts for strategic growth in the later stages (see Willard, 2010).

Stage 1: *Pre-Compliance*. Here, the company cuts corners, and tries not to get caught if it breaks the law or uses exploitative practices that cheat the system. This behaviour ignores notions of sustainability; environmental; health; and safety regulations. This stage can be the norm in corrupt jurisdictions. In developed countries, it is a risky stage and less encountered. Most companies move quickly to Stage 2, not least to avoid potential fines, prosecution, and public embarrassment for illegal acts.

Stage 2: *Compliance*. Here, the business follows labour, environmental, health, and safety regulations. As discussed above, it reactively does what it is legally bound to do. Companies at this stage may well install pollution abatement equipment, for example, and provide a safer, healthier, more respectful workplace for employees. However, environmental and philanthropic social actions are treated as costs, pollution abatement projects are likely to be peripheral, and corporate social responsibility is not a high priority item.

A Stage 2 company's actions are legal but they're still unsustainable. Companies at stage 1 or 2 are based on a linear 'take-make-waste' or 'make-use-dispose' model of commerce. In a typical manufacturing organisation the sequence of activity is:

1. Extract raw materials

2. Parts supply

3. Manufacturing

4. Distribution

5. Consumer use

6. Incineration and landfill

This process, and the waste generated, violate the fundamental principles of sustainable enterprise. According to Bob Willard: *"They treat Nature as a dump site for the waste created when extracting the natural resources required for their products. They treat Nature as a dump site for the waste created from their manufacturing processes. Nature's dump site fills with the end-of-life disposal of their goods when consumers are finished with them."* (See Willard, 2010).

What we see here is how companies externalise many of their ecological and social impacts that arise from this model of business. There are increasing societal demands for businesses to be more accountable for their collateral social and environmental damage.

Stage 3: *Beyond compliance*. A company may come to realise that it can save money with proactive, operational eco-efficiencies in four ways:

1. Saving energy and reducing its associated carbon footprint

2. Saving water

3. Saving materials in its products and packaging

4. Saving waste-handling costs

By these actions, a company will increase its community investment, thereby enhancing its reputation and maximising shareholder value. However, in Stage 3 organisations it may well be that sustainability initiatives are still marginalised within specialised departments. They appear as 'green housekeeping', rather than being institutionalised in the company's governance systems. This is still an unsustainable business, just less so.

Stage 4: *Integrated Strategy.* By this stage, the firm has transformed its business model into a sustainable 'borrow-use-return' design. This is to help to build a '**circular economy**'. A circular economy is one that is restorative and regenerative by design, and which aims to keep products, components and materials at their highest utility and value at all times, distinguishing between technical and biological cycles (see Figure 3.1). This involves practices such as recycling, refurbishing, servicing rather than disposal, with the focus on reuse and minimising waste.

At this stage the company re-brands itself as a company committed to sustainability. It injects sustainability principles into its core organisational values, demonstrating this by coordinating sustainability approaches with the key business strategies. The business can capture added value from sustainability initiatives that benefit all stakeholders. Instead of seeing 'green' costs and risks, it sees investments and opportunities. These firms make cleaner products, apply eco-effectiveness and life-cycle stewardship, and gain competitive advantages from their sustainability initiatives.

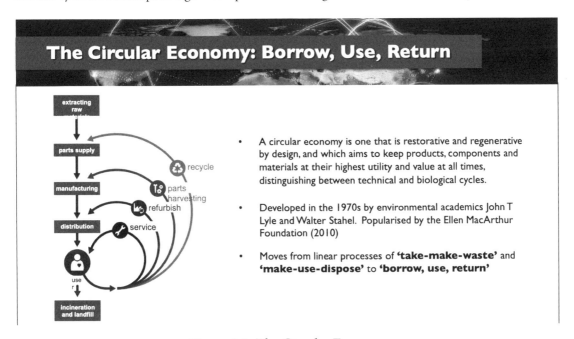

Figure 3.1: The Circular Economy

Stage 5: *Passion and Purpose.* Driven by a passionate, values-based commitment to improve the well-being of the company, society, and the environment, a Stage 5 company would help to build a better world because it is the right thing to do. (Stage 4 companies do most of the things a Stage 5 company does but 'do the right things' so that they are successful businesses). At Stage 5, company values reflect founder/CEO values. Some founder-owned and founder-led companies start and end in this stage without ever entering the other four stages—such as Seventh Generation led by Jeffrey

Hollander, and Patagonia led by Yvon Chouinard. While there are few such public companies operating, one might see an increasing number evolve once business communities support the legitimacy of social and environmental metrics and practices.

3.8.3. Dealing with Corruption

Every organisation establishes some sort of moral 'climate' for operating. Its senior management establishes a framework of business ethics for employees. There will be broadly agreed norms, which enable the business to act as an organisation and with its many stakeholders. The moral climate will be imbedded, however informally, in the organisational form; governance; strategy pursued; and daily operations. All business decisions will have a moral component. But none of this indicates **how** moral the organisation is, and **how** ethical its practices are. The 'moral climate' of the organisation can be quite loose, weak, ambivalent; or may be contradictory, rather than strong, consistent, and showing high corporate social responsibility. Moreover the country, culture and environment in which you are operating can have big influences on the ethics you adopt.

We have seen how this plays out in the context of devolving corporate social responsibility, and adopting sustainability strategies. But how do international businesses deal with the challenges of experiencing differing degrees of corruption in countries and business practices across the world?

Transparency International, an anti-corruption, non-governmental organisation that monitors levels of corruption across the globe, define **corruption** as *the abuse of entrusted power for private gain*. This is usually in the form of bribery. In *Coping with Corruption in Foreign Markets*, Doh et al (2003) suggest two dimensions of corruption—pervasiveness and arbitrariness (see Figure 3.2). Note that the countries in the diagram are listed in alphabetical order ***not*** in degree of corruption. Also note that the diagram represents the situation in 2003, and not the most recent assessments.

Corruption has been well documented in most societies, whether it is in banks of the Congo; Japanese politicians; Brazilian banks; the New York city police department; oil companies of every nationality; or government officials in Zimbabwe and the Philippines, as just a few examples. According to the Transparency International Corruption Perceptions Index, in 2019 a majority of countries were showing little or no improvement in tackling corruption. Transparency International has estimated that businesses and individuals spend in excess of $400 billion a year worldwide on bribes related to government procurement contracts alone. It suggests that reducing big money in politics, and promoting inclusive political decision-making, are essential to curbing corruption. Looking at 180 countries and their perceived levels of public sector corruption, the report found more than two-thirds of countries scoring below 50 out of 100 (where 100 is 'very clean'). No country recorded a perfect score, the highest being 87.

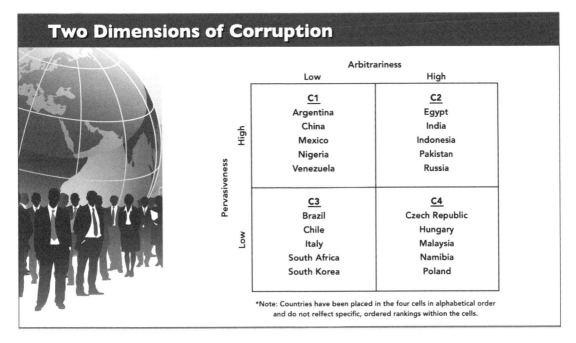

Figure 3.2: Two Dimensions of Corruption

Source: 'Coping with Corruption in Foreign Markets', The Academy of Management Executive, 17(3), 2003

The most transparent and least corrupt countries were New Zealand; Denmark; Finland; Switzerland; Singapore; Sweden; Norway; Netherlands; Luxembourg; and Germany. The most corrupt countries were Somalia; South Sudan; Syria; Yemen; and Venezuela.

In *Corruption in International Business*, Cuervo-Cazurra, (2016) has provided a neat framework for analysing corruption, and the points of leverage for governments and companies wanting to behave more ethically, (see Figure 3.3). The author argues that while the definition, types and measurement of corruption remain under-researched and need development, it is possible to identify the causes of corruption, in terms of demand and supply; reduce the risks from corrupt behaviour; and lower the rewards for acting corruptly. If proper controls and punishments are put in place at government and company level, it is possible to gain more desirable outcomes in terms of country development and company profitability.

Corruption is not just a government-business phenomenon; it also occurs massively in markets and in transactions between businesses. Undoubtedly, corruption needs to be combatted by businesses, not least because it can be inordinately costly, and can also do irreparable damage to the brand and business relationships. Amongst the costs of poor corporate governance of corruption for a company are:

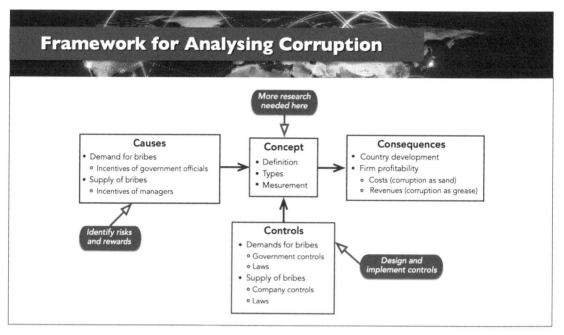

Figure 3.3: Framework for Analysing Corruption in International Business

Source: Adapted by Susan Scott from Journal of World Businesses, 51, pp.35-49, Cuervo-Cazurra, A. *(2016)*

- Business losses
- Reputational damage or weakened competitive position
- Deadlines not met
- Higher costs and lower productivity
- Poorer quality than expected
- Failure to realise benefits
- Barriers to innovation

There are many ways forward for reducing corruption in international trade. These include:

- **Policy**—national and international—acknowledging multi-jurisdictional issues and bridging the problems of jurisdictions' differing rules, if not resolving them. For example, in the 1970s the USA passed the Foreign Corrupt Practices Act, following revelations that US companies had bribed government officials in foreign countries to gain lucrative contracts. Walmart sparked an investigation when evidence emerged, in 2012, that the firm violated this Act in its eagerness to expand in Mexico. By 2016 the company was negotiating a settlement with the US government estimated to be at least $600 million. In 1997 the then 34 major economies of the Organisation for Economic Cooperation and Development (but not Russia, India or China) adopted the convention on Combating Bribery of Foreign Public Officials in International Business Transactions, obliging member states to make such bribery a criminal offence—though exceptions were allowed for facilitating or expediting payments made to speed up routine governmental action. However some companies, for example an oil multinational, has a zero-tolerance approach towards such facilitating payments, while others have a more nuanced approach—discouraging them but allowing them as long as properly documented.

- *Non-state actors* such as the International Standards Organisation (ISO) who develop and publish international standards to guide best practice.

- *Organisational goals and directives*: from written policies, to governance processes and strategic priorities.

- *Communicating a sense of stakeholding*, *developing commitment to values*, and providing motivation for all organisational members to act in non-corrupt ways. A start might be the publishing of corporate codes and principles.

3.9. PESTEL Factors

Now that you have read Chapters 2 and 3, it is worth introducing a summary framework for understanding and analysing formal and informal institutions. This is **PESTEL**, which, as you can see in Figure 3.4, categorises environmental influences into six areas ...

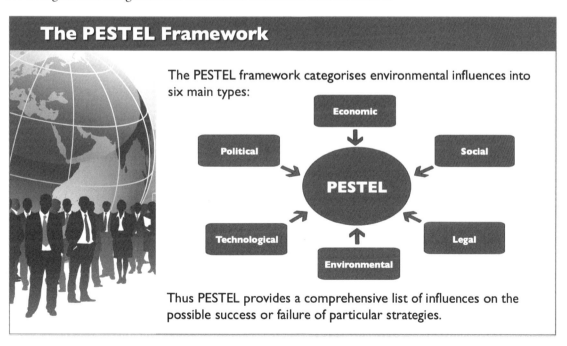

Figure 3.4: The PESTEL Framework

Here is an example of PESTEL analysis carried out by my colleague Dr. Susan Scott.

IKEA is a Swedish chain store selling home furnishings. In the 1960s it opened its first stores outside Sweden—in Norway and Denmark. It continued expansion into many countries throughout 1970–2000. In 2000 it opened stores in Russia. The two PESTEL analyses in Figure 3.5, comparing the Swedish and Russian business environments, revealed them as very different ...

Ikea – Sweden PESTEL Analysis

POLITICAL	TECHNOLOGICAL
Stable environment and low level of corruption	High technological advancement and good overall infrastructure
ECONOMIC	**ENVIRONMENTAL**
Sound macroeconomic fundamentals; small and saturated market	Sound balance between economic growth and environmental standards
SOCIAL	**LEGAL**
Well-trained labour force but ageing population	Strong legal system with high level of business freedom

Overall, the Swedish environment has been highly conductive to business but, given its small market size, expansion was inevitable

Ikea – Russia PESTEL Analysis

POLITICAL	TECHNOLOGICAL
Federal structure; power centres on supply of natural resources/energy; high level of corruption	Good IT but lack of infrastructure
ECONOMIC	**ENVIRONMENTAL**
Increasing demand but below average growth; high inflation/unemployment	Cold war/WWII debris but increasing environmental awareness
SOCIAL	**LEGAL**
Increasing middle-class but section of population below poverty line is still high	Underdeveloped legal system and slow implementation

The political and environmental landscape in Russia was, and still is, challenging

Figure 3.5 IKEA PESTEL Analysis for Sweden and Russia

Source Dr Susan Scott, LSE, 2021

The Russian market was clearly going to be challenging! Subsequently IKEA made a $4 billion investment into the Russian market over 10 years. It established a chain of stores and a distribution network throughout Russia; some large-scale 'mega' shopping centres; and outsourced production to Russia as well—taking advantage of abundant natural resources and cheap labour in that country. As of 2021 IKEA still operated in Russia. We will follow the IKEA story further in Chapter 4.

PESTEL is discussed further in Chapter 4, in the context of business strategy. The technological dimensions are considered in detail in Willcocks, (2021).

3.10. Conclusion

In this chapter we have looked at cultural differences across countries and workplaces, and how firms need to take into account cultural issues within their own organisations as well as in the countries and markets in which they operate. It becomes clear that cultures systematically differ from each other. They are deeply rooted and need to be worked with carefully, in an adaptive mode, in international settings. We have reached an understanding of what culture is and detailed several useful frameworks that attempt to delineate the dimensions of culture. We have also highlighted two of culture's creators and manifestations—namely language and religion—and pointed to the importance of taking these into account when undertaking international business.

The chapter has also introduced the subject, and importance, of business ethics, and the challenges likely to be experienced on the international stage. A related set of challenges, but also ways forward, were identified with the topic of corporate social responsibility. Through 2018–2021 this had become a global high-profile issue with regard to the major companies like Google, Facebook, Apple and Amazon, with particular reference to their collection and use of data from their users and customers. In early 2018 Facebook ran into problems with the use of its data by Cambridge Analytics, ostensibly to target political advertising during the 2016 US elections. Was this a socially responsible way of leveraging the data? Issues of sustainability, climate change and corruption have also gained much profile in recent years. Firms can be reactive, defensive, accommodative, or pro-active on corporate social responsibility. Failing to take the CSR issues on board is to ignore both the wider stakeholder community, to which international businesses are increasingly answerable in a globalising world, and the power of the formal and informal institutions described in this chapter and in Chapter 2, to shape the path international businesses can take, when they embark on the task of strategy—the subject we turn to in the next chapter.

References

Collinson, S. Nerula, R. and Rugman, A. (2017), *International Business*, Pearson Education , Harrow, UK

Cuervo-Casurra, A. (2016), 'Corruption in International Business', *Journal of World Businesses*, 51, pp.35-49

Doh, J., Rodriguez, P., Uhlenbruck, K., Collins, J. and Eden, L. (2003), 'Coping with Corruption in Foreign Markets', *The Academy of Management Executive*, 17(3), pp.114-129.

Donaldson, T. (1996), 'Values In Tension: Ethics Away From Home', *Harvard Business Review*, September-October

Friedman, M. (1970), 'The Social Responsibility of Business Is To Increase Profits', *The New York Times Magazine,* September 13th

Hall, E. (1990), *Understanding Cultural Differences - Germans, French and Americans*, Yarmouth, Maine, USA

Hill, C. and Hult, T. (2019), *International Business*, McGraw Hill, New York, USA

Hofstede, G. (1997), *Culture and Organisations*, McGraw Hill, New York, USA

Hofstede, G., Hofstede, G. J. and Mankov, M. (2010), *Cultures and Organisations*, McGraw Hill, New York, USA

Huntingdon, S. (1996), *The Clash of Civilisations and The Remaking of World Order*, Simon and Schuster, New York, USA

Peng, M. and Meyer, K. (2019), *International Business*, Cengage Learning, London, UK

Ronen and Shankar (1985), 'Clustering Countries On Attitudinal Dimensions', *Academy of Management Review*, 10, pp. 435-454

Trompenaars, F. (1993), *Riding The Waves Of Culture*, Nicholas Brealey, London, UK

Willard, B. (2012), *The New Sustainability Challenge*, New Society Publishers, London, UK

Willcocks, L. (2021), *Global Business Management*, SB Publishing, Stratford-upon-Avon, UK

'All can see these tactics whereby I conquer, but what none can see is the strategy out of which victory is evolved'

Sun Tzu

'However beautiful the strategy, you should occasionally look at the results'

Sir Winston Churchill

Chapter 4

Strategy in a Global Context: One Size Fits All?

4.1. Introduction

This chapter provides an introduction to international business management strategy. In order to go international all firms must first develop a strategy and identify how to create more value by operating in foreign, as well as domestic, markets. An important part of strategy is to design the firm's value chain of primary and support activities to ensure that it has the processes and activities necessary to create and optimise value. The managers of a firm must also understand the economics of international enterprise, and in particular how they can achieve economies from location, scale, and from experience effects.

With this in place, the firm needs to carry out an environmental analysis to identify the key factors that can support or constrict strategic action in different markets. This is a way of linking our learning from the first three chapters to generating strategic options. We provide three frameworks—PESTEL, CAGE, and SWOT—to facilitate such an analysis. We also refer you to Chapter 7 where further methods for analysing uncertain future environments are presented, the main one being scenario planning.

Finally, the firm needs to choose a strategy. We introduce four types of strategy commonly pursued in international business, how such strategies evolve, and detail Ghemawat's **A**ggregation, **A**rbitrage, and **A**daptation (AAA) strategy triangle as a basis for designing strategy for international contexts. Some argue that, following the 2020–2021 crisis and the volatility and uncertainty prevalent in the global economy, perhaps permanently, strategy as long-term planning becomes more or less redundant. The reality is that it is more necessary, but has to become much more adaptive, based on a variety of scenarios, and needs to be founded on organisational operational resilience capable of delivering on different plans, and responsive to changes in strategic direction.

4.2. Strategy and Value Creation

A firm's strategy has been defined variously as a long-term plan, a set of actions and/or as an integrated set of commitments. For example:

- *"A set of concrete plans to help the organisation accomplish its goal."* (Oster, 1994)

- *"The creation of a unique and valuable position, involving a different set of activities ... making trade-offs in competing ... creating fit among a company's activities."* (Porter, 1996)

- *"The determination of the basic long-term goals and objectives of an enterprise, and the adoption of courses of action and the allocation of resources necessary for carrying out these goals."* (Chandler, 1962)

- *"An integrated and coordinated set of commitments and actions designed to exploit core competencies and gain a competitive advantage."* (Hitt, Ireland, and Hoskisson, 2003)

Here, we will work with the Hitt et al. (2003) definition, recognising that strategy looks at long term (3 years or more) direction, while planning actions for short (1 year) and medium term (3 year) goals. Strategy asks, and seeks to answer, three fundamental questions:

1. Where are we now?
2. Where do we want to be/must we be?
3. How do we get there?

These questions form the essence of strategy as shown in Figure 4.1. You can apply this framework to identify, analyse and make strategy recommendations for any organisation.

Note that in Figure 4.1 not all espoused strategies work, and some aspects may be modified or dropped (unrealised strategy). On the other hand, not all strategies that eventually get enacted appear in the original plan. They may emerge in the course of events, as managers respond to circumstances, take opportunities, or have to react to unexpected events (emergent strategy). Expect to see a lot of changing, dropped and emergent strategies in international businesses over the next five years! You can test the usefulness of Figure 4.1 now. Take a large company you know well, (e.g. SingTel in Singapore, Tata in India, Barclays Bank in the UK.), and apply the framework to the period 2015-2020. Strategically, where was the company in 2015? Where did it want to get to? What strategy did it follow to get there? You can use the company's annual reports, available on the Internet, to help you with this task. If you want to extend your analysis, consider how the 2020 pandemic and economic crises made the company change direction. Looking at Figure 4.1., what are their strategies today,?

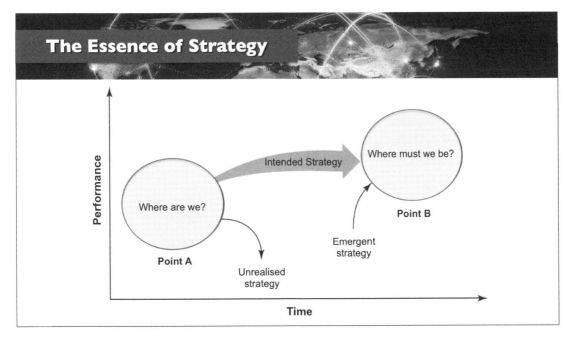

Figure 4.1: The Essence of Strategy

Value creation and the value chain

A business needs to pursue strategies that increase profitability and profit growth. Profitability is the rate of return the firm makes on its invested capital. Profit growth is the percentage increase in net profits over time. In general, higher profitability and profit growth increases the value of a firm to its owners. A firm can increase profitability by adopting strategies that (a) reduce costs, and/or (b) add value to the firm's products/services, thus allowing it to raise prices. A firm can increase the rate of profit growth by selling more products/services in existing markets, or pursuing strategies to enter new markets. Generally speaking, firms expand internationally because they experience restrictions and competition in their domestic markets, and see international business as a way of increasing profitability and their profit growth rates.

In practice, a firm is always trying to find the optimal—that is the most profitable—balance between: (a) keeping its own costs low, and (b) differentiating its products/services in ways that allow it to increase prices to levels at which enough customers will still buy those offerings. The trick is to identify the market segment, that is the group of customers, to whom your product/ service and price is more attractive than those offered by the competition. This is not easy! Take US hotel chains that operate internationally. The Four Seasons positions itself as a luxury chain and stresses the high value of its product offering. It can thus charge a premium price for its differentiated product, but at the same time will incur increased costs of operation, e.g. more service staff per customer, better quality of food and restaurant. The Marriott and Sheraton and Westin chains aim to offer sufficient value to attract international business travellers but do not compete in the luxury market, though they do compete against each other. Cutting costs can enhance profitability, but will this affect the quality of the product/service and so the customer experience? Will this then drive customers to rival hotels? Improving the product/service and customer experience could attract customers, allowing price increases, but at what point do higher prices drive customers elsewhere? And what are the adverse cost impacts of improving quality? We will revisit these issues in the next chapter when discussing Michael Porter and Cost versus Differentiation strategies.

The Firm as a value chain

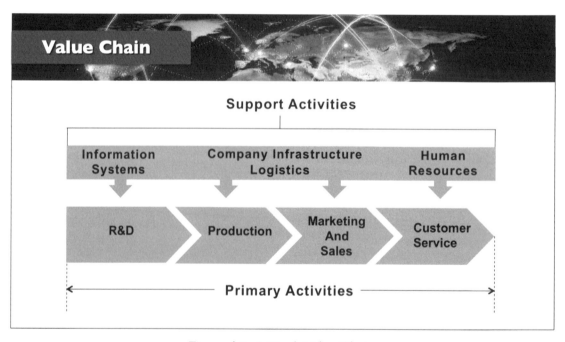

Figure 4.2: A Firm's Value Chain

The international hotel chains mentioned above, like all businesses, will only create superior value if they organise their operations efficiently. Operations here are defined as the different value creation activities a firm undertakes. These include, in a manufacturing firm, production, marketing and sales, R&D, human resources, information systems, logistics and infrastructure. Figure 4.2 is an example only and does not exhaust possibilities. For instance, a service organisation like Singapore Airlines or British Airways will have its primary activities organised around producing its services—selling the right seat, providing responsive service to or at the airport, during and after the flight.

Primary activities have to do with the design, production and delivery of the product/service; its marketing; and its support and after-sales service. All create value in various ways:

- *R&D*. Value is added through the design of products, services, and production processes, e.g. banks compete by designing new financial products like mortgages, insurance policies, and processes like on-line banking, smart money cards.

- *Production* adds value to a product by converting raw materials into an item, e.g. a car, a computer. In a service like health care 'production' consists of delivering the service, e.g. a heart operation, a prescription.

- *Marketing and Sales* can increase the perceived value of a product/service through global branding ('your promise to the customer') and advertising, e.g. Gillette differentiating its razors from non-branded razors or more local products.

- *Customer service* can give support through the whole customer's buying experience from awareness of the product/service through to the actual buying event, to after-sales support. As one example, US-based Caterpillar manufactures heavy earthmoving machines and vehicles, and can get spare parts to a customer anywhere in the world within 24 hours after a malfunction.

The support activities of the value chain provide inputs that allow the primary activities to occur. Typical support activities that we will deal with in detail in later chapters are:

- Logistics (sourcing and supply chain management)

- Information Systems management

- Human Resource management

Do not be misled. These can be as important, and sometimes even more important, than 'primary' activities. That is why we have a companion book focusing entirely on them (see Willcocks, 2021). For example, Amazon began making worldwide sales through being an internet 'pure play' in the 1990s and, with no retail outlets, dominates the book market and has been able to move into other business lines—CDs, electrical goods, household items, for example. Its IT infrastructure capability has allowed it to develop a 'cloud' (internet) based business renting digital storage space to other businesses worldwide. Major consultancy companies like McKinsey, PA Consulting Group, and Bain and Company, are crucially dependent on their HR capability in the so-called 'war for talent', i.e. getting the best, skilled and motivated employees in sufficient numbers to service clients' needs. Logistics deals with sourcing decisions and, in a semi-conductor manufacturer based in Taiwan, for example, sourcing refers to the transference of physical material through the value chain from procurement, through production into distribution. Efficient logistics creates value by lowering costs. When computerised, the cost reductions can be dramatic. But better still, excellent logistics can provide raw materials, components and finished goods to where they are needed faster, reducing bottlenecks in internal operations, and improving end service, and even creating a point of competitive differentiation by 'delighting' the customer. The firm's infrastructure provides the support for all these other activities, and includes finance and accounting, organisation structure and control systems, and IT infrastructure services.

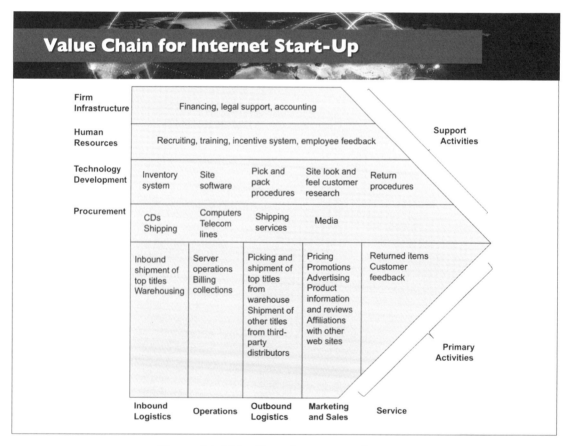

Figure 4.3: Vale Chain for Internet Start-up

To show the relevance of value chain analysis in the age of the Internet, Figure 4.3 portrays the value chain of an Internet start-up company looking to compete against Amazon. Note that it is a service rather than a manufacturing firm, and that, like most organisations with international, or even global, ambitions it is highly dependent on information and communications technologies throughout the value chain.

4.3. Going International - Economies of Scale, Location, and Experience

Firms operate on the international stage in order to expand their markets. The success of firms that expand internationally depends first on the goods or services they sell, i.e. the competitiveness of their value proposition or offering to international customers. In Chapter 5 we shall see that carrying out **competitive positioning analysis** can enhance this. Second, international success depends on core competencies—skills within the firm that competitors cannot easily match or imitate. Core competencies enable the firm to reduce the costs of value creation and/or to create perceived value so that premium pricing is possible. In the next chapter we shall see the importance of taking a **resource-based approach** to competitiveness. In addition, in domestic and international business, three ways of achieving cost advantage regularly come up in management thinking. We note them here because the terms will occur frequently in subsequent chapters.

1. *Economies of scale* refer to the reductions in unit cost achieved by producing a large volume of a product. Sources of economies of scale include: spreading fixed development and production costs over a larger volume of output; utilising production facilities more intensively; increasing bargaining power with suppliers. Going international can help economies of scale in several ways. For example the cost to a pharmaceutical company like Pfizer of developing a new major drug and bringing it to market can exceed US$900 million and take 12 years. Companies like Pfizer therefore look to sell their products worldwide to reduce average unit costs by spreading fixed costs over an increasing sales volume. The highly competitive global automobile industry faces intensive cost pressures in every product type, from luxury cars to the cheapest. An efficient factory needs to scale at, say, 200,000 units per year. The only way to sell cars in that number is to serve international as well as domestic markets, so using its factory assets more intensively.

   Growth in output and size, fuelled by international sales, may also have another scale benefit. As demand for resource inputs increases so does bargaining power with suppliers. Thus retailers like Wal-Mart generate huge sales volumes and so can negotiate down prices it pays to suppliers of goods sold in Wal-Mart stores.

2. *Location economies.* Here value creation activities are dispersed to locations where they can be performed most efficiently and effectively. Location economies arise from performing a value creation activity in the optimal location for that activity, wherever in the world that might be. A location might be more attractive cost-wise because of favourable political, legal, and economic factors, for example. Also due to differences in factor costs certain countries have comparative advantage when producing certain products, for example, historically, pharmaceuticals in Switzerland; semiconductors in South Korea; computer software in the USA. This was one reason why initially so many firms moved their IT work to Indian centres like Bangalore and Mumbai, though relative labour costs there have been rising in recent years. By achieving location economies, firms can lower the costs of value creation and achieve a low cost position, and can also differentiate their product offering. Firms that take advantage of location economies in different parts of the world create a global web of value creation activities. Different stages of the value chain are dispersed to locations where perceived value is maximised or where the costs of value creation are minimised. An example is Lenovo, the Chinese computer company that bought IBM's personal computer operations in 2005. The products are designed in the USA, case keyboard and hard drives are made in Thailand, the memory and display screen in Thailand, the wireless card in Malaysia and the microprocessor in the USA. Meanwhile the ThinkPad is assembled in Mexico, and then shipped to the USA for final sale. Note that location economies can vary over time and this Lenovo setup may well change in the future. Furthermore the 2020–2021 crisis accelerated corporate rethinking of sourcing strategy and supply chain design.

3. *Experience curve effects.* This refers to systematic reductions in production costs over product lifetime. Studies have tended to show, for example in the airframe industry, that whenever output doubles, the cost per unit can decline to 80 percent of the previous cost. This comes mainly from learning effects, as people learn to work more productively and management achieves efficiencies in how work is organised. Where learning falls off after a few years, then economies of scale—whereby increasing the scale of production spreads costs more thinly over each unit produced—will also contribute to this cumulative effect.

The utilisation of any of these three sources of economies can have significant strategic impacts for a firm. In certain industries, once a firm establishes a profitable low cost position, this can form a real barrier to new competitors. For example, in the 1970s Matsushita, the Japanese electronics company, at first lagged behind Philips and Sony in the race to get a commercial videocassette recorder on the market. Matsushita's strategy was to build sales volume world wide and fast by producing from one Japanese factory, which reaped huge learning effects and economies of scale. The objective was to get its VHS standard for videocassette recorders accepted worldwide (Sony and Philips had Betamax standard). Lower costs of production enabled Matsushita to drop its prices by 50 percent within five years of launching its first VHS videocassette recorder. By 1983 it controlled 45 percent of the global market and had a major scale and cost advantage over its rivals.

4.4. Analysing the International Environment

So far you have gained an understanding of strategy, and the economics and activities that underpin any strategy. We now focus more specifically on how firms can move into internationalising their businesses. There are three very helpful frameworks for diagnosing the environment, and the national and international factors likely to have a high impact on the success or failure of a firm's strategy.

The PESTEL Framework

Recall Chapters 2 and 3. To recap, the **PESTEL** framework categorises environmental influences into six main types:

- **P**olitical
- **T**echnological
- **E**conomic
- **E**nvironmental
- **S**ocial
- **L**egal

PESTEL provides a comprehensive list of influences on the possible success or failure of particular strategies. PESTEL summarises for international management purposes, i.e. from the firm's perspective, the critical factors discussed in Chapters 2 and 3:

- *Political Factors.* For example, Government policies; taxation changes; foreign trade regulations; political risk in foreign markets; changes in trade blocks (e.g. the EU in 2020).

- *Economic Factors.* For example, business cycles; interest rates; personal disposable income; exchange rates; unemployment rates; GDP trends.

- *Socio-cultural Factors.* For example, population changes; income distribution; lifestyle changes; consumerism; changes in culture and fashion.

- *Technological Factors.* For example, new discoveries and technology developments; ICT innovations; rates of obsolescence; increased spending on R&D.

- *Environmental ('Green') Factors.* For example, environmental protection regulations; energy consumption, global warming; waste disposal; re-cycling.

- *Legal Factors.* For example, competition laws; health and safety laws; employment laws; licensing laws; IPR laws.

Here are some rules for using PESTEL:

- Apply **selectively**—identify specific factors that impact on the industry, market and organisation in question.

- Identify factors that are **important currently**, but also consider which will become **more important** in the next few years.

- Use **data** to support your points, and analyse trends using up-to-date information.

- Identify **opportunities** and **threats**.

- Revisit the analysis very regularly. The 2020–2021 crisis demonstrated the importance of regular PESTEL updates, given today's unpredictable, volatile, connected global economy.

Now is also a good time to carry out a preliminary **SWOT** analysis:

- **S** – **S**trengths of the firm.
- **W** – **W**eaknesses of the firm.
- **O** – **O**pportunities for the firm.
- **T** – **T**hreats to the firm.

Here 'SW' refers to the internal firm's **capabilities**, while 'OT' refers to the **PESTEL environment**, plus (as discussed in Chapter 5) **competitive rivalry** at industry level. There is a neat way of performing a SWOT analysis and deriving some provisional views on strategy. It is called a **'MiniMax' analysis** (see Figure 4.4).

Here ask yourself four questions:

1. How can the firm maximise its strengths to take advantage of its opportunities?

2. How can a firm leverage its strengths to minimise threats?

3. How can a firm maximise opportunities to minimise its weaknesses?

4. What actions do the firm need to take to minimise its weaknesses and threats?

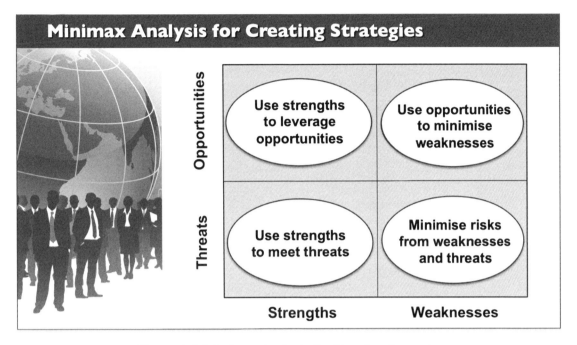

Figure 4.4: Minimax Analysis for Creating Strategies

Here you can see the firm is at its strongest using its strengths to take advantage of opportunities. For example Amazon is very good at running an online book service. Here Amazon's strength is being used to take advantage of an opportunity. Many bookstores have not been so good. One solution has been to use Amazon to run their online book service. A business can also use its strengths to meet and minimise threats. In a very competitive industry like newspaper publishing, in some countries your strength just might be control of the distribution chain and speed of delivery. Potentially you could make life quite difficult for a new start-up newspaper! However, increasing on-line news has eroded these possibilities in many markets, though physical newspapers still remain popular. If your business has weaknesses, for example a call centre facility that is costly and underutilised in the Netherlands, then maybe the opportunity is to outsource it to South Africa, especially given South Africa's Dutch heritage. The firm is at its weakest where weaknesses and threats come together. Typically this arises because another firm is attacking you at your weakest point. For example you offer a poor, or at least a very variable and high-priced service to your customers in a hotel chain across the world. Local hotels are eroding your market share. A response is needed! One might be to sell the non-competitive parts of the hotel chain. Another might be to institute radical improvements to establish standards and pricing that customers will appreciate and that are competitive in different countries.

The CAGE Distance Framework

We mentioned Ghemawat's work on *Distance Still Matters* in Chapter 1. He developed a CAGE framework to provide a richer understanding of what he means by distance—it is not just geographical distance he is referring to. You will recall that Ghemawat argues, and produces evidence for the fact that, for global strategy, distance still matters. Despite Thomas Friedman's 'The World Is Flat,' (see Chapter 1) there are important differences between countries. The world is not globalised but semi-globalised. In practice firms recognise this by trading less in parts of the world that are more distant from them in cultural/administrative/political/institutional, geographic, or economic terms. As one example, Ghemawat notes in his book, *The Laws of Globalisation and Business Applications* (2018, Cambridge University Press) that the United Kingdom does more than 50 percent of its trade with the European Union and Switzerland. He notes that a common language between countries, together with colony-coloniser ties (as the UK and USA have) boosts trade by 341 percent and FDI by 656 percent. His research shows that even just sharing a common language can double the trade between two countries. Firms need to pay attention to

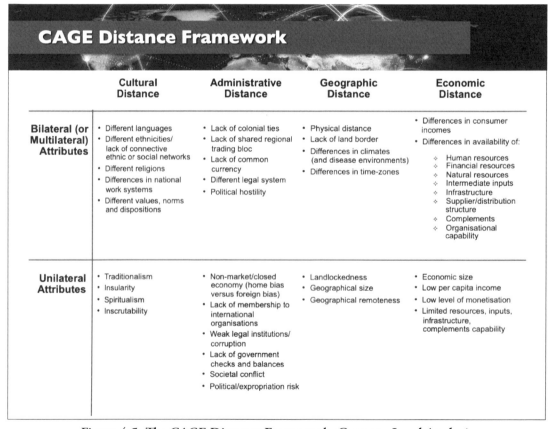

Figure 4.5: The CAGE Distance Framework: Country-Level Analysis

the distinctively large differences that arise at national borders, and devise international business strategies that take these differences into account. Ghemawat argues that pure global standardisation and localisation strategies will not work. International business strategy always needs to take into account the CAGE factors shown in Figure 4.5. CAGE, as you can see, stands for **C**ultural, **A**dministrative, **G**eographical, and **E**conomic differences. Note that the figure shows typical bilateral differences between the USA and several Asian mainland countries.

Clearly, distance and differences between the USA and these Asian mainland countries are not just geographic. There are also cultural differences for example language; race/ethnicity; social norms and values; administrative, political and institutional differences; and economic differences, e.g. personal incomes, infrastructure, human talent. Each country will also have what Ghemawat calls 'unilateral' CAGE attributes—distinct attributes that a PESTEL analysis would highlight, and which will influence the design of international business strategy. For example, Singapore has English as its official language; is multi-ethnic; has strong legal institutions is a small island (that has been made bigger!) but strategically located; has historically had strong government intervention in the economy; and a protected bank system.

Ghemawat also points out that a CAGE distance analysis at country level may not suffice. In Ghemawat (2010) he argues also for a CAGE industry-level analysis and discusses the case of Mexican-based multinational CEMEX and its internationalisation strategy. One of the notable parts of CEMEX's rise to globalism over 25 years has been the care with which it entered markets that shared affinities with Mexico on several of the CAGE dimensions. Its international excursions began in 1992 with the acquisition of two Spanish companies (Mexico is Spanish speaking). Then it acquired small cement companies in Latin America and the Caribbean, then in Colombia and Venezuela. Note that its acquisition policy over the years recognises that CAGE factors are so important that local companies are needed in order to gain local market share. By the mid-2000s CEMEX had become Mexico's top multinational with operations in 30 countries across five continents, and was the first firm from a developing country to enter the list of the world's top 100 transnational firms.

How to manage across CAGE distance factors? Ghemawat, in the Laws of Globalisation and Business Applications, suggest the four 'Cs' are useful to firms wanting to become better at bridging external distances. These are:

1. *Configuration*. The configuration or architecture of an international firm's value-adding activities has to take into account the trade-offs between internal and external distance. For example, locating R&D in a major foreign market, like India, may be advantageous to a US multinational in terms of reducing external costs to customers, but entails costs in stretching a strategically important function across

greater internal distance. Some general guidelines can apply. Thus some decisions will be highly centralised/coordinated, for example, for back-end IT platforms and global networks for high R&D spenders. Meanwhile front-end activities will tend to be more decentralised. But even a highly centralised activity does not need to be located in the home country. Wal-Mart, for example, secured the benefits of both scale (Aggregation) and global sourcing (Arbitrage—see below) by locating its global procurement headquarters in Shenzen, China. Meanwhile it may well be that advances in IT—software driven assets; larger streams of data; developments in the internet of things; cloud services; and other emerging technologies, including machine intelligence—are tilting more activities towards centralisation. The rapid globalisation of Airbnb, Uber, Amazon and Facebook, for example, point to the development of platforms that instead of residing at the back-end of organisations, can be taken to market globally.

2. *Coordination*. Given a decision on degrees of centralisation and decentralisation for various activities, how can these activities be coordinated effectively? Modern technologies have a big, and ever-increasing role to play in facilitating such coordination, especially over geographic distance. But formal reporting structures and informal systems, routines and relationships, as well as the interplay between formal and informal coordination methods, all still have a vital role to play—as discussed in more detail in Willcocks, (2021) on the subject of organisation architecture. The firm has also to take into account what will be a suitable structure for coordinating activity in the light of the business strategy chosen

3. *Culture*. A strong organisational culture can serve as a bridge across national cultural differences. Organisational culture as a unifier is particularly prevalent amongst, for example, management consultancies, investment banks and other professional service firms. But this practice is not limited to professional service firms. For example, Johnson and Johnson, producing health care products, has had a strong customer-focused culture for decades, while a more recent firm like Google, also has developed a strong unified culture. A common corporate language can also help. Thus Cemex implemented English as the single global operating language, despite being a Mexican firm whose native language in that country is Spanish. However, a strong culture does not necessarily breed openness to diverse ideas and people, though these may be the very qualities you want to take advantage of by becoming international. Also too closely aligning the strong culture with a firm's home country may be poor signalling, and reduce the firm's capacity to bridge distance. (See also Chapter 3).

4. *Cosmopolitanism*. This is linked to culture, but also important are the people who lead international businesses, especially multinationals. Amongst the top teams of the world's largest corporations there is quite a lot of evidence of limited diversity in terms of ethnicity and sex, amongst the top teams of the world's largest corporations. In 2013, for example, 87 percent of the top Fortune 500 companies were led by a native CEO, and 85 percent of their top team members were also natives. There is some evidence that boosting diversity amongst these top teams has the potential to unlock large benefits in terms of increasing firm performance. One 2012 study found that companies with high executive board diversity produced ROE on average 53 percent higher than those firms in the lowest quartile. Selecting a non-native can also be a powerful signal. For example, Satya Nadella, born in India, was appointed Microsoft's CEO and this must have been seen as particularly inspiring to the estimated one third of the workforce of Indian ethnic origin. That said, some studies show that top management diversity becomes advantageous only in firms with a high degree of internationalisation. A strong corporate culture that encourages openness can help to strengthen the benefits of top team national diversity. Also boosting the cosmopolitanism of organisational members, and their education and experience helps in reducing the distance sensitivity of the company.

4.5. Ghemawat's AAA Model for Strategy Development

How does one deal with the international environments-regions, countries, and industries-and the characteristics and differences uncovered by analyses like PESTEL and CAGE? Ghemawat provides an answer in his AAA framework. When looking to globalise, the firm will experience a tension between the need to be responsive to local conditions and markets (**Adaptation**), and the need to achieve economies of scale and other advantages through global integration (**Aggregation**). At the same time it will want to take advantage of any absolute economies it can get from operating in a different country (**Arbitrage**). Let's look at these concepts in more detail (see Figure 4.6). In a foreign marketplace:

- *Adaptation* provides the most obvious strategy for dealing with differences. The strategy is to *adjust* to those differences. Faced with different customer preferences, a company can offer different or modified products or services, and tailor policies, positioning, advertising, and pricing. But such variation can be expensive, and sub-strategies will be needed to reduce the costs of such variation. Given the limitations imposed on other strategies by cross-country differences and distance, nearly every company operating internationally needs to engage in at least some adaptation. Variation needs to extend beyond the blunt matter of

Ghemawat's AAA Model

AAA Strategy	Adaptation	Aggregation	Arbitrage
Competitive Advantage: Why globalize at all?	To achieve local relevance through national focus (while exploiting some scale)	To achieve scale and scope economies through international standardization	To achieve absolute (nonscalar) economies through international specialization
Configuration: Where to locate overseas?	To limit the effects of cultural – administrative-geographic-economic differences by concentrating on foreign countries that are similar to home		To exploit (selected) differences by operating in more diverse countries
Coordination: How should international operation be organized?	By country: emphasis on adjustments to achieve a local face within borders	By business: emphasis on horizontal relationships to achieve economies of scale across borders	By function: emphasis on vertical relationships, including across organizational boundaries
Checks: What to watch out for strategically?	Excessive variety or complexity	Excessive standardization	Narrowing spreads
Corporate Diplomacy: Which public issues need to be addressed?	Potentially discreet and robust given emphasis on cultivation of a local face	Appearances of and backlash against homogenization or hegemonism (especially on part of US companies)	The exploitation or displacement of suppliers, channels, or intermediaries: potentially most prone to political disruption

Figure 4.6: Integrating Adaptation, Aggregation and Arbitrage Strategies

deciding on degree of centralisation or decentralisation in terms of structure and decision-making. Product variation is the most visible aspect of adaptation.

Japan's Panasonic corporation, for example, launched a new clothes-washing machine in India in 2017, designed specifically to handle stains especially common in India, for example curry and hair oil. Unilever has over 100 variants on its global Lux soap brand. The Apple iPhone may look the same everywhere, but the devices user interfaces are localised. Companies can also localise aspects of their marketing and internal operations. In 2015 the world's largest marketing services company, WPP, estimated that only 15 percent of its marketing methods was truly global. Where products might not vary much, a lot of variation can be added to how they are sold. But the costs of variation can be substantial. Thus Panasonic spent two years analysing curry and other distinctive Indian stains, and assigned a Japanese-Indian study team to tweak the machines appropriately. Beyond the upfront investment, the machines probably cannot be sold in many other markets. One solution might be to focus on products or services that need less variation, that is by narrowing scope of product. India's IT service companies, for example, have focused on application development and maintenance where they have captured 25 percent of the world's market. Another approach is to externalise making the variation. For example on the Airbnb platform, those who are offering rooms for rent have a great deal of latitude on how they wish to customise the offering. The thinking here is that those offering rooms have much more local knowledge than Airbnb.

Another approach is to design products in a modular way, knowing what is standard, and what has to be customised for different markets. Motor cars are an obvious example. Thus, in 2016, Ford simplified from 26 car and truck designs, or platforms, down to nine. Within each design what was visible to the customer was customised to local requirements. What was invisible to the customer was standardised—an approach called mass customisation. Another approach is to innovate. IKEA, the Swedish home furnishing company, innovated with its flat pack design, thus reducing transportation costs, while Cemex, the Mexican cement manufacturer, offered marketing innovation by time-based delivery guarantees.

- *Aggregation.* The strategy here is to *overcome* differences. Use grouping devices and intragroup coordination mechanisms to create greater economies of scale/scope than country-by-country adaptation can provide. Standardisation of products/services is just one Aggregation strategy amongst many other possibilities. Particularly important are regional strategies that aggregate based on geography. This involves establishing, for example, regional hubs, shared service centres, and marketing and sales platforms regionally. Recall that more than one half of international trade and foreign direct investment (FDI) takes place within regions. One reason is that countries in a region often have commonalities in the cultural, administrative and economic, as well as geographic, dimensions of the CAGE distance framework. But firms also aggregate along other dimensions. For example, Tata Consultancy Services (TCS)—based in India, and one of the largest Indian IT services companies— aggregates partly by language. Uruguayan operations service Spanish-speaking markets; Hungarian operations service German-speaking countries; while TCS has also set up in Morocco to service French-speaking markets. Recall CEMEX, and how initially it focused on emerging markets—representing an aggregation strategy along an economic dimension. Later it shifted to an aggregation strategy based on geography.

119

Many major multinationals tend to compete abroad primarily on the basis of aggregation, especially by scaling their intangible assets. One case in point is US-based multinational GE whose strengths in aggregating technology, brand, talent and R&D in international business underpin strategies that are more difficult for international and local competitors to copy (see the ***resource-based perspective*** in Chapter 5). Leading pharmaceutical companies also exemplify global strategies based on aggregating intangibles, in their case primarily R&D assets. However, Ghemawat's laws of globalisation (see Chapter 1) do impose limits on aggregation. The constraining power of borders and distance implies that strategies of pure aggregation are rarely feasible or desirable. Aggregation is typically most effective within the confines of similar groups of countries. You can apply the CAGE framework here as a useful indicator. Thus, companies can use aggregation among countries with cultural similarities (e.g Ibero-America); administrative linkages (e.g. via free trade agreements); geographic proximity (e.g by region); or economic similarity (e.g. advanced versus emerging economies).

- ***Arbitrage***. As a strategy, this *exploits* differences between national or regional markets by locating different parts of the supply chain in different places. As such, arbitrage represents a production strategy, where the firm focuses on absolute economies rather than scale economies gained through standardisation. Find the location where there are lower labour costs, lower resource (minerals, raw materials) or assembly costs or cheaper capital, and/or perhaps tax advantages. Arbitrage strategies treat differences across borders as opportunities rather than constraints. Arbitrage strategy classically sees a firm produce where costs are low, and sell where prices are high.

Labour cost arbitrage is particularly powerful, and explains the initial impetus for China's long-time global lead in manufacturing, and for the lift-off in India's offshore services boom. By 2018, for example, India's offshore IT sector was generating nearly 8 percent of India's GDP, and 49 percent of India's service exports, as well as employing directly and indirectly about 14 million people. The labour arbitrage figures show how India, amongst many other locations, remained attractive. In 2014, mid-career IT professionals in India averaged only 15-25 percent of US pay for similar jobs. Despite these sorts of figures, there has been a more recent backlash, a lot of it perceptual, against arbitrage strategies and offshoring in advanced economies. However, arbitrage opportunities exist not just because of labour market differences, but also across all the four dimensions of the CAGE distance framework. In practice, firms in every industrial and service sector have multiple arbitrage opportunities across the world.

The key to successful global competitiveness is to look at the trade-offs between the three As when entering a specific country and industry, and form an integrated AAA strategy. Figure 4.6 summarises Ghemawat's views on what each strategy offers and how they often pull in different directions. You can see first of all that there are real tensions between the three strategies in terms of the objectives of going international; where best to locate overseas; how international operations should be organised; what to watch out for strategically; and which public issues need to be addressed. International business management is about clarifying and dealing with these tensions inherent in the strategic choices made.

In his book *Redefining Global Strategy* (2007), Ghemawat helpfully discusses the example of De Beers, the Africa-based diamond mining and retail multinational. He argues that, even before a major strategy shift, De Beers used all three AAA strategies to engage with cross-country differences. Thus De Beers *adapted* to adjust to country differences by focusing on owning mines in 'weak governance countries'; presented different marketing campaigns for different countries while obscuring the country of origin; strove for market and product development in different markets; and tended to have a global mind-set in its management cadre. De Beers also *aggregated* to overcome country differences. Infrastructure and other activities were subject to large-scale economies. Global demand was managed by stockpiling to keep the price up and by global advertising. And it built up bargaining power over its distribution channels through leveraging size and control. At the same time De Beers undertook *arbitrage* to exploit differences. For example, it sourced where material costs were low, for example Africa, Russia, and Australia. On labour costs, it used India for absorbing the smallest stones. It gained attractive terms from certain countries needing contracts. It arbitraged to reduce its tax burden. And it retained superior information on optimal locations for its range of activities.

4.6. Choosing a Strategy for International Business

We have one more framework to look at! There are four basic strategies to compete in international markets (see Figure 4.7). The appropriateness of each strategy depends on the pressures for cost reduction and local responsiveness in the industry. Let us look at the vertical axis first. Pressures for cost reductions are greatest:

- In industries producing **commodity type products** that fill universal needs (needs that exist when the tastes and preferences of consumers in different nations are similar if not identical) where price is the main competitive weapon.

- When major competitors are based in **low cost locations**.

- Where there is persistent **excess capacity**.

- Where **consumers are powerful** and face low switching costs.

Figure 4.7: Four Basic International Business Strategies

Pressures for local responsiveness arise from:

- **Differences in consumer tastes and preferences**. Strong pressure emerges when consumer tastes and preferences differ significantly between countries.

- **Differences in traditional practices and infrastructure**. Strong pressure emerges when there are significant differences in infrastructure and/or traditional practices between countries.

- **Differences in distribution channels**. There is a need to be responsive to differences in distribution channels between countries.

- **Host government demands**. Economic and political demands imposed by host country governments may require local responsiveness.

- **Rise of regionalism**. In recent years there has been a tendency for convergence of tastes, practices, infrastructure, distribution channels and host government demands, not just across one nation, but two or more, forming what we can call a **region**. The European Union provides the most obvious example, where, indeed, there are institutional forces pushing for convergence. The recently revised USA, Canada and

Mexico trade agreement also provides and example of a degree of convergence at a regional level (see Chapter 2). One could also argue that there is a Latin American region where there is a shared Spanish language, (except Brazil, where Portuguese is spoken), history and cultural heritage, which can moderate national differences within the region. Taking a regional perspective is important because it suggests that localisation at the regional, rather than the national, level forms a better strategic response.

Pressures for local responsiveness suggest that it may not be possible for a firm to realise the full benefits from economies of scale, learning effects and location economies; or to leverage a firm's core competencies from one country's markets to those of other countries. What strategies can we choose, then, and when is each most suitable? Firms typically choose between four strategic positions when competing internationally:

1. *International (home replication) strategy,* which stresses the advantages of replication internationally of home country-based competencies, e.g. brand, distribution network, products, and services. Taking products first produced for the domestic market and selling them internationally with only minimal local customisation makes sense when there are low cost/global integration pressures and low pressures for local responsiveness. Successful firms using this strategy tend to be selling a product that serves universal needs, but do not face significant competitors, and so do not face pressures to reduce cost. When it invented and commercialised the photocopier, Xerox protected the product with patents and hence did not face strong competition for many years. As a result Xerox was able to sell the same basic product in most developed economies, and, for an in-demand product, charge a relatively high price. A business pursuing an international strategy tend to centralise product development and R&D at home, while head office keeps tight control over marketing and product strategy. However, the same business may also evolve into establishing marketing and manufacturing functions in the country/region in which they are doing business, as a part localisation and arbitrage strategy.

2. *Localisation (multi-domestic) strategy,* which considers each country or region as a stand-alone local market worthy in itself of significant adaptation and attention. This responds to Ghemawat's Adaptation requirements in strategy. The strategy involves increasing profitability by customising goods or services so that they match tastes and preferences in different national markets. This makes sense when there are substantial differences across nations with regard to consumer tastes and preferences and when cost pressures are not too intense. The benefits of standardisation are

lost, additional customisation costs are incurred, but these downsides may well be outweighed where local customisation supports higher pricing, and/or leads to higher local demand. Cost have to be carefully managed, and, whenever possible, it is important to capture some scale economies from the firm's global reach. As we noted earlier, automobile companies try to achieve this tricky balancing act by applying a mass customisation philosophy—standardising what is invisible to customers, and customising what is visible.

3. **Global standardisation strategy**, which seeks to develop and distribute standardised products/services worldwide to reap the benefits of economies of scale and shared product development. This is Ghemawat's Aggregation goal, namely to increase profitability and profit growth using economies of scale, learning effects, and location economies. This makes sense when there are strong pressures for cost reductions and demands for local responsiveness are minimal. Production, marketing, R&D, and supply chain activities will be concentrated in a few favourable locations. Customisation will be minimal. Increasingly the conditions most suitable for a global standardisation strategy include many industrial goods industries, where products often serve universal needs and operate under global standards. One example is the semi-conductor industry, where Intel, Motorola and Texas Instruments, for instance, all pursue a global standardisation strategy.

4. **Transnational strategy**, which aims to capture the 'best of both worlds' by endeavouring to be both cost efficient (Aggregation focus) and locally responsive (Adaptation focus). This tries to simultaneously achieve low costs through location economies, economies of scale, and learning effects, differentiate the product offering across geographic markets to account for local differences, and foster a multidirectional flow of skills between different subsidiaries in the firm's global network of operations. This makes sense when cost pressures are intense and pressures for local responsiveness are strong. An important part of transnational strategy is to leverage skills, innovation and product offerings from every location and foreign subsidiary, rather than there being just a flow one way from home country to foreign subsidiary. While all this sounds attractive, it is not that easy to pursue! One of the problems it that it creates conflicting demands. Differentiating the product to respond to local demands in different geographic markets raises costs, which runs counter to the goal of *reducing* costs. Companies like 3M, and the engineering conglomerate ABB, have found transnational strategy difficult to implement. On the other hand, Caterpillar had faced significant pressures for cost reduction and local responsiveness—not least from intense low-cost competition from, for example,

Komatsu of Japan. Caterpillar reduced costs by redesigning its product to use many identical components, and built a few large-scale component manufacturing facilities in favourable locations. By building assembly plants in each of its major global markets—where local product features were added, and the product finished off—augmented centralised manufacturing. Caterpillar also managed to double output per employee—significantly reducing its cost structure in the process. Meanwhile Hitachi and Komatsu adhered to a Japan-centric global strategy, and saw their cost advantages disappear, while losing market share to Caterpillar.

How do these strategies evolve? For each strategic posture, over time, competitors inevitably emerge. The company's own strategy may change. Senior management may become more ambitious internationally. We mentioned Xerox above. Eventually Canon invented their way into producing their own photocopiers in efficient manufacturing plants, priced their products lower, and took global market share from Xerox. In Xerox's case the problem was really Xerox's failure to manage its cost structure against efficient emerging competition, and its failure to face the need to change its strategic positioning. Some typical changes in positioning are shown in Figure 4.8.

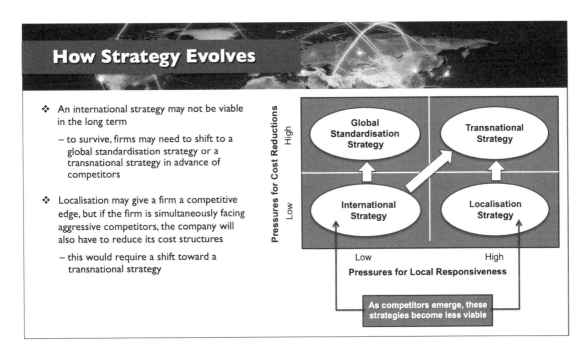

Figure 4.8: How Strategy Evolves

To survive, firms may need to shift to a global standardisation strategy or a transnational strategy in advance of competitors. A **localisation strategy** may give a firm a competitive edge, but if the firm is simultaneously facing aggressive competitors, the company will also have to reduce its cost structures. This would require a shift toward a more **transnational strategy**. This is what Procter and Gamble did from 1999, when it moved from localisation to a more global strategy. As competition intensifies, managers need to move from less viable international or localisation strategies, and direct their companies towards a global standardisation or transnational strategy. Procter and Gamble achieved annual cost savings of $800 million, which it used to cut prices and increase market share, thus achieving further cost reductions through scale economies. However, there needs to be constant evolution in today's global business climate. For example, Procter and Gamble put in strong performances on profit and growth during the 2000s, while its competitors struggled. But since 2014 P&G once again saw a decline in sales. International strategies become out-dated and inevitably evolve to fit with changes in strategic choices and environment. Another issue is 'fit', or alignment, with the organisation structure and operations (see Willcocks, 2021).

4.7. Conclusion

Through this chapter we have arrived at an understanding of what strategy is, how it is a design for value creation, and how the value chain of a firm is vital to deliver on the value promise inherent in the strategy. These concepts have been applied to firms operating internationally with worked examples illustrating the concepts and principles. You were also introduced to economies from location, scale and experience effects, and should be able to apply these ideas to strategy development in international business. This chapter stressed the importance of your learning from Chapters 1, 2, and 3 and described the major components of an environmental analysis capturing this learning through PESTEL and CAGE frameworks.

We also showed you how to apply these frameworks to actual cases, and generate strategies from the analyses, not least by using the simple but powerful MiniMax box. This chapter introduced a major means for developing international business strategy for an organisation in detailing Ghemawat's AAA model. We also discussed the four basic international strategy types, namely **International** (home replication), **Localisation**, **Global Standardisation**, and **Transnational** strategies and the inevitability of evolution from these simple models to deal with changes in strategic choices, levels of success and environmental dynamism.

By 2021, and going forward, the frameworks detailed in this chapter had become vital tools for arriving at international business strategy. With these you can pick up the fact that economies of scale had been eroding for some time—global firms have big overheads, while complex supply chains tie up inventory. With more mergers and acquisitions, sprawling organisations become increasingly more difficult to run. Some arbitrage opportunities were deteriorating. For example, Indian and Chinese wages continue to rise, and increased protectionism in the form of tariffs, and informal barriers can make foreign locations less attractive. Local firms are becoming more sophisticated. Tax bills have been reduced as far as they can go as a result of managing tax avoidance internationally. Governments are looking to take more of the value generated by the multinationals. One corporate response to all this has been to put down deeper roots in the countries in which they operate. General Electric and Siemens, for example, have been localising supply chains, production, jobs, and tax into national or regional units. Another strategy has been to become more 'virtual' as an organisation, focusing on intangibles, moving, for example, from running fast-food chains or hotels, to selling branding rights.

This sets us up for the next chapter, which looks at how firms can compete internationally. We will look at competitive positioning as well as resource-based, and institution-based, perspectives on this issue.

References

Chandler, (1962), *Strategy and Structure*, MIT Press, Boston, USA

Ghemawat, P. (2007), *Redefining Global Strategy*.

Ghemawat, P. (2018), *The Laws of Globalisation and Business Applications*, Cambridge University Press, Cambridge, UK

Hitt, M., Ireland, D. and Hoskisson, R. (2003), *Strategic Management* (5th edition), Thomson South Western, Cincinnati, USA

Oster, (1994), *Modern Competitive Analysis*, Oxford University Press, Oxford, UK

Porter, M. (1996), 'What Is Strategy?', *Harvard Business Review*, 74, 6, 61-68

Willcocks, L. (2021), *Global Business Management*, SB Publishing, Stratford-upon-Avon, UK

"You may not be interested in strategy, but strategy is interested in you."

Leon Trotsky

"The essence of strategy is choosing what not to do."

Michael Porter

"'If you know the enemy and know yourself, you need not fear the result of a hundred battles. If you know yourself but not the enemy, for every victory gained you will also suffer a defeat. If you know neither the enemy nor yourself, you will succumb in every battle."

Sun Tzu

Chapter 5

International Competitive Strategy: Debating Approaches

5.1. Introduction

At this point, we make a distinction between three types of strategy. **Business-level** or competitive strategy—the subject of this chapter—focuses on how individual businesses should compete in their particular markets. There is also **corporate level** strategy that concerns the overall scope of a firm, and how value is added, and synergies achieved across the firm's several business units if taken as whole. We deal with this issue in Chapter 6. Then there are the operational strategies, where the focus falls on how the components of an organisation deliver effectively the corporate and business level strategies in terms of resources, processes, and people. **Operational** strategies are covered in a companion book (Willcocks, 2021) that deals with the primary functional areas—marketing; R&D; organisation and structure; sourcing; information systems; international finance; human resources; and project and change management.

An *industry* is a group of firms producing goods (products/services) that are similar to each other. There may be thousands of firms offering similar goods/services in perfect competition. Here entry barriers are low, there are many equal rivals each with similar products, and information about competitors is freely available. An example is taxicab services in large cities throughout the world. More typically, there are relatively few organisations in direct competition. At the other extreme, a *monopoly* is where only one firm provides the goods/services for an industry. A *duopoly* is where two firms dominate the industry. An *oligopoly* is where a few firms control an industry. A *market* is a group of customers for specific products or services that are similar to each other. Thus Honda operates in the world's automobile market and will sell its range of cars in markets like USA, Europe, Japan, with intensive competition from other automakers like Toyota, BMW, GM (General Motors), Citroen, across its entire car range. To compete successfully, Honda needs to understand the competitive dynamics of its industry, globally, the strategies available to it, the resources it needs to create and leverage to compete, and where it needs to cooperate with other firms in its competitive effort and in its supply chain. In this chapter we focus on the three major approaches to competitive strategy—the competitive positioning, resource-based and institution-based perspectives. We discuss how they can be used in a complementary way, and debate and offer insights into the usefulness of each. We argue that, in the dynamic, complex, uncertain global business environment we find ourselves, these approaches remain as relevant as ever.

5.2. Porter's Five Forces Framework

Michael Porter has been a pioneer in developing the competitive positioning perspective. His five forces model identifies an industry's structure, and whether or not it is an attractive industry for a business unit to compete in. It provides a useful starting point for identifying whether competing will be profitable, and if not, what actions a firm can take, what levers to pull, as it were, to become more profitable. Porter's framework helps a business to position itself advantageously relative to its competitors (Porter, 1985). The five forces are shown in Figure 5.1.

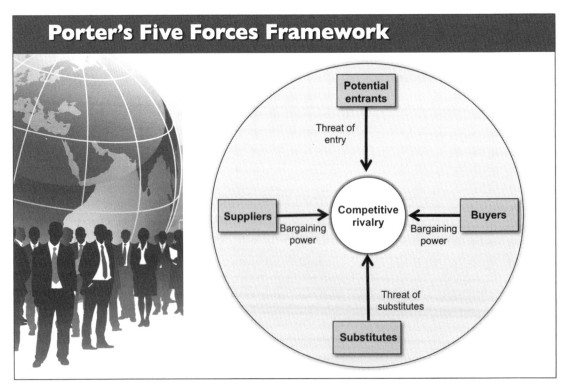

Figure 5.1: Five Forces Framework for Competitive Analysis

5.2.1. Rivalry Between Competitors

Competitive rivals are organisations with similar products and services aimed at the same customer group, and are direct competitors in the same industry/market (they are distinct from substitutes.) For example, Air France and British Airways compete for airline passengers in Europe. Trains are a substitute service. The degree of rivalry is increased when:

- Competitors are of roughly equal size. This leads to more intense struggles for dominance between the firms.

- Competitors are aggressive in seeking leadership.

- The market is mature or declining. Think about this. If the market is expanding, the strong growth rate in sales allows firms to grow with the market. But if the products/services are mature, or the market is declining, then firms are competing for a shrinking share. As a result there may be high price competition and low profitability, involving intensive rivalry.

- There are high fixed costs. Industries requiring high capital equipment costs, e.g. the steel industry, or high research and development costs, e.g. pharmaceuticals, will seek to spread their fixed costs across increased sales, thus competing intensely with rivals.

- The exit barriers are high, for example, due to high costs of redundancy or the decommissioning of capital equipment that is not easily resaleable. In a declining industry this puts pressure on rivals to fight to maintain market share.

- There is a low level of differentiation. Differentiation can be made, for example by providing goods/services with different attributes, e.g. colour and shape of tennis racquet, battery length in a portable computer, or by pricing the goods/services differently, or by branding—customers are willing to pay more for Adidas or Nike sports shoes than for non-branded shoes.

Figure 5.2 gives a simplified example of competitive rivalry in the global automobile industry. Note that there are different markets for different types of car, and that products and related services are differentiated from one another by factors like price and prestige. Looking at Figure 5.2 from a customer perspective, there are three markets—mass, luxury, and ultra luxury. We call each a *market segment*, i.e. a group of customers with similar needs, different from customer needs, in other parts of the market.

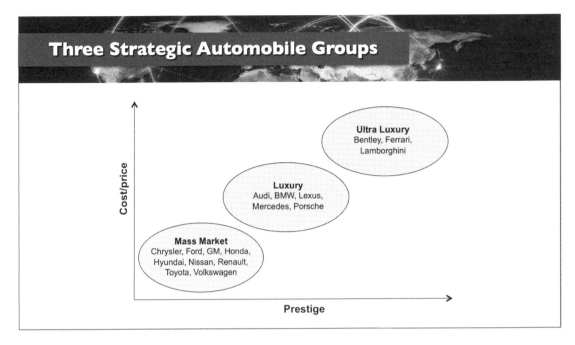

Figure 5.2: Three Strategic Groups in the Global Automobile Industry

5.2.2. The Threat of Entry by New Rivals, and Barriers to Their Entry

Barriers to entry are the factors that need to be overcome by new entrants if they are to compete in an industry. The threat of rival entry is low when high entry barriers keep them out, such as:

- Economies of scale/high fixed costs. The steel, semi-conductor, and pharmaceutical industries are just three examples.

- Non-scale-based advantages, for example patents, difficult to imitate know-how, superior information about customers; such factors are resource-based. See below for more discussion.

- High experience and learning needed to succeed in the industry.

- Difficult access to supply and distribution channels. In many industries firms have built control over their suppliers, by contracts, or by direct ownership for example large supermarket chains in Europe and the USA. This can be overcome of course. For example, in the 1990s Dell Computers built a highly successful global business selling computer equipment on-line, with no retail outlets, and focused on controlling manufacturing and the supply chain.

- High differentiation and market penetration costs—typical for the products shown in Figure 5.2.

- Difficult government restrictions (e.g. licensing, tax regimes). For example, the Indian government historically, has banned large-scale entry by foreign retailers like Wal-Mart and Tesco.

- Possible retaliation by incumbent (existing) firms in the market, for example slashing prices against a new rival setting up in the UK newspaper industry.

5.2.3. Threat of Substitutes

- Substitutes are products or services that offer a similar benefit to an industry's products or services, but by a different process. For example, in India Tata's 'one lakh' car could substitute for motorcycles and rickshaws, initially in Indian cities, but then as an export abroad. Customers will switch to alternatives (and thus the threat increases) if:

- The price/performance ratio of the substitute is superior, e.g. aluminium may be more expensive than steel but it is more cost efficient for some car parts.

The substitute benefits from an innovation that improves customer satisfaction, e.g. high-speed trains can be quicker than airlines from city centre to city centre—London to Paris, in Europe, for example. But note in this example that the price Eurostar can charge for train travel, despite Eurostar being a monopoly, is still limited by the cost of air travel to the same destination. Note also that the substitute may come from outside what you have defined as the industry—in this case, air travel.

5.2.4. The Bargaining Power of Buyers

Buyers are the organisation's immediate customers, not necessarily the ultimate consumers. For example, for companies like Unilever and Proctor and Gamble (that make detergents, shampoos, and hundreds of related products) their customers are stores like Carrefour, Marks and Spencer. If buyers are powerful, then they can demand cheap prices or product/service improvements to reduce profits. Buyer power is likely to be high when:

- Buyers are concentrated, that is where a few buyers account for the majority of sales. Thus hundreds of automobile component suppliers try to sell to a small number of carmakers like Honda, BMW, Ford, and Citroen. This can give the automakers a lot of bargaining power.

- Look at Toyota in Guangzhou China, where more than 30 supplier factories surround the Toyota factory. Suppliers had to locate this closely because Toyota wanted low transaction costs, and strong control over its suppliers.

- Buyers have low switching costs, meaning they can switch easily between suppliers. For example, a global retail chain like Starbucks could switch between coffee suppliers easily. Switching costs are low when the item bought is a weakly differentiated commodity, and is easily available, e.g. sugar.

- Buyers can supply their own inputs (this is called backward vertical integration). For example, some Chinese steel companies have gained power over their iron ore suppliers by acquiring iron ore sources for themselves, which puts them in a strong bargaining position relative to their existing suppliers.

5.2.5. The Bargaining Power of Suppliers

Suppliers are those who supply what organisations need in order to produce the product or service. Powerful suppliers can eat into an organisation's profits. Supplier power is likely to be high when:

- The suppliers are concentrated, that is, there are very few of them. Or suppliers provide a specialist or rare input. For example, for Coca-Cola bottlers there is only one supplier of Coke syrup—Coca-Cola. If Coca-Cola changes the price, there is little the bottlers can do but pay.

- Buyers represent only a small part of sales by the supplier. Thus Boeing will not offer lower prices for new aircraft to small airlines, but may well offer large discounts to Singapore Airlines, Malaysian Airlines, Emirates, or British Airways.

- Switching costs are high, that is where it is disruptive or expensive to change suppliers. Thus Microsoft is a powerful supplier in the PC industry because of the high switching costs of moving from one operating system to another. Likewise Intel for microprocessors.

- Suppliers can integrate forwards. For example, low cost airlines can cut out the use of travel agents. Nike supplies shoes to traditional footwear stores, but has also established a number of retail outlets, such as Nike City, in major cities.

5.2.6. Use and Criticisms of The Porter Five Forces Framework

With the Five Forces Framework you are trying to assess the attractiveness of an industry, and how to make it more attractive, from a business perspective. It is important, therefore, to ask:

- Should we enter or leave this industry?

- What leverage can we exert to improve our chances of success?

- How are competitors reacting to the five forces, and how will they react to moves we make?

The Five Forces Framework is a useful tool but must be applied carefully:

1. Apply the framework at the most *appropriate level*—not necessarily the whole industry. For example, the European low cost airline industry must be separated out from the airlines industry globally.

2. A Five Forces analysis may assume too much stability. In most modern competitive environments, especially in the 2020s, there is a higher dynamism than Porter assumed when he designed the framework back in the 1980s. For example, there is the phenomenon of *hypercompetition* where the frequency, boldness, and aggression of competitor interactions create constant disequilibrium and change. Think of the global mobile 'phone industry from 2008-12 (Samsung, Nokia, Apple iPhone, Google's Nexus One) and its destabilising innovation, aggressive price cuts, and expensive marketing efforts.

3. Industry boundaries are constantly changing. Many industries, especially in hi-tech areas, are converging. Think of digital industries and convergence between mobile 'phones, cameras, and MP3 players, for example. This leads to blurred industry boundaries, rendering the Five Forces analysis more difficult, and needing constant updating. As one example, which industry is Amazon in? What industries has it moved into? Remember, it started life as an online bookseller! Technology and business platforms build millions of customers, and can then move into selling them products and services previously the preserve of other industries. Thus, Amazon started moves into banking in 2018. It was well positioned to move into US banking because of its frequent purchaser and customer reviews; a full commercial credit card on file; integration into customers' computers, smartphones, tablets, TVs and home audio devices; excellent service; and no major security breaches. Once established as a co-branded basic banking service, Amazon can then move into other financial products like lending; mortgages; property/casualty insurance; wealth management; and term life insurance. Imagine the threat this can represent to incumbent banks and insurance companies, but also to less well-branded fintech start-ups.

4. Five Forces analysis tends to neglect the growing importance of *complementors*. Some commentators argue that, in fact, complementors represent a sixth force. An organisation is your complementor when (a) customers value your product more if they use it along with the other firm's product/service than when they use your

product alone, and (b) it is more attractive for suppliers to provide resources to both you and the other organisation, rather than to you alone. Thus Microsoft Windows and McAfee computer security systems have been type (a) complements. Boeing, in its relationships to airlines, is a type (b) example. Here, Boeing invests huge sums in innovation because it has so many airlines as potential customers. Boeing and its customers find it advantageous to cooperate on aircraft development in order to compete on other activities. The complementors to the PC industry are firms that produce software applications. When a complementor produces a new winning computer game, for example, then demand for both PCs and the game increases. In the Amazon banking example above, the company sought to co-brand with JP Morgan Chase as its complementor.

5. Are all Five Forces potential threats? This neglects the rise of strategic alliances between firms to achieve wider goals together, for example a foreign and local firm trying to dominate the Chinese market in a specific industry. Also, because of the costs of competition, even competitors are found these days cooperating. Thus GM and Toyota manufacture cars together. South Korean based Samsung provides computer chips to Japan-based Sony. Such firms cooperate in order to compete— not the prime message of the original Five Forces Framework!

6. The view of competition inherent in the Five Forces Framework assumes that in conditions of high market uncertainty the firm is best advised to integrate backward to compete with suppliers, or forward to compete with buyers, in order to lessen the threats from these two sources. But is such integration advisable? It can be costly, and acquisitions to achieve integration can fail all too easily. Moreover, critics argue that in conditions of high uncertainty, less integration is advisable, because it is easier to get rid of suppliers than one's own internal capability. This gives the firm more flexibility in the face of uncertainty. Furthermore, it is argued, outsourcing can give you closer control over suppliers and over cost and quality. The interesting example, historically, has been to compare Toyota with a company like US-based GM. The Japanese company has always had a lot fewer full-time employees than GM, but has used its keiretsu network of strategic suppliers with whom it has very strong relationships to, for example, co-develop technologies, deliver materials just-in-time, and support the financial position of Toyota in times of market difficulty.[1]

---

[1] A **keiretsu** is a set of companies with interlocking business relationships and shareholdings. In the legal sense, it is a type of informal business group that are loosely organized alliances within the social world of Japan's business community.

5.3. Generic Strategies

Having analysed the macro-environment and the competitive forces in industry and marketplace, the firm needs to make strategic choices. Porter's work again is a useful starting point. He suggests three generic strategies to choose from (see Figure 5.3). Let us look at these in more detail.

Generic Competitive Strategies

	PRODUCT DIFFERENTIATION	MARKET SEGMENTATION	KEY FUNCTIONAL AREAS
Cost Leadership	Low (mainly by price)	Low (mass market)	Manufacturing and materials management
Differentiation	High (mainly by uniqueness)	High (many market segments)	Research and development, marketing and sales
Focus	Low (mainly by price) or high (mainly uniqueness	Low (one of a few segments)	Any kind of functional area

Figure 5.3: Three Generic Competitive Strategies

Cost leadership

This competitive strategy centres on competing through low costs and prices. It is achieved through approaches such as the relentless pursuit of cost reductions and overhead control, avoidance of marginal customers, and cost minimisations in non-key areas like R&D, marketing, service, and perhaps advertising. The idea is to offer better value to customers through the same value at a lower price. Following this strategy, a firm will target average customers in a mass market and offer little product/service differentiation. The firm takes a high volume, low margin approach. The important issue here is to become the cost leader, if at all possible. One example is Primark, the low-price clothing retailer in several markets worldwide. A second example is Wal-Mart. Both drive their cost bases down low so they can sell at lower prices and still make higher profits than their rivals. Buying in massive bulk also gives such firms leverage over their suppliers, whose dependence is increased, while their bargaining power is reduced.

The strategy has some weaknesses. A relentless drive to cut costs might compromise value that customers desire. Competing on price alone leaves little room for competitive manoeuvre if a competitor finds ways of reducing its own costs, e.g. innovating in its supply chain, or finding a substitute product. Consider the impact on world markets if Tata exported its 'one lakh' car mentioned above. The Tata Nano car sold initially for US$3,000 in India, while abroad, competitors' cheapest cars were selling for US$8,000 – US$10,000.

An example of cost leadership strategy is Micromax. Its smart 'phones and mobile 'phones provide good quality products at an affordable price, and contain all the features of a premium 'phone like Apple or Samsung.

Differentiation

A differentiation strategy delivers products/services that customers perceive to be valuable and different, even unique. Here a firm targets customers in smaller, well-defined segments who are willing to pay premium prices. It takes a low volume, high margin approach. The strategy is dependent on products/services with unique attributes (actual or perceived), for example in terms of quality, sophistication, prestige, or luxury. Of course, it can be quite a challenge to identify unique attributes that are valued by customers in each market segment, especially if the firm is selling into a mature market where most differentiation has already been tried or delivered. Thus key functional areas are research and development (as a source of innovation), marketing/sales, and after-sale services.

Note that differentiation also erodes and becomes commoditised as competitors find ways of replicating the original product. In the fashion industry, new designs of dresses can sometimes be replicated by competitors and on the High Street at much lower prices within a few days of the original design being launched. Firms competing on differentiation will need to continually revisit customer preferences, and find ways for differentiating products/services that are valuable to the customer and firm alike. Shiv Mathur and Alfred Kenyon, in *Creating Value: Shaping Tomorrow's Business* (2015) help here in suggesting that differentiation can be established by looking at the offering to the customer along two different dimensions—merchandise and support:

1. **Merchandise** represents two sources of differentiation—content and aura. With the content of the product/service, differentiation here can be through better technical, physical, or aesthetic features. You can also differentiate an offering by 'aura', i.e. what the offering 'says' about the customer. For example, what does being seen with an Apple iPhone say about you, as opposed to being seen carrying a cheaper, less well known make. *'It will say the right things about you'* is the message conveyed by aura, regardless of content features. Offerings differentiated by 'aura' are often symbols of status and good taste, or even ethical behaviour. Think for example of companies that advertise that they do not use real animal fur in their clothing, and cosmetic firms that turn away from using animal experiments to test their products. Remember that many products/services these days might be very standardised, so, in the minds of customers, 'aura' can add a lot of perceived value and differentiation to the offering. This is true in most markets these days, whether it is cosmetics, cars, food delivery services, financial products, or supermarkets—as some examples.

2. **Support** is the way the business helps the customer to choose, obtain and use the offering. This has two dimensions: personalisation and expertise. 'Personalisation' is a measure of the pleasing personal attention paid to each individual customer—perhaps with a welcoming smile, or extra care to establish personal circumstances and specific requirements. These are just some examples amongst many. A high degree of personalisation can result in considerable valuable customer loyalty. **Expertise** measures the extent to which the customer regards the supplier as proficient in brainpower, skills and knowledge, when specifying, delivering and implementing the offering.

Combining all these dimensions creates 16 permutations for differentiation, leading to four main competitive strategies, based on differentiation, which will appeal to different customers or at different times and situations:

a. **Commodity buy** – low support, low merchandise

b. **Service buy** – high support, low merchandise

c. **Product buy** – low support, high merchandise

d. **System buy** – high support, high merchandise

BMW provides an example of differentiation leadership: BMW offers cars that are different from other car brands. BMW cars are more technologically advanced, have better features and have personalised services. The BMW brand—as 'the promise to the customer'—is also a valuable differentiator. With these attributes, BMW cars and motorbikes, for example, offerings are most often a 'system buy', being high on content, aura, personalisation and expertise. With so much differentiation, BMW can charge higher prices—one of the advantages coming from strong differentiation that the customer values. Note that in all this, what makes the product/service competitive is the relative perceived differentiation, that is how the customer perceives and experiences the differentiation. This attribute is also sometimes known as relative perceived quality. For example, I play tennis. Tennis racquets can vary in price from say US$40 to US$300. What extra am I paying for at $300? Well, probably the materials and design are superior; it will be a branded product; it might offer a refund guarantee if I dislike the 'feel' of the racquet; maybe it has a microchip in it that controls vibration when the ball hits the racquet. Is this worth paying an extra $260 for? Objectively, probably not, but relative perceived quality will be high, and the high price itself will be an indicator of quality. The advantage to the producer is that they can charge a high price even though the cost of producing and selling the item might be relatively low. Thus differentiation—distinctive qualities that are not replicated—has the powerful advantage of creating flexibility on the price you can charge.

Focus (or niche) strategy

Here a firm concentrates on serving the needs of a particular segment or niche of an industry such as a geographical market, type of customer, or product line. A specialised differentiator has a smaller, narrower, and sharper focus than a large differentiator. For example, Japanese shipbuilders tend to build high quality vessels at premium prices for the global market. Scandinavian shipbuilders narrow their focus to building icebreakers, cruise ships, and other specialised vessels.

There are two forms of focus. One is being a cost leader in a defined segment. The other is being a differentiation leader, also in a scope-limited segment. A specialised cost leader deals with a narrower segment compared with the traditional cost leader. Focusing will be particularly successful when a firm possesses intimate knowledge of a particular market segment. India's large IT outsourcing firms such as TCS, Wipro, and Infosys competed successfully, throughout the early and mid 2000s, against much larger firms such as Accenture, Hewlett Packard, and IBM (and still do) because they focused on providing good quality at lower costs for IT support, maintenance, and development work. Lower costs came from lower labour costs in India, and the adoption of process methodologies. Another firm with a cost leadership focus strategy is Sonata. Sonata watches are focused towards providing wrist watches at low cost compared to competitors like Rolex, Titan and Omega. An example of a firm that operates a focus strategy through differentiation leadership is Titan. Titan makes watches but concentrates on a premium segment, which includes jewels in its watches.

Looking across these strategies, one principle that Porter always argued for is *'don't get stuck in the middle!'* In other words do not get compromised by adopting more than one of these strategies. This has probably played well in a lot of strategic situations over the years, but in more modern environments increased competitive pressure has meant that firms have tended to have to **both** reduce costs and differentiate—even in the same market segment. This has become true across a number of industries, not least the car industry where even cheap cars are expected, in many global markets, to be reliable and good quality. Firms in the supermarket industry regularly stress 'value for money'. For a time UK-based Sainsbury's had as its motto *'Good food costs less at Sainsbury's.'* If this is a product of increased competitive pressure, not least from foreign firms, then 'middle' strategies are also massively enabled by the more advanced technologies now available. For example, in the car industry, scale economies used to be everything in terms of establishing low price. These days flexible manufacturing systems and advanced automation have made mass-customisation possible, whereby quality cars can be produced in smaller batches at highly competitive prices.

5.4. A Resource-Based Perspective on Competitiveness

Figure 5.4: Examples of resources and capabilities

The industry-based view detailed so far focuses on competitive positioning in relation to external **Opportunities** and **Threats**. The resource-based view we now discuss focuses on the resources and capabilities needed to compete, and deals with the internal **Strengths** and **Weaknesses** of the firm. The most fundamental questions asked by the resource-based view are: do the resources add value? Do they enable a firm to exploit an external opportunity and/or neutralise an external threat?

Resources are the tangible and intangible assets a firm uses to choose and implement its strategies. Capabilities are a firm's capacity to technically deploy those resources to deliver strategy. Look at Figure 5.4.

- **Tangible assets** are those that are observable and more easily quantified. Financial assets include internal funds such as shareholders' capital and retained profits, as well as external capital, like loans provided by banks.

- **Physical assets** include plants, offices, infrastructure, and equipment, as well as inventories of raw materials, components, and finished goods.

- **Intangible assets** are also found on companies' balance sheets, but they are harder to value, difficult to codify, and tough to observe. Reputational resources are the firm's goodwill, brand names, and business relationships.

- **Reputation** can be regarded as an outcome of a competitive process in which firms gain and signal prestige in specific areas important for competing effectively, e.g. reputation for quality (cars), for corporate responsibility (banking), as a good employer (management consultancy).

- **Innovation capabilities** are increasingly highly valued across industries, though prevalent in hi-tech firms like Samsung, IBM, and Microsoft.

Human resources (or human capital) are embedded in the individuals working in an organisation:

- Individual employees' skills, talent and knowledge.

- Individual employees' capacity for collaboration and communication, and their abilities for interpersonal interaction that are not captured by the firms' formal systems and structures.

- Employees' shared values, traditions, and social norms within an organisation.

Financial analysts may take human resources for granted, but many firms regard them as a foundation of all their capabilities. Knowledge and associated routines and practices are known as capabilities. These days, knowledge capabilities are highly valued as firm-specific intangible abilities to use resources to achieve organisational goals.

Now here is a critical point about global competitiveness in the second and third decades of the 21st century. According to Jonathan Hastel and Stian Westlake, (see *Capitalism Without Capital*, 2018), by around 2008, in the EU countries and the USA, intangible investments by firms were exceeding tangible investments, and the disparity has increased since. This has also become true of many other economies and multiple sectors. Microsoft is an interesting example. Its 2006 market value was US$250 billion. But its balance sheet records a valuation of $70 billion, of which $60 billion is cash and various financial instruments, while $3 billion was plant and equipment. On this analysis Microsoft had some $180 billion in intangible assets (much more since) but these were not accounted for in traditional accounting reports! What are these intangibles, for Microsoft? Examples include ideas generated by its investments in R&D and product design; the value of its brands; its internal structures; its supply chains; and the human capital built up by training.

So why this increasing dependence on intangibles for competitive advantage? A lot of it correlates with the rise of technology-driven developments producing data, software, virtual business and communication processes, as just some examples. The other aspect is that intangible investments have different economic features from tangible assets. Hastel and Westlake (2018) summarise these as fours S's:

1. Sunk costs
2. Scalability
3. Spillovers
4. Synergies

They represent **sunk costs** in that they are harder to sell than say, a tractor, and more likely to be specific to the company that makes them. Thus Toyota invests millions in its lean production systems, but it would be very difficult to separate these investments from their factories, and sell them off. But intangible assets are also more likely to be **scalable**. Thus Coca Cola's most valuable assets are brands, licensing agreements, and the recipe for making Coke taste like Coke. These can be scaled around the world, while manufacturing and bottling and distribution can easily be outsourced, with no discernible loss in competitive advantage. But intangible investments also generate what economists call '**spillovers**'. Many, but by no means all, intangible investments are difficult to protect from others benefiting from what was meant to be a private use item. You can protect a factory and its use fairly easily; software and data are much more difficult. Intangible investments also create **synergies** with one another. They can be complementary; they are more valuable together, at least in the right combination. For example, the MP2 protocol, together with the miniaturised hard disk and Apple's licensing agreements with record labels, and design skills, created the iPod—in international business terms a very valuable innovation. The rise of intangible investments with these different economic characteristics is having major effects not only on how firms behave, compete, and but also on how economies operate.

Let's return to the issue of capabilities. No firm can generate competitive advantage by relying only on primary resources. As we saw in Chapter 4, most goods and services are produced through a chain of vertical activities (from upstream to downstream) that add value—in short, a value chain. Many of the most important capabilities in today's business world relate to abilities to connect different stages of the value chain. Here are some examples:

- **Capabilities in innovation.** A firm's assets and skills to (1) research and develop new products and services, and (2) innovate and change ways of organising.

- **Capabilities in operations.** A firm's ability to effectively implement its regular activities, notably the manufacturing process.

- **Capabilities in marketing** enable firms to develop and sustain brand's awareness and values and to induce consumers to buy these brands.

- **Capabilities in sales and distribution** enable firms to manage interactions with (potential) customers and bring products to the right customer at the right time.

- **Capabilities in corporate functions** include a firm's planning, command, and control systems, and structures.

While all such capabilities can contribute to competitive advantage, some may become primary for a firm in specific circumstances. For example, Wal-Mart today is the biggest retail company in the world. It does not make a single thing. All it 'makes' is a hyper-efficient supply chain. Its logistics capabilities were born from being initially located in low cost Arkansas, USA. Its logistics capabilities give Wal-Mart speed, scale, and cost advantages over rivals, and also enable Wal-Mart to provide logistics advice and services to other companies.

One of the critical questions on capabilities a firm must answer is whether a capability is critical enough to be kept in-house, or whether it is not a core critical capability and can be outsourced, or be the subject of a strong partnering relationship with another firm, or service supplier. As one example, many booksellers found they could not develop the capability to run an online book service. So they hired Amazon to run their websites and service. It is an interesting question whether this was a good move in terms of long-term competitiveness. What do you think?

5.5. Resource-based Competition: The VRIO Framework

Peng and Meyer (2019) propose a resource-based framework that focuses on the value (V), rarity (R), imitability (I), and organisational (O) aspects of resources and capabilities. This is called a VRIO framework. You may also come across the VRIN framework. The difference here is the N! In the VRIN framework N stands for non-substitutability. This refers to products/services, but also importantly to non-substitutable competencies. Peng (2001) argues for the need to replace this attribute with the more general one of Organisation, thus profiling the distinctive characteristics and abilities of the organisation built over years as a guard against easy competence substitution. Here we work with Peng's VRIO framework. VRIO poses four fundamental questions:

1. *Value.* Do resources and capabilities exist that are valued by customers and provide potential competitive advantage? Adding value is necessary for achieving competitive advantage. For example, throughout the 1980s and 1990s IBM sold PCs but this became highly competitiveand its focus on hardware became a disadvantage. IBM moved into the more lucrative software and services areas, and indeed sold its PC division to China's Lenovo in 2004.

2. *Rarity.* How rare are the valuable resources and capabilities? Do capabilities exist that no, or few, competitors possess? Valuable but common resources do not give an advantage, e.g. water as a cooling agent in wet weather countries. However, in hot, dry countries water might be both valuable, rare, and access to water prized. Valuable and rare can give a temporary advantage. Advantage is temporary because competitors catch up, and the differentiation becomes commoditised. An interesting example is the quality advantage Japanese cars had in US and European markets for many years. The quality across carmakers is now comparable but quality is no longer rare, and has become a minimum requirement to compete in the industry.

3. *Imitability.* How easy is it to replicate the resources/capability? Generally, it is easier to imitate tangible resources/capabilities, for example a manufacturing plant, than intangible ones, for example tacit knowledge, managerial talent, superior motivation. There are two ways to imitate—direct duplication and substitution:

   a) **Direct duplication** is the more difficult: It is hard to acquire in a short period of time what competitors have developed over a long period of time. It is also difficult for a competitor to identify the causal determinants of your firm's performance. An interesting case is Toyota (Qumar 2010). Until recently Toyota was the number one automaker in the world and was much admired and studied over many years for something called 'The Toyota Way', i.e. the way it combined all factors and resources in a distinctive way that other organisations tried and rarely succeeded in replicating.

   b) **Substitution** is less challenging, but not always easy. For example, the substitute resource or capability might not be as good, and this could differentiate the competitor as inferior.

4. *Organisation.* How is a firm organised to develop and leverage the full potential of its resources and capabilities? For example, in the movie business, film stars are valuable, rare, and hard to imitate, but they need a studio and an organisation to make the film into a success. This involves using complementary assets—film crews,

directors, make-up artists, business managers. This can be a long list! It also involves socially complex ways of organising, for example overcoming cultural differences, establishing strong human relationships by which activity can be facilitated. Thus distinctive organisation that gives competitive advantage is dependent on using complementary assets effectively; managing social complexity successfully; and leveraging invisible relationships that can add value—because this makes imitation much more difficult.

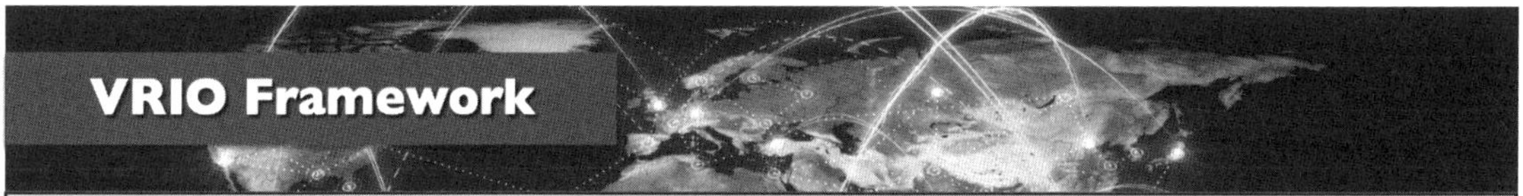

VRIO Framework

Criterion	Question	Resource 1	Resource 2	Resource 3	Resource 4
Value Creating	Does the resource add value?	No	Yes	Yes	Yes
Rare	How rare is the resource	-	No	Yes	Yes
Imitability	How difficult is it for others to imitate the resource	-	No	No	Yes
Organization	Are other policies and procedures organized to support the exploitation of this resource	No	Yes	Yes	Yes
		↓	↓	↓	↓
Competitive implications		Disadvantage	Parity	Temporary advantage	Sustained advantage

Figure 5.5: The VRIO Framework

Source: Adapted from Peng & Meyer, 2019

Figure 5.5 shows the growing competitive advantage from developing firm-specific resources and capabilities that are valuable, rare, non-imitable and are supported by distinctive organisational capabilities. Valuable, rare, but imitable resources/capabilities can give temporary advantage. Only valuable, rare and hard-to-imitate resources/capabilities backed by distinctive organisation can provide a sustained competitive advantage.

Are there limitations to the resource-based perspective? Critics point to several issues:

- The first is the conceptual blurring of the notions of resources and capabilities. At what point do resources convert into capabilities, and how is the combination arrived at? It is all too easy for managers to look at a group of resources and say they add up to a capability; but what makes them a capability rather than just a group of resources?

- Secondly, and relatedly, a capability is potential. It can only be proven in performance. Firms can mislead themselves into believing they have distinctive competitive capabilities because they have not really had to utilise them, or do not know the capabilities of competitors very well. The US car industry felt it had world-class capability in building cars in the late 1980s until comparisons were made with Japanese factories both in Japan and the USA in the early 1990s. The inferior US performance led to much analysis of Japanese capabilities and the distinctiveness of their work practices, labour policies, and supplier network systems.

- Thirdly, resource-based competition involves building from the bottom-up, and capabilities, as Peng and Meyer (2019) point out, may take a long time horizon in which to develop and achieve differentiation. Do modern firms have the time to do this? Basically a firm has to make a strategic bet on a capability. But by the time it is built, the dynamic competitive marketplace might have moved on and the capability is no longer needed, and/or does not differentiate in any meaningful way.

5.6. Bringing Environment and Strategy Together: Which Strategy, When?

Beyond the competitive positioning, resource-based and institution-based approaches to strategy and competitiveness, Christopher Bingham, Kathleen Eisenhardt and Nathan Furr (in the 'Strategy Guidebook', *Sloan Management Review*, 2015) look at '*Which Strategy, When?*' The authors found that 'competitive strategy' has to be disaggregated into three kinds: strategies of **position**, strategies of **leverage**, and strategies of **opportunity**. What's right for a company depends on three factors: its circumstances, its available resources and how management links those resources. They suggest a process similar to one detailed earlier: look at the environment and the industry in which you are competing (see Chapter 4 and above), then establish your resources, and also how these connect up (see resource-based view). Once this external and internal assessment has been completed, then choose a strategic positioning from three main possibilities. Let's look at this in more detail:

- **The first step: understand your circumstances.** Is your industry stable, dynamic or somewhere in between? If you can map Porter's five industry structure forces in your industry and these tend to stay largely the same, then you are probably operating within a stable industry. If the industry is too unsettled to map (think mobile Internet applications), or the basic rules for competing are in flux (think clean or nano technology), then you most likely inhabit a dynamic industry.

Where do your products fit in the product life cycle? In stable industries, standards are well-defined; product expectations clear; product life cycles known and often long; and a limited number of competitors may push slowly on innovation. However, in dynamic industries standards may not yet exist; product life cycles will be short; products are diverse; and no clear dominant technology or product has emerged. Some industries are in between. The auto industry was historically a relatively stable industry. But new technologies (for example, hybrid and electric-powered engines); compressed product development times; volatile oil prices; and regulatory pressure have increased dynamism.

- **The second step: take stock of your resources.** As we have seen with the resource-based approach, resources lie at the heart of strategy. They enable companies to set themselves apart from competitors. Tangible resources (such as Intel's fabrication facilities or Starbucks' locations) are relatively easier to assess than intangible resources (for instance, Amazon's patents or Procter & Gamble's brands). Beyond these, organisational processes (for example, the acquisition process of India's Tata Group) can provide a critical basis for advantage.

  Now find out how advantageous they really are. Taking a VRIO, resource-based approach, the most strategically important resources are valuable (i.e. useful in your industry); rare (i.e. possessed by only a few); inimitable (i.e. difficult to copy); and supported by distinctive organisation capability. These resources are a potential source of competitive advantage. Yet even if they can provide advantage, they are not absolutely necessary for competitive advantage. Indeed, even common resources can be a source of advantage depending on how they are linked with other resources.

- **The third step: establish the relationships among resources.** A secret to picking the right strategic framework is assessing how a firm's resources relate to one another. Some resources are tightly linked. Thus, Wal-Mart's low-cost strategy in the United States depends heavily on its physical resources (often rural locations); sophisticated information technology (such as maximising selling space in stores and quickly replenishing inventories); efficient logistics (for example, cross-docking); and cost-conscious culture—all of which reinforce each other. By contrast, Google's resources are more loosely linked. Here human capital and technical resources are recombined as needed to tackle different markets and products. There are trade-offs. Wal-Mart's tightly linked resources create more defensible strategic positions, but resist change.

Google's loosely linked resources are easier to change, but they can be inefficiently deployed and become redundant.

Once this analysis has been carried out, it becomes more clear as to which strategy to choose. The three choices and rationales are detailed in Figur

	POSITION STRATEGY	LEVERAGE STRATEGY	OPPORTUNITY STRATEGY
STRATEGY	Build mutually reinforcing resource systems with many resources in an attractive strategic position. Deepen their links.	Build strategically important resources for current markets. Leverage them into attractive new products and new markets.	Pick a few strategic processes with deep and swift flows of opportunities. Learn simple rules to capture opportunities.
Circumstances Best for	Stable environments	Moderately dynamic environments	Dynamic environments
Resources	Often mundane	Strategically important (i.e., valuable, rare, inimitable and nonsubstitutable)	Opportunity-rich strategic processes guided by simple rules
Relationships	Tightly interlocked resources	Moderately linked resources	Loosely linked resources
Basis of Competitive Advantage	A cost leadership or differentiated strategic position that is defensible	Ownership of specific strategically important resources that can be leveraged	Capture of attractive opportunities before rivals
Sustainability of Advantage	Long term	Medium term	Unpredictable
Inimitability of Advantage	Through causal ambiguity of tightly linked resources plus time to develop the resource system and path dependence	Through property rights, path dependence and time needed to develop the same resources	Through first-mover advantage and the challenge of inferring rules from partially improvised outcomes
Challenges	Adjusting system of tightly linked resources quickly enough and without producing negative synergy	Adjusting resource portfolio without being blocked by cognitive and political rigidities	Maintaining "edge of chaos" with the right number and types of rules. Timely pivoting to better strategic processes

Figure 5.6: Choosing the Right Strategy

Source: Adapted from Bingham et al., 2015

5.6.1. The Position Strategy

With a position strategy, competitive advantage depends, firstly, on choosing a valuable and unoccupied strategic position in a given industry, and, secondly, on creating and linking company resources to defend that position. This strategy is commonly associated with Five Forces Framework analysis and depends on a relatively stable competitive environment so that, once established, the competitive advantage is sustainable. Note that the resources do not need to be superior; tight linking of resources might be more important. As one example, JetBlue, the low-cost US airline has common resources: Airbus A320 and Embraer 190 aircraft; comfortable passenger seats; DIRECTV access and SIRIUS XM satellite radio; e-mail and instant messaging services; and fast turnaround capability at airport gates. But packaged and tightly linked, they produce capability and competitive advantage that are difficult to imitate. However, resources need to be continuously updated. For example, over the years Spanish clothing company Zara has added better small-batch production that links to air shipment logistics, allowing it to send new designs to any international store in under two days.

The weakness of the positioning strategy is its vulnerability to change. Moving an organisation locked into a defensive position with tightly linked resources is difficult! For example, apparel company Liz Claiborne had a positioning strategy with production; distribution; marketing; design; presentation; and sales resources were all tightly linked. The industry changed, and the company's relationships with department stores were disrupted. They tried changing their 'no reordering' process that had upset department stores. But this was tied tightly with overseas logistics and distant manufacturing locations, and a systems change was needed, impacting, for a while, on performance, until new resource connectivities were established. A firm can establish a positioning strategy by combining elements of both the competitive positioning and the resource based approaches discussed above. For example, in the US mutual fund industry, The Vanguard Group built its strategy around the competitive positioning of low risk investment management and low costs. Vanguard had a mutual funds average expense ratio much lower than its competitors. The company defends its position with mutually reinforcing resource choices, including low commissions, modest management perks and an absence of retail branches. Thus, the key to advantage with a position strategy is not just having a valuable strategic position, but also linking resources to defend successfully against challengers.

5.6.2. The Leverage Strategy

Companies that pursue leverage strategies achieve competitive advantage by using their strategically important resources in existing and new industries at a pace that is consistent with moderate change in the market. This strategy is associated with the resource-based view. Here, unlike with position strategies, resources are often only moderately interconnected. Pepsi provides an example over the years. It has several strategically important resources (for example, brand, product formulae, distribution system). More important is how Pepsi has leveraged them to support new products that fit with increasingly health-conscious Consumers. These include waters, juices, teas and sports drinks, all of which leverage the company's existing strategically important resources, while refreshing these.

The leverage strategy can be used in existing markets or new ones. For example, Intel's short-term success depended on extracting value from its existing microprocessors products, but long-term growth depended on using its well-known design capabilities, branding and manufacturing resources in future generations of microprocessors. Amazon.com is a prime example of a company that has utilised its core capabilities to spread into many different markets. But early on it did experience difficulties because it failed to reassess the importance of its resources. Thus when Amazon tried to leverage its online book and music ordering and inventory fulfilment capabilities to include other product categories such as toys, it ran into problems. The inventory systems were not well suited to the extreme seasonality of toys, and the fact that toys come in all shapes and sizes.

An obvious difficulty with a leverage strategy is the timing and updating of the resource portfolio as industries change. This relates to sourcing decisions—do you acquire, partner or develop key resources in-house? One successful example was Toyota's Prius, which leveraged existing resources, especially brand and electronics technology, while developing and acquiring new resources for hybrid technology, engine control software and regenerative braking. Compare Chrysler. Introducing the first minivan in the 1980s, Chrysler had 20 years of sales, introduced successful pickup trucks and SUVs and refreshed its Jeep line. But the auto industry changed. Competitors like General Motors and Ford adapted their engine technologies to emphasise fuel efficiency and retooled their manufacturing plants for small cars; Chrysler failed to update its resource portfolio, and eventually became controlled by Fiat.

5.6.3. The Opportunity Strategy

This strategy is suitable for dynamic industries characterised by fast-moving but often unpredictable opportunities, where competitors change fast, likewise customer preferences and business models. Competitive advantage may last for only a short time. Bingham, Eisenhardt and Furr compare the opportunity strategy to surfing, with performance resulting from catching a great wave at the right time, even though the duration of that wave is likely to be short and the ride a precarious 'edge of chaos' experience and falling off is always a possibility! Timing and capturing successive waves faster and better than competitors are what matters. They cite the video game console industry as an example—in just a few years, companies like Sega, Nintendo, Sony and Microsoft 'caught the wave' and for a time led the industry.

This strategy is commonly associated with the 'simple rules' philosophy that Kathleen Eisenhardt and her colleagues have promoted for 'managing on the edge of chaos' (see for example, Brown and Eisenhardt, 1998, *Managing on The Edge*). This requires combining two elements: choosing a focal strategic process and developing simple rules to guide that process. Consider Tata Group in the first decade of the 21st Century. With diversified operations, high market capitalisation and ready access to corporate debt, Tata depended heavily on quick and effective acquisitions as its focal strategic process. Meanwhile Apple focused on a different strategic process—product development—to produce valuable new designs. Both were successful, and both build on processes that are loosely coupled. In place of strategic planning, managers also need to learn and deploy simple rules. These provide enough structure for action while also allowing flexibility to capture unanticipated opportunities.

Let's look at Pixar Animation Studio, producer of the *Toy Story* movies, *A Bug's Life*, and *Finding Nemo*, which operates simple rules. One rule is 'no studio executives'. Pixar is run by creative artists, now able to create without middle management interference. A second rule is 'great story first, then animation'. Another rule stipulates 'in-house original ideas only'. A further rule at Pixar is 'one new movie per year'. The rules provide strong corporate guidance but do not stifle much needed creativity.

With an 'Opportunity' strategy, where to compete is driven primarily by the opportunities rather than by fit with the company's strategically important resources. Two examples:

- When product development opportunities slowed, Google placed more emphasis on internationalisation opportunities, aiming at one point to enter more than 55 countries with more than 35 languages by supporting localised search. Google now gains most revenue from outside the USA.

- LinkedIn reached sufficient scale in its user network, then switched from emphasising its strategic process for acquisition to one for developing new revenue-producing services.

Opportunity strategies have their vulnerabilities. The risks of getting timing and focus wrong are higher in fast moving environments. For entrepreneurial start-ups it may be that too little structure is riskier than too much. They tend to need more rules and structure than they are comfortable with. However, for large companies, the greater risk is having too much structure. Managers need to limit the number of rules, and not just focus on the content of the rules. Managers also need to watch for signs that they are slowing their responses to opportunities, or, conversely, for signs that the industry is slowing. This could be, for example, due to consolidation; standardisation; and longer product life cycles. A shift to a leverage strategy might then be more suitable.

5.7. Debating Strategy and Competitiveness

Finally, there are a number of controversies that are worth pointing to when it comes to the different approaches to competitiveness:

1. One interesting question is whether the competitive industry positioning approach that Michael Porter and others advance helps a firm compete better than the firm-

specific resource-based approach. While many arguments and much evidence are marshalled to answer this question, the truth is that they are probably best seen as complementary lenses. Both provide different, useful insights on how a firm can compete successfully in international business.

2. In the last 10 years there has been much greater emphasis on the need for dynamic capabilities that are most frequently knowledge-based. There are dangers in investing in static capabilities whose differentiating, valuable, rare and organisationally-supported attributes commoditise and become less valuable over time. Dynamic capabilities are needed in fast moving and highly competitive environments typical of most industries in emerging and developed economies today.

3. Should the firm's resources and capabilities be retained in-house or can they be outsourced? Can they be offshored? What are the limits to offshoring and outsourcing? How can we avoid 'hollowing out' the organisation?

4. What about international capabilities? Do firms that are successful domestically, have what it takes to win internationally? In the mid-2000s the US fashion retailer Limited Brands had 4,000 stores throughout the USA, held brands like Victoria's Secrets, and Bath & Body Works, but still refused to go abroad, even to Canada. This scepticism is backed by some evidence showing that it takes additional capabilities to move into overseas markets. Thus in the mid-2000s Wal-Mart withdrew from Germany and South Korea. Its main, French-based competitor, Carrefour, also exited Japan, Mexico, Slovakia, and South Korea.

   The recent de-globalisation trend discussed in earlier chapters has seen businesses, faced with declining sales and profits abroad, retrench to home or regionally based markets and operations. At the same time, the Scandinavian furniture company IKEA has found its style of flat-pack packaging and method of selling are popular in many global markets. Companies like Zara, United Colors of Benetton, and Gucci have been successful in major cities around the world. Reasons for success can be found in Chapter 6 when we discuss modes of entry and the factors and choices that render international business performance effective.

5. We dealt with an institution-based view of competition in Chapters 2 and 3. Peng and Meyer (2019), and Peng, Wang and Jiang (2008) are particularly strong on this perspective. They point out that, especially when it comes to international competitiveness, formal and informal institutions greatly affect and shape the strategies that are possible in specific countries and markets—something that the

industry positioning and resource-based approaches tend to downplay, and even neglect. Institutions create formal and informal constraints on industry conditions and firm behaviours, and there is always dynamic interaction between a firm's specific resources, capabilities and strategic choices, the institutional setting, and firm behaviours.

6. There has been some new thinking on strategy. For example, in *Connected Strategy* (Harvard Business Review Press, 2019), Siggelkow and Terwiesch argue that leading businesses are gaining an advantage over rivals in two ways. Firstly, they are changing how they connect with their customers, moving from occasional interactions, to continuous contact, and providing services and products as the customer needs them or even anticipating the need. Secondly, they do it at lower cost. For example, Amazon is able to deliver goods (often ordered by Alexa) within hours without the need for expensive retail premises. Likewise, the publishing company McGraw-Hill provides personalised digital learning experiences to students through automation-based tutoring rather than expensive instructors. Thanks to the availability of technology, many companies have the opportunity to forge such connections. The key is to not just make the connection but to maintain it. To do this, the authors advocate a continuous cycle that depends on four **R**s:

   • **Recognise** a customer need; help the customer to identify a solution, leading to a customer ...

   • **Request**; in turn this will trigger the company to ...

   • **Respond**; those that are able to ...

   • **Repeat** these interactions and learn each time will be able to build lasting connections with customers that competitors will struggle to match.

   To a large extent these ideas are not that new, but the stress on getting digitally connected and intensifying customer interaction and company responsiveness to achieve competitive advantage, does usefully highlight where strategic value has been migrating to in contemporary markets.

7. Stephen Bungay, writing in the *Harvard Business Review* (April 19, 2019) added to the debate by pointing to '**Five Myths About Strategy**'.

   • The **first myth** is that strategy is about the long-term. Strategy is not about the long-term or the short-term, but about the **fundamentals** of how the business works: the sources of value creation, the drivers of the cost to deliver it, and the basis of competition. To get a grip on strategy, we do not need to lengthen the time horizon of our thinking, but its **depth**.

- The **second myth** is that disruptors change strategy, and invent new strategies all the time. Do they? In the case of Amazon and the rest of Big Tech, most of the innovative new products and services reflect a single, consistent strategy, familiar since since the 1960s, namely 'cut price and add capacity' reflecting that costs would decline as more products were sold. By pricing ahead in anticipation of those cost declines, a company could sacrifice current margins to gain share, achieve market leadership and then reap the gains. For today's platform businesses, the imperative could be called 'give it away and add users'. But it's just a more radical version of an old strategy.

- The **third myth**—not believed by those advocating the competitive frameworks discussed in this chapter—is that competitive advantage is dead. But the competitive advantages of Amazon, Alphabet, Apple, Facebook and Microsoft are so massive and the barriers to overcoming them so high, that many believe that regulation is needed to break them up to break them up to reduce their power. The full truth that can be learned from these companies, though, is not that competitive advantage is dead, but that you need to rely on multiple advantages rather than just one. And part of the reason that Amazon etc. will be hard to unseat is that they have realised this.

- The **fourth myth** is: you don't need a strategy; you just need to be agile. But agility is a capability, not a strategy. A strategy is a framework for decision-making; a set of guiding principles, which can be applied as the situation evolves. Look at successful, as opposed to failing start-ups. These actually do a lot of hard thinking about fundamentals, questioning and testing basic assumptions with a rigour that incumbents would do well to emulate.

- Finally the **fifth myth**: you need a digital strategy. In fact you don't want a strategy for digital, IT, finance, HR or anything else—just a strategy for the business. You cannot develop a strategy for the digital part of your business and leave the rest alone. Digital technology and the more specific technologies to which it gives rise fundamentally change the sources of customer value and the cost of delivering it. The way to address digital is to think through and lay out all the fundamental assumptions you have about how your business works and ask yourself if they are still valid.

5.8. Conclusion

In this chapter we have focused on competitive business strategy, as applied to international contexts. We saw the usefulness, but also the limitations of competitive positioning frameworks and approaches. In particular we looked at Porter's work on the Five Forces and generic strategies. While Porter's frameworks have been much criticised, they have also been much used over the years, not least by practising strategists. Much of the criticisms come from the original frameworks (developed in the 1980s) not always addressing the realities of the global marketplace of the 2020s. Thus we see how some have argued for a sixth force—complementors—being added to the framework for industry analysis. Such improvements can always, must always, be made in the fast-moving, globalising management field. This should not detract from the importance of carrying out competitive positioning analysis when embarking on international business.

By 2015 it had already become clear that the next ten years would see businesses become increasingly digital. The major global players in terms of net worth, such as Apple, Google, Amazon and Facebook were already heavily digitised. Studies continued to show that moving from place and goods to space and information brought with it higher profits and return on investment. Many, but by no means all, of the contextual and environmental factors detailed in Chapters 1, 2, and 3 could be circumvented, or at least mitigated. Not surprisingly sectors that were heavily based on information, either as a product or as a basis for essential transactions, for example financial services, insurance, utilities—with their millions of customers—have been all trying to become digital businesses and investing in information technologies to support this. One probable outcome from the 2020–2021 crises was that this process of digital transformation will be accelerated. This is discussed in detail in our companion volume (Willcocks, 2021). Becoming increasingly technologised through applying information and communication technologies is fundamentally challenging, especially in international contexts. The good news is that the frameworks discussed in this chapter all help us to analysis and develop digital business strategies.

The chapter also gave an understanding of the resource-based approach to competition, in particular the VRIO framework, and how tangible and intangible resources and capabilities can be utilised to achieve competitiveness. To some extent the resource-based view of the firm is also a critique of competitive positioning approaches as represented by Porter, but it is best to see the perspectives as working in tandem, as it were, along with an understanding of the PESTEL and CAGE environments that comes from an institution-based perspective. To put it another way, a practising manager would gain much from applying only one of these perspectives, but the real advantage will come from applying all three when designing and crafting strategy for international business. This point was brought out when we discussed the contingency approach in 5.6., which showed how to draw upon these different approaches in arriving at a position, leverage or opportunity strategy. Finally we pointed to a range of debates and controversies in strategy, demonstrating shifts and also the ongoing importance of the subject. We now move on to consider another dimension of international strategy: how to enter and evolve in foreign markets.

References

Bingham, C., Eisenhardt, K. and Furr, N. (2015), *Which Strategy, When?* Sloan Management Review Strategy Guide Book, SMR, Boston, USA

Brown and Eisenhardt, K. (1998), *Managing on The Edge,* Harvard Business Review Press, Boston, USA

Bungay, S. (2019), 'Five Myths About Strategy', *Harvard Business Review*, April 19.

Hastel, J. and Westlake, S. (2018), *Capitalism Without Capital,* Princeton University Press, Princeton, USA

Mathur, S. and Kenyon, A. (2015), *Creating Value: Shaping Tomorrow's Business,* Butterworth-Heinemann, Oxford, UK

Siggelkow and Terwiesch (2019), *Connected Strategy*, Harvard Business Review Press, Boston, USA

Peng, M. Wang, D. and Jiang, Y. (2008), 'An Institution-Based View of International Business Strategy', *Journal Of International Business,* 19, 920-936

Peng, M. and Meyer, K. (2019), *International Business*, Cengage Learning, London, UK

Porter, M. (1985), *Competitive Advantage*, Free Press, Boston, USA

Willcocks, L. (2021), *Global Business Management*, SB Publishing, Stratford-upon-Avon, UK

'Before you journey, observe the wind carefully, detect its direction, and then follow it. You will get to your destination twice as fast with half the effort'

Chin-Ning Chu

'The relationship between commitment and doubt is by no means an antagonistic one. Commitment is healthiest when it is not without doubt, but in spite of doubt'

Rollo May, *The Courage to Create*

'And the day came when the risk to remain tight in a bud was more painful than the risk it took to blossom'

Anais Nin

Chapter 6

Market Entry and Evolution: Commitment *versus* Risk

6.1. Introduction

Throughout earlier chapters you read about foreign direct investment. FDI occurs when a firm invests directly in facilities to produce and/or market their products or services in a foreign country. Once a firm undertakes FDI it becomes, by definition, a multinational enterprise or MNE. However, entering a foreign market is not that simple. And the 2020-2021 global pandemic did not make it any simpler. There are major choices: why enter a foreign market, which market(s) to enter, when to enter the market(s), and on what scale? What kind of products and services, and how are they customised? There are also major options available as to how to enter a foreign market.

In this chapter, we discuss foreign direct investment in detail and the conditions under which it becomes a viable strategy. However, we also discuss options and their advantages and disadvantages. You will learn about exporting, turnkey projects, licensing, franchising, joint ventures, as well as fully owned subsidiaries. You will also learn about when to establish strategic alliances, and how to make these work. Finally, and connecting back to chapter 4 you will learn how firms evolve their international strategy in order to seek optimal location, organisational arrangements and returns.

6.2. The Decision to Enter Foreign Markets

The decision to enter a foreign market breaks down into four decisions that we will discuss here. If you are a small or medium enterprise (SME) your reasons and decisions may well be very different from those of a multinational (MNE). We will consider both kinds of enterprises here, though the main focus will be on MNEs.

Why enter a foreign market?

The obvious reason to seek foreign markets is to expand sales revenues. The home market may be too small to grow the business, but foreign markets for the product or service, when added together, could represent an enormous business opportunity, and also a source of funding. Increased sales may well provide increased production economies of scale feeding into lower costs and more competitive pricing. Increased profits, and profitability can lead to further investment in the development of the business and its products/services. Consider the Russian company Kaspersky Lab. The product here is anti-virus software for home and company use, which is easily adaptable for international markets. The company started very small in 1997 but by 2008 was the fourth largest supplier in the world. They did this by gaining funding initially through foreign licensing agreements, expanding using foreign sales partners, then launching local offices, initially in the UK, Poland, Holland, and China, but then other countries were gradually added. Its dramatically successful growth is one that many SMEs would seek to replicate, though each would have its own distinctive set of challenges on the road to internationalisation.

Some MNEs, on the other hand, may well have sufficient financial resources and be mature enough to act on a larger-scale and longer term basis and be able to invest directly in establishing subsidiaries abroad. Peng and Meyer (2019) suggest that such investments have one or more of four common objectives:

- *Natural resource seeking.* For example oil exploration in the Middle East, Russia, minerals in Africa, where the issues are quality, quantity, and cost of resources.

- *Market seeking.* For example luxury consumer goods in emerging countries, where the objective is to find strong market demand and customers willing to pay.

- *Efficiency seeking.* For example manufacturing in Guandong, China, logistics in Rotterdam, where the objective is to achieve economies of scale, use low-cost skilled labour, with sufficient transport, supplier, and communications, plus energy infrastructure.

- *Innovation seeking.* For example information technology (IT) in Silicon Valley USA, and Bangalore India, biotech firms in Cambridge UK, where the objective is to seek out clusters of innovatory firms or individuals, or educational institutions.

More often, a firm's first entry into foreign markets is the start of a long-term evolution towards internationalisation, and becoming a multinational. In this respect, consider the history of Pearl River Piano. Founded in 1956, it became China's leading brand, but by the 1980s faced strong competition in its domestic market. It started exporting to US importers, and only in 1999 established a US subsidiary, in California. In 2000 it also bought a prestigious German brand piano company (Ritmuller) to position itself in the higher priced end of the European Market. Global competition pushed a strategy of exports, Greenfield investments, and acquisitions over time. Pearl River is now capable of producing over 100,000 pianos a year, and exports them to more than 80 countries. By 2021 Pearl River pianos were being manufactured under a wide range of brands and levels. The Hallet & Davis line produced by Pearl River is the oldest United States piano name still in production. Acquisitions have been a key mode of entry. For example, in January 2016, the company took over 90 percent of the shares of Wilhelm Schimmel, a German piano manufacturer in Braunschweig. After getting control of the Schimmel's factory in Braunschweig, Pearl River Piano Group Europe tidied up its sourcing strategy by switching Ritmuller production to this factory.

Which markets to enter?

With over 196 countries and more than 60 territories globally there are all too many markets to choose from! These will often be very different so: which markets are preferable? The answer to this question depends on the firm's objectives. A ***market seeking*** firm looks at size of market, and the present and future purchasing power of consumers there. Large markets such as India, China, and Indonesia will still differ in terms of living standards and economic growth. Thus weak economic growth in Indonesia makes it a less attractive target for foreign investment than India or China. Our earlier chapters established a range of factors that shape the overall attractiveness, or otherwise, of a particular regional, national, or intra-national marketplace (see also Willcocks, 2021, on global sourcing and location attractiveness). Also important is the level of domestic and foreign competition experienced in that foreign market.

Tesco, the British grocery chain, was, in 2017, the second largest retailer in the world, after Walmart, with sales of US$70 billion. Tesco has been a market seeking firm. It expanded its foreign operations in recent years in emerging countries, especially in Eastern Europe and Asia where markets lacked strong local or multinational competitors, and where there may be large potential demand. Tesco entered Hungary in 1995, gaining a majority share in a state-owned grocery chain there. By 2017 it was the market leader in that country. In 1996 it acquired 31 stores in Poland; by 2017 this had increased to 450 stores. The pattern continued in Czech Republic, Slovakia, Ireland, and also across Asia, including into China, via a joint venture in 2004, and another in 2014. By 2017 Tesco was generating a $21 billion of its revenues from outside the

United Kingdom. All its foreign ventures have been making money. Success seems to be based on careful transfer of core capabilities to the new ventures; hiring local managers, rather than using expatriates; effective choice of partners who understand the market, though lack Tesco's complementary retailing capabilities and financial strength; increasing ownership stakes in the joint ventures; and a focus on markets with growth potential but lacking strong local competitors. By 2020, after five years of turnaround, including selling its businesses in Thailand and Malaysia, during 2019-2020 Tesco was making sales of £56.5 billion and profits of £2.959 billion. *Other firms will have different objectives from Tesco. Natural resource seeking* firms, for example, looking for oil or gas deposits, seek quantity, quality, and low cost resources, as do efficiency seeking firms wanting - typically - low cost, productive and reliable local workforces, e.g. software developers and engineers in India, call centre operatives in South Africa. But for ***efficiency seeking*** firms total cost, not just labour costs, is a vital calculation.

When to enter?

Entering a market in advance of competitors can give first mover advantages. These include:

- The ability to pre-empt rivals by establishing a strong brand name.

- The ability to build up sales volume and ride down the experience curve ahead of rivals, and gain a cost advantage over later entrants.

- The ability to create switching costs that tie customers to products or services, making it difficult for later entrants to win business.

- Avoidance of clash with dominant rivals at home

- Building early relationships with customers and governments

- Pre-emption of scarce resources at home that may be available abroad

- Bringing technological leadership into the foreign market

However, being a first mover can also have risks and disadvantages, including:

- The risks and costs of business failure if inexperience in the foreign market leads to major mistakes, e.g. underestimating costs or cultural differences in customer preferences.

- Pioneering costs where the foreign business environment is so different that major time, effort, and expense has to be incurred in learning from experience.

162

- Costs of promoting and establishing a product offering and brand, including cost of educating customers.

- Regulations may change, or other aspects of the environment, in ways that reduce the value of an early entrant's investments, thus creating disadvantage relative to later entrants, e.g regulations require changes in your costly operating model.

As one example of the advantages of being a late entrant, look at McDonald's' experience in China. As an early US fast food chain into China, KFC incurred considerable costs in setting up the business, but its US rival McDonald's learned from KFC's experience, and as a later entrant has capitalised on the market in China. Late movers, then, can gain certain advantages that first movers may not enjoy. Examples include taking advantage of a first mover's investments in educating customers, and learning about the market, and what works managerially; letting the market and technological uncertainties be sorted out by the first mover before entering the market; being able to leapfrog the early mover by being in a position to differentiate its products/services more precisely.

Scale and ownership

Clearly, entering a foreign market incurs risk. Therefore it is important to decide whether you are making a strategic commitment, i.e. committing large resources and investments rapidly or wish to proceed incrementally, taking less risk. A strategic commitment can have long term impacts, be difficult to reverse, and may mean that fewer resources are available to support entry into other desirable markets. One result may well be strategic inflexibility. Small-scale entry has the advantage of allowing the firm to learn about the foreign market while limiting financial exposure, opportunity costs, and risk. However, it is less likely than a large-scale entrant to capture first mover advantages. If the decision is to seize a large market opportunity and make a strategic commitment, then MNEs will look at the importance of ownership and control. To maintain control they might choose to start a new business in the foreign country as a ***wholly owned Greenfield site.*** Alternatively they might acquire, that is buy, an existing business with market presence in the country they wish to enter – this would be a ***full acquisition,*** giving better control, protection of know-how, and ability to coordinate globally.

Less control and ownership can be had from choosing a ***newly created joint venture*** with another business, to share costs, risks and profits, and gain access to the partner's knowledge, assets, and market presence. ***Partial acquisition*** of another business will give less ownership and control, and the potential of conflicts with the co-owners, but is a means of getting size, presence, and existing know-how in the foreign market.

'Born global' businesses: different decisions?

What is similar about Skype (Internet/software application), Mavi (clothing), HTC (smartphones), and Cochlear (medical devices)? It's not country of origin—they come from, respectively, Estonia, Turkey, Taiwan and Australia. Well, they are all 'born global' companies—enterprises whose genesis stems from a major, even exclusive, focus on foreign markets rather than their own ones. 'Born global' firms have their own answers to the 'why, which, when and how' market entry questions. A pure born-global firm is a venture launched to exploit a global niche from the first day of its operations. The term is also used to describe any firms that target global niches and develop global presence within one or two years of their founding, i.e. early in the product life-cycle. Born-global firms begin exporting their products or services during the couple of years after their founding and may export a quarter or more of their total production. Most of them advance through subsequent stages of internationalisation, collaboration with foreign partners, or undertaking of direct foreign investment.

Tanev (2012) suggests that 'born global' firms have the following characteristics:

- tend to be small, with limited financial and tangible resources;

- present in most sectors, not just hi- tech;

- managers have a strong international and entrepreneurial outlook;

- emphasis on differentiation and superior product quality;

- leverage of information and communications technologies (ICTs;

- use of external, independent intermediaries for distribution in foreign markets.

Such characteristics shape and constrain market entry decisions significantly. Such relatively small firms cannot compete directly with MNEs on risk and commitment, nor on the resources and time that can be invested in building up international markets. Typically, they take advantage of ICTs to process information efficiently, and interact and transact with partners and customers worldwide at very low cost. They tend to go for a niche differentiation strategy (see Chapter 5), and in foreign markets rely on astute use of third party intermediaries and contactors. Not surprisingly, many of these firms operate in knowledge-intensive or high-technology sectors. Having a technically advanced differentiated offering is key to the firm's competitive advantage, especially if the firm's product or service category faces few trade barriers. It also helps if the firm's product or service has high value relative to its transportation and other logistics costs.

The approach of a 'born global' firm, especially in its initial stages, tends towards what we might call '**lean internationalisation**'. Typical practices in lean internationalisation are:

- Running as much of the business as possible using ICTs and the Internet;

- focusing on smaller market segments they can dominate with differentiated, high value products/services;

- being lean on committing resources;

- using intermediaries.

All this leads to market entry taking the low risk approaches we discuss below, with exporting playing a very prominent role (see section 6.5).

6.3. Foreign Direct Investment

Having spelt out the decision points on market entry, let us look in more detail at foreign direct investment as an option. Foreign direct investment, or FDI, occurs when a firm invests directly in facilities to produce and/or market their products or services in a foreign country. Once a firm undertakes FDI it becomes, by definition, a multinational enterprise or MNE. There are two main forms of FDI. As we said above, Greenfield investment involves establishing a wholly owned new operation in a foreign country. The second type of FDI is an acquisition or merger with an existing firm in the foreign country. Most firms make their investments either through mergers with existing firms, or acquisitions. Firms prefer this route because mergers and acquisitions tend to be quicker to execute than Greenfield investments, it is usually easier to acquire assets than build them from the ground up, and because firms believe they can increase the efficiency of acquired assets by transferring capital, technology, or management skills.

Before we look at firm level decisions, let us look at the bigger picture. The flow of FDI refers to the amount of FDI undertaken over a given period of time. Outflows of FDI are the flows of FDI out of a country, while inflows of FDI are the flows of FDI into a country. The stock of FDI refers to the total accumulated value of foreign-owned assets at a given time. There has been a marked increase in both the flow and stock of FDI in the world economy. In 1975, the outflow of FDI was about US$25 billion; by 2008 it peaked at US$2.2 trillion! Together, six countries accounted for almost 60 percent of all FDI outflows from 1998 to 2006—USA, UK, Netherlands, France, Germany, and Japan. However FDI has declined since, with FDI outflows reaching US$1.6 trillion in 2016. Nevertheless, companies still have a massive presence abroad. For example, in 2016 American MNEs had US$6.4 trillion of assets under control around the world. Together the largest five European countries matched this. Why are FDI outflows so large, even in an era of growing de-globalisation?

- Firms are worried about protectionist measures, and see FDI as a way of getting around trade barriers.

- Changes in the economic and political policies of many countries have opened new markets to investment. Think, for example, of the changes in Eastern Europe that have made it possible for foreign firms to expand there. This is likely to continue after the 2020-2021 crisis as international trade remains, for many countries, a key to national prosperity.

- Many firms see the world as their market now, and so have expanded wherever they felt it made sense. For example, Spain's Telefónica has pursued opportunities in Latin America and in Europe. This, again, is likely to continue in the 2020-2025 period, though on a more selective basis.

- Many manufacturers and service companies have expanded into foreign countries to take advantage of lower cost labour, or to be closer to customers, amongst other reasons. For example, China has become a hot spot for firms that are attracted to the country's low wage rates, and very large markets. Into the 2020s, these sunk investments in time, resource and money will be reviewed carefully, but in many cases the rationale for FDI is likely to be still convincing.

We place FDI and market entry into the bigger 2021–2025 global picture in Chapter 7.

Why do firms become MNEs by engaging in FDI?

The answer to this question will help you understand how firms choose between the different foreign modes of entry - exporting, licensing, turnkey projects, franchising, joint ventures, fully-owned subsidiaries - discussed below. Dunning and Lundan (2009) developed a useful OLI framework that says firms will undertake FDI if there are:

Ownership advantages – resources of the firm transferable across borders that enable the firm to obtain competitive advantage abroad. Ownership advantages arise when a firm finds resources it owns that are not location-bound, but are internationally transferable, e.g. managerial capability to manage large hotels like Marriott, or a brand and product that travels well, e.g. IKEA and its style of furniture.

Locational advantages – location-specific advantages available to the firm in the foreign locality, conditions that it would not enjoy at home, e.g. raw materials, human resources. These advantages are not constant but grow, evolve, and even decline. Here we will mention four types of locational advantages:

Markets

There are often advantages in being close to existing or potential markets – one reason why so many firms have sought to set up in the rapidly developing, hugely populated country of China. These advantages include:

- Avoidance of local protectionism.

- Reduction in transportation costs; where direct interaction with the local customer is essential, e.g. after sales service, component manufacturer needing to be close to the foreign car plant it supplies.

- Dealing with services where production and sale cannot be separated, e.g. hotels, consultancy, Spanish banks using local branches in South America to serve their clients there.

- Local marketing assets, e.g. acquiring local distribution networks and brand names.

Dunning's Theory – O and L Advantages

Types of O-Advantages	Examples
• Resources created in one country that can be exploited in other countries	• Proprietary technology and managerial know-how (e.g. VW)
• Sharing of resources across business units	• Sharing of business model and brand name across stores (e.g. IKEA)CVCV
• Capabilities arising from combining business units in multiple countries	• Logistics based on superior co-ordinations between business units in different locations (e.g. Wal-Mart)
• Capabilities arising from organizational structures and culture	• Operation manuals, codes of conduct, organizational norms and practices (e.g. IKEA, Carrefour)
Types of L-Advantages	**Examples**
• Markets	• Size and growth consumer demand (e.g. China), presence of key clients (e.g. Antolin), high income consumers (e.g. Haier in the USA)
• Location-bound resources	• Human capital, such as a skilled labour force, natural resources, such as oil and gas deposits (e.g. Shell, BP) and agriculture (e.g. land in Africa)
• Agglomeration	• Geographic cluster of potential customers and suppliers (e.g. cars in Slovakia)
• Institutions	• Incentive schemes to attract FDI (e.g. Hungary)

Figure 6.1: Dunning's Theory—O and L advantages

167

Resource endowments

The locality may have specific resource advantages that the MNE can tap into, e.g. in land, labour, weather, infrastructure. For example, the last 15 years have seen Chinese MNEs increasingly seek natural resources around the world in oil, gas, minerals, and also agriculture and land. Other companies from India and China buy technology and brand names in Europe and the USA to combine these with their own resources and compete on the global stage.

Agglomeration

This refers to the location advantages arising from the clustering of economic activity in certain locations. Think of Silicon Valley in the USA and the cluster of suppliers, manufacturers, research firms, and market leaders there. Think of the City of London as a global financial centre. Advantages arise from:

- Knowledge spillovers whereby knowledge flows amongst closely located firms.
- Locally transferable skilled labour force.
- The creation of co-located specialised suppliers and buyers.

Dunning's Theory – Internalisation advantages

I-Advantages: Types of Market Failure	Examples
• Asset specificity	• FDI versus exports (e.g. aluminium industry)
	• FDI versus outsourcing (e.g. Flextronics, Wipro)
• Information asymmetry	• FDI versus exports where assessing the quality of the goods is difficult (e.g. database access in consultancy
	• FDI versus outsourcing where monitoring of the actual process is important(e.g. Nike, adidas)
• Dissemination risk	• FDI versus licensing of technology (e.g. automotive components)
	• In-house versus outsourcing of complex manufacturing processes (e.g. consumer electronics manufacturing)
• Tacit knowledge transfers	• FDI versus licensing/franchising of complex knowledge (e.g. Marks & Spencer)
• Strategic control	• FDI versus licensing as market entry strategy (e.g. Starbucks)

Source: Based on Multinational Enterprises and the Global Economy, 2nd ed. By J.H.Dunning & S. Lundan, 2008, Reproduced with permission from Edward Elgar Publishing Ltd and Professor S. Lundan

Figure 6.2: Dunning's Theory—Internalisation advantages

Institutions

A country may well offer tax advantages, business opportunities, legal recourse, subsidies, access and the like in order to attract foreign direct investment from multinationals.

Internalisation advantages

These arise if the MNE can organise activities better and cheaper internally, within the MNE, than if using a third party that incurs prohibitive transaction costs.

The OLI framework and the advantages accruing are shown in Figures 6.1. and 6.2.

6.4 Governments and Foreign Direct Investment

Let us return to an institution-based perspective on this subject for a moment. How does a government's attitude affect FDI? You can think of ideology toward FDI as being on a continuum where at one end is the radical view that is hostile to all FDI, and at the other end is the non-interventionist principle of free market economies. In between these two extremes is a more pragmatic nationalism. In the recent past more countries have adopted friendlier FDI policies, though the 2010-2020 period saw cross-border investment, trade, bank loans and supply chains all shrinking or stagnating relative to world GDP. Global companies have been retrenching more activity to their domestic or regional bases. For example, in 2016 alone multinational cross-border investment fell by up to 15 percent (see Chapter 1, 1.10). Countries not only retain but some have strengthened institutions that restrict and regulate FDI:

- Outright banning, e.g. nationalisation of the oil industry in Venezuela in the new century; the US government's 2019, and on-going, restrictions on Huawei, Chinese-based provider of information and communications technology infrastructure and smart devices

- Case-by-case approval of FDI with registration and authorisation requiring a range of conditions and negotiations to be gone through.

- Ownership requirements which disallow full foreign ownership but allow joint ventures perhaps, or minority foreign ownership, e.g. for security reasons the USA does not allow majority foreign ownership of domestic air transportation.

- Local business regulations will have to be complied with and may be restrictive if applied inflexibly.

Local content conditions requiring that a certain part of the value of the goods made or sold in the country should originate from that country, e.g. European countries introduced legislation demanding that Japanese automakers use components that had partly originated in the host country rather than being made wholly in Japan and assembled in the host country.

Benefits and Costs of FDI

	Possible benefits of FDI	Possible negative effects of FDI
Consumers	• Access to international quality products and brands • Lower prices due to scale economies and competition	• Reduces variety of traditional local brands (if local firms are crowded out)
Suppliers	• Technology transfer enhancing productivity • Opportunity to become an international supplier	• Crowding out by international sourcing
Competitors	• Technology spillovers enable learning • Competition may trigger upgrading and innovation	• Crowding out by overwhelming competition
Workers	• Employment opportunities • Typically higher labour standards than local firms • Training and knowledge transfer	• Often less labour intensive production (thus less work places) than local firms
Government	• Tax revenues • Economic growth	• Costs of subsidies and other incentives
Natural environment	• MNE's often have higher environmental standards than local firms	• MNE's may locate highly polluting activities in places with less stringent regulation

Note: These are possible effects that vary across FDI projects

Sources: (1) 'Perspectives on Multinational Enterprises in Emerging Economies', K.E. Meyer, 2004, *Journal of International Business Studies,* 34, pp. 259-277, Palgrave Macmillan; (2) 'When and where does foreign direct investment generate positive spillovers?' K.E. Meyer and E. Sinani, 2009, *Journal of International Business Studies,* 40, pp. 1075-1094, Palgrave Macmillan; (3) 'Multinational corporations and spillovers' Blomstom M. and Kokko, A., *Journey of Economic Surveys,* 12, pp 247-277, 1998, Blackwell; (4) Editors' Introduction in *Multinational Enterprises and Host Economies,* K.E. Meyer, ed., 2008, Edward Elgar Publishing. Reproduced and permission of Palgrave Macmillan, Wiley-Blackwell and Edward Elgar publishing Ltd.

Figure 6.3: Benefits and costs of FDI

Clearly Governments may be very suspicious of FDI and will need to weigh up the costs and benefits of FDI to the host country as shown in Figure 6.3. Quite a useful exercise for you is to also think through what the advantages and disadvantages for the home country might be if the home MNE makes foreign direct investments elsewhere. What do you think?

If the host country sees FDI as beneficial it might encourage FDI. It might reduce MNE risk by offering a government-backed programme covering the major forms of risk like the risk of expropriation, war losses, or the inability to repatriate profits. Some countries have also developed special loan programmes for companies investing in developing countries, created tax incentives, and encouraged host nations to relax their restrictions on inward FDI.

To discourage outward FDI, countries regulate the amount of capital that can be taken out of a country, use tax incentives to keep investments at home, and actually forbid investments in certain countries – for example, as the USA has done for companies trying to invest in Cuba and Iran. In Sweden for example, foreign companies are not allowed to invest in the tobacco industry. In Japan, until the early 1980s, most FDI was prohibited unless the foreign firm had valuable technology. Then, the foreign firm was allowed to form a joint venture with a Japanese company because the government believed this would speed up the diffusion of the technology throughout the Japanese economy.

6.5. Major Modes of Entering Foreign Markets

OK, so government may be favourable or not favourable towards FDI. But FDI does not exhaust the options. There are six major ways we see firms entering foreign markets. These are (with variants): exporting, turnkey projects, licensing, franchising, establishing joint ventures with a host country firm, or setting up a new wholly owned subsidiary in the host country. Each mode of entry has its advantages and disadvantages. As a firm's positioning in a foreign market evolves, you will also see shifts in ownership and modes of operating in order to achieve further revenue growth and competitive advantage.

Exporting

Exporting is the sale of products made by firms in their home country to customers in other countries. Exporting is a common first step for many manufacturing firms. Later, feeling limited in terms of revenue growth and lack of control, such firms may switch to another mode. Exporting is attractive because:

- It avoids the costs of establishing local manufacturing and service operations.

- It helps firms achieve experience curve and location economies.

- Lack of trust on payment can be overcome by a ***letter of credit***. For example if a US exporter does not trust a Chinese importer, it can draw up a financial contract that states that the importer's highly reputable bank will pay a specific sum of money to the exporter's bank on receipt of the goods/service.

- Export intermediaries are usually available in the exporting country with the expertise to help facilitate exports to a range of other countries. These are especially used by SMEs. The exporter can also employ its own sales agents, on commission fees, in the foreign country, or sell the products to a distributor, who is a local intermediary in the foreign country trading on their own account.

However, exporting may also be unattractive because:

- There may be lower cost locations for manufacturing the products abroad that are not being taken advantage of. Exporting from a home market base may not be the most effective policy.

- High transport costs and tariffs can make it uneconomical.

- Agents in a foreign country cannot be closely controlled, and may not act in an exporter's best interests.

- There will be restrictions on the amount of revenue growth that can be achieved using this channel.

Turnkey projects

In a turnkey project the foreign contractor agrees to handle every detail of the project for a local client, including training personnel. After designing and constructing the new facility, the contractor completes the contract by handing the client the 'key' to the plant that is ready for full operation – thus the term *turnkey.* A variant is the build-operate-transfer model, which includes the contractor managing the facility for fees after the construction has been completed. Turnkey projects are most common in the metal refining, pharmaceutical, petrol refining, and chemical industries. All these use complex and expensive production technologies. Turnkey projects are a means of exporting such know-how to foreign countries that lack these competencies. The approach is also popular in the construction and engineering industries for large infrastructure projects – for example airports (a Spanish firm Ferrovial has operated London Heathrow and other British airports; Athens airport was built largely by German companies), power stations, and motorways.

Turnkey projects are attractive because:

- They are a way of earning economic returns from the know-how required to assemble and run a technologically complex process.

- They can be less risky than more conventional forms of foreign direct investment.

However the problems with turnkey projects include:

- The contractor firm has no long-term interest in the foreign country so market growth may be small.

- The contractor firm may create a local competitor that can grow to compete globally.

- If the contractor firm is supplying process technology or know-how that is its own source of competitive advantage, then selling this through a turnkey project is also selling competitive advantage to potential competitors.

Licensing

A licensing agreement is where a licensor grants the rights to intangible property to another entity (the licensee) for a specified period, in return for a royalty fee paid by the licensee. Intangible property includes patents, inventions, formulas, processes, designs, copyrights, and trademarks. As one example, Xerox signed an agreement with Fuji Photo in order to enter the Japanese market, creating Fuji Xerox. Xerox then licensed its xerographic know-how to Fuji Photo in exchange for a royalty fee of 5 percent of net sales revenue, earned from photocopier sales. The agreement was for 10 years and was extended several times, with direct sales restricted to the Asia Pacific region.

Licensing has several advantages:

- The firm avoids development costs and risks associated with opening a foreign market.

- The firm avoids barriers to investment, e.g. in the Xerox case above, the Japanese government prohibited Xerox from setting up a fully owned subsidiary in Japan.

- The firm can capitalise on market opportunities without developing additional marketing, administrative, and operational capabilities itself.

At the same time licensing may be unattractive because:

- The firm does not have the tight control over manufacturing, marketing, and strategy needed to gain economies from an experience curve and location advantages.

- For a technology-based firm, lack of control over the technology and intellectual property (IP) may become a problem.

- The firm's ability to coordinate strategic moves across countries is constrained.

- Proprietary or intangible assets could be lost. This risk can be lessened by using cross-licensing agreements. These are increasingly common in hi-tech industries. Here a firm licenses use of its proprietary know-how in exchange for a license to use the other firm's know-how. For example, US biotechnology firm Amgen licenses Japanese sales of its product Nuprogene to Japanese firm, Kirin. In exchange Kirin licenses Amgen to sell some of Kirin's products in the USA. Risks can also be reduced by forming a joint venture as was the case with Fuji Photo (above).

Franchising

Franchising is a specialised longer-term form of licensing where the franchiser not only sells intangible property to a franchisee (e.g. a trademark), but also insists on tight rules on how it does business. The franchiser will also often assist the franchisee to run the business on an ongoing basis. Like licensing, typically the franchiser receives a royalty payment, usually a percentage of the franchisee's net revenues. Whereas licensing is used primarily by manufacturing firms, franchising is used primarily by service firms. The obvious example globally is McDonald's, whose strict rules include control over the menu, cooking methods, staffing policies, design, and location. McDonald's also organises the supply chain for its franchisees, and provides management training and financial assistance.

The advantages of franchising include:

- It avoids the costs and risks of opening up a foreign market.

- A firm can quickly build a global presence.

However a firm needs to take into account certain risks, including:

- It may inhibit the firm's ability to take profits out of one country to support competitive attacks in another.

- Geographical and administrative distance from the franchisee may make it difficult to detect poor quality; likewise if there are many thousands of franchisees across the world. One way in which US firms like KFC and McDonald's have reduced these risks is by establishing a joint venture with a local firm in each country or region. This firm then acts as a master franchisee, controlling the local firms' performances.

- Poor quality at one branch can hurt the brand globally. For example, travellers expect the same quality of experience in a Four Seasons Hotel in Hong Kong as in New York. If they experience variable quality they may be dissuaded from staying in this brand hotel in the future.

Joint ventures

A joint venture (JV) involves establishing a firm that is jointly owned by two or more otherwise independent firms, e.g. Fuji Photo described above. US multinational General Electric has in recent years used joint ventures to enter foreign markets like Spain and South Korea where its units lacked a strong presence. GE switched its policy in the 2000s because of the rising costs of foreign acquisition, and because it recognised it could lower risks and gain local knowledge through JVs, while navigating difficult legal, political, economic, and cultural markets like China. JVs are typically 50-50 owned by the partners, but minority ownership is also frequent, although sometimes creating issues around power, direction and control.

Joint ventures can be attractive because:

- Firms benefit from a local partner's knowledge of local conditions, culture, language, political systems, legal know-how, and business systems.

- The costs and risk of opening a foreign market are shared.

- JVs often satisfy local political considerations for market entry.

But joint ventures run a number of risks, which we will discuss in more detail below when we look at strategic alliances:

- The firm risks giving control of its technology to its partner.

- The firm may not have the tight control needed to realise economies from the experience curve, or from location economies, or to coordinate attacks against rivals on a global basis. Thus Texas Instruments (TI) instead established a fully owned subsidiary in Japan to check Japanese market share of the world semi-conductor market. TI required the subsidiary to take instructions from TI's US-based corporate centre and run at a loss if necessary – something few JV partners would be willing to accept.

- JVs can be difficult to coordinate globally.

- Shared ownership can frequently lead to conflicts and battles for control if goals and objectives differ or change over time, or power imbalances develop between the parties.

Fully owned subsidiaries

Here the firm owns 100 percent of shares in the subsidiary. A fully owned subsidiary can be defined as a subsidiary located in a foreign country that is entirely owned by the parent multinational.

Wholly owned subsidiaries are attractive because:

- They reduce the risk of losing control over core competencies.

- The firm gains 100 percent of the profits earned in the foreign market.

175

- They can help in protection of key technologies and intellectual property – particularly important in hi-tech, pharmaceutical, and electronics industries worldwide.

- They give a firm tight control over operations in different countries necessary for engaging in global strategic coordination.

- They may be required in order to gain location and experience curve economies. This is important where a firm wishes to establish a fully optimised global production system, or where there are intense cost pressures in the specific industry.

- Firms pursuing global standardisation or transnational strategies (see chapter 8) tend to prefer establishing wholly owned subsidiaries, which allow them more opportunity for creating an integrated global strategy.

Wholly owned subsidiaries may also be unattractive because:

- The firm bears the full risk and cost of setting up overseas.

- Entry speed may be slower than alternatives, for example acquisition.

One additional decision a firm needs to make if going down the wholly owned subsidiary route is whether to adopt a ***Greenfield*** or ***Acquisition*** strategy. In a Greenfield strategy the firm builds the subsidiary from the ground up, as opposed to acquiring an existing company.

The main advantage of a Greenfield venture is that it gives the firm a greater ability to build the kind of subsidiary company it needs, and that fits with the parent company. Firms also often discover that it is very difficult to transfer organisational culture and ways of operating to acquired firms. A wholly owned greenfield venture also gives control over equity and operations, and better protects company know-how. But Greenfield ventures are slower to establish, and are also risky in terms of high capital investment and long payback periods. They also might lead to market entry being pre-empted by a rival who uses an acquisition strategy to gain a quicker foothold in the same market.

Alternatively, as we mentioned above, a firm can acquire an established company in the host nation and use that firm to promote, or even manufacture its products/services. As one example, insurance major ING entered the US insurance market by acquiring existing US firms rather than trying to build an operation from scratch. Acquisitions can be attractive as a mode of entry because:

- They can be quicker to execute.

- Full acquisition offers equity and operational control. Part acquisition can still offer access to operations the previous owner resisted giving up, and also the previous owner's continuing commitment.

- They enable firms to pre-empt their competitors in the foreign market.

- They do not add unnecessary new capacity.

- They may incur less risk than Greenfield or other options. You buy a set of assets that are producing a known revenue and profit stream. You also gain tangible assets – factories, logistics systems etc., and also intangible assets, e.g. brand name, managers' local knowledge of markets, existing customer relationships.

However, acquisitions have been known to fail due to:

- The acquiring firm overpaying for the acquired firm, resulting in disappointment in realised value, and sometimes even failure.

- High up-front capital needs.

- Clash of cultures between the two firms.

- Attempts to realise synergies running into roadblocks (for example incompatible technologies and human resource policies) and take much longer and are more expensive to realise than forecast. In partial acquisitions, such problems are made worse by limited control.

- There is inadequate pre-acquisition screening.

- Political sensitivities in the host country

For these reasons firms that are frequently on the acquisition trail – for example Cisco Systems and Cemex, develop a core expertise in carefully screening the firm to be acquired, ensuring they do not pay too much for the acquisition, and moving rapidly to implement a pre-developed integration plan. Another approach to reduce risks might be to carry out staged acquisitions. These often occur where the owner does not want to sell the whole business, and where the owner and senior executives and specialist staff remain a vital part of future success. The acquiring company may also see this as a way of reducing the initial risks of foreign market entry. A staged acquisition can create uncertainty over the future ownership structure, however.

Part of this will be a human resources (HR) plan to allay the fears of the management and talented staff of the acquired firm, and to deal with other HR issues (for example resistance to change, the need for redundancies) that are likely to arise (see Willcocks, 2021).

6.6. Assessing the Relevance of Strategic Alliances

Strategic alliances (SAs) are collaborations between independent firms using equity modes, non-equity contractual agreements, or both. SAs can form between potential or actual competitors. Formal joint ventures are one form of strategic alliance. But an SA may also take the form of business unit joint ventures, R&D joint ventures, or short-term contractual agreements for operational collaboration, to cooperate on a particular strategic task, for example joint marketing, production, or distribution arrangements. An example of a successful business unit JV is Japanese-American Fuji Xerox, which manufactured printers together since 1962. By 2018 Fuji Film was looking to take over the Xerox company. More often, companies end the JV when its original purpose has been achieved. An R&D JV may be formed with direct competitors or with technology specialists as complementors (see Chapter 5) and can be useful when trying to develop industry standards or new eco-systems. For example, BMW and Daimler made a JV to develop new eco-systems for its car sharing and mobility services. They also collaborated with Intel and Mobileye to develop technology for self-driving cars. IBM and Maersk began collaborating to devlop blockchain applications for transforming international trade practices like negotiating, accounting, and enacting automated transactions. Operational collaboration does not need equity investment to be successful. Consider how international airlines collaborate with each other—for example code-sharing, mutual frequent flyer programmes, sharing of facilities at airports—to connect up all major travel destinations for the customer.

The number of strategic alliances has exploded in recent decades as firms have sought to expand, and recognised that they do not necessarily have all the resources available to do so at the desired speed. Why choose a strategic alliance? Because it:

- Facilitates entry into a foreign market.

- Can be a stepping-stone to a full acquisition, allowing the parties to learn how to work together, so smoothing the path to full acquisition.

- Allows a firm to share the fixed costs and risks of developing new products or processes.

- Helps a firm to establish technological standards for the industry that will benefit the firms.

- Brings together complementary skills and assets that neither partner could easily develop on their own.

But SAs have been criticised as an entry mode because:

- An SA may give the competitor you ally with a low cost route to technologies and market. For example, many US companies in the semiconductor and machine tool industries were criticised for their SAs with Japanese firms which, it was argued, allowed the Japanese companies to keep high paying high value-added jobs in Japan while gaining valuable US project engineering and production process skills, thus reducing US firms' competitive advantage. At the same time some US-Japanese SAs clearly work, for example the Microsoft-Toshiba alliance and the Boeing-Mitsubishi alliance to build the 787 aeroplane.

- The failure rate for SAs is very high. Historically, two thirds run into serious financial and managerial trouble within two years of their formation, and one third of these are subsequently rated as failures. As one example, in 2011 Nokia, a major smartphone manufacturer, allied with Microsoft to use Microsoft's Windows mobile operating system, the aim being to make this the industry standard against Apple's iPhone and Google's Android. But Nokia did not get enough market share so its mobile phone operation was acquired by Microsoft in 2013 to continue the push into the mobile phone business. Unfortunately this proved unsuccessful, and resulted in Microsoft writing off some US$7 billion, and the loss of 7,800 jobs in 2015.

This suggests that SAs need to be carefully entered into and managed. One approach is to look for a limited SA first. Thus some firms enter into a business unit JV, where existing business units from two firms are merged. This works if the two firms can achieve something, e.g. market leadership, technological innovation, which neither could achieve on their own. It may also be a sensible option if a full takeover is not practicable. Also where the merged unit depends on inputs (such as technologies) from both parties that would be disrupted by legal separation. Another form of SA is operational collaboration, consisting of collaboration in operations, marketing, or distribution. For example, in the airline industry, national airlines form alliances to connect to all major travel destinations, and also share frequent flyer programmes, and share facilities and resources such as passenger lounges.

Summarising the research studies, the success of an alliance is a function of:

- *Partner selection.* An effective partner helps the firm achieve its strategic goals and has capabilities the firm lacks and values; has a shared vision on the alliance's purpose; and does not exploit the alliance just for its own ends.

- *Alliance structure.* This should make it difficult to transfer technology not meant to be transferred; have contractual guarantees to guard against partner opportunism; and allow for swapping of skills and technologies with equal gains.

179

- ***Management capability.*** This requires the building of strong interpersonal relationships - called relational or social capital - amongst the two managements. It also seems to require learning from the alliance partner. Successful SAs see the partners perceiving the SA not just as a cost-sharing or risk-sharing device, but also as an opportunity to learn from a potential competitor how to do business better. This learning then needs to be diffused throughout the organisation.

6.7 Going International: Growth Through Evolution

It is important to understand that foreign market entry is only the start of what is often a very long journey for a firm. If you refer back to Chapter 4, you will recall how a firm will seek to evolve and grow its international business. An ***international strategy*** will seek to sell domestic products in foreign markets with minimal customisation. Or a firm may choose a ***localisation strategy*** to give itself a competitive edge in the foreign market. However, pressures to reduce costs together with the requirement to grow market size may well lead to the development of a ***global standardisation strategy***. Alternatively where there are pressures to reduce costs, retain local responsiveness, and grow the market globally, the firm may well move to a ***transnational strategy***. In chapter 5 we saw that competitive markets are highly dynamic, and firms are continually seeking to match, outpace, or respond to competitors, these days increasingly on a global stage. Firms have to also continually adjust their structure and operational models to fit with their emerging strategies to expand operations, revenues and profits, and adjust to changes in location and market attractiveness.

All this means that the initial mode of entry may well be only the temporary starting point for a firm's globalising strategy. Much depends on the assessment of costs, risks, and benefits and how the changing trade-offs between these three factors suggest to a firm changes in commitment of resources, scale of operations, and ownership in the foreign market. A firm can make a relatively low commitment to a market through exporting, licensing and franchising, or by small-scale or partial acquisitions, or by limited joint ventures/alliances.

They may also see a low risk approach, for example, such as using the internet to extend their business beyond national boundaries. However, to grow further they may need to make bigger commitments through wholly owned subsidiaries, large-scale joint ventures, and/or large mergers/acquisitions. In doing so they will need to integrate their internet business strategy relative to their other modes of operating in foreign markets. Figure 6.4 provides a useful summary of major, typical modes of market entry, and their attributes in terms of control, resource commitment, strategic flexibility and levels of risk.

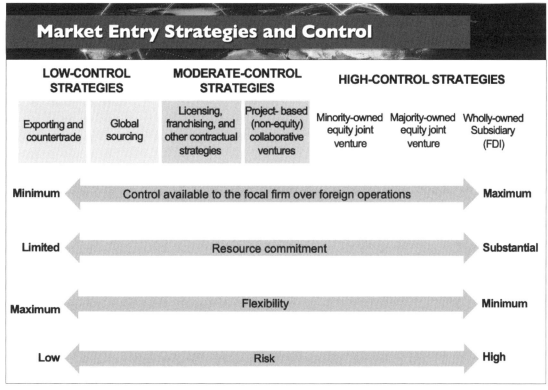

Figure 6.4: Market entry strategies and control

Source: Adapted form several sources

6.8. Conclusion

Between 2017–2021 there were more than 100,000 MNEs around the world, driving some 80 percent of world trade. While this represented only 0.1 percent of the companies in the world, these MNEs had some 890,000 foreign affiliates. These affiliates generated 33 percent of the world's exports of goods and services (in 2014). Large firms are more international than small and medium enterprises, but even the world's largest firms by revenue generate on average around 54 percent of revenues in their home countries, and 65 percent in their regions—Asia Pacific, Europe Middle East and Africa (EMEA), or North/South America.

However, by 2021, over several years, there had been amongst multinationals moves away from going abroad. In 2016 multinationals' cross-border investment had dropped by 10-15 percent. The share of trade accounted for by cross-border supply chains has stagnated at 60 percent since 2007. The proportion of sales Western firms make outside their home region has been shrinking, while multinational profits have been falling relative to those of domestic-based firms.

The flow of new multinational investment has been declining relative to Gross Domestic Product. As a result firms with a domestic focus were winning market share. For example, in Brazil local banks—Bradesco and Itau—were beating global lenders. In India, multinationals like Bharti Airtel and Vodaphone, have been losing customers to Reliance, a domestic firm. In China, a multinational like KFC has seen its sales being eroded by local dumpling brands. By 2017, multinational share of global profits—35 percent in 2007—declined to only 30 percent. The lack of advantage is revealed by the fact that, by 2018, roughly 50 percent of the stock of foreign direct investment made a return on equity of less than 10 percent. Companies like Ford and General Motors were making more than 80 percent of their profits in North America, suggesting that their foreign returns were very poor. Many industries that tried to globalise seem to work best when national or regional. As Ghemawat (2018), in the Laws Of Globalisation, pointed out, truly global companies are less frequent than you think. But clearly, despite the 2020–2021 economic crisis, international trade was likely to return to being vast and busy, and foreign market entry and evolution will be a perennial, critical challenge.

In this chapter we have looked at the major decisions a firm needs to address when considering entry into foreign markets. A firm needs to answer four questions – why enter, which market(s) to enter, when to enter, and at what scale and level of ownership. The objectives of the firm, whether it is natural resource seeking, market seeking, efficiency seeking, or innovation seeking, will shape greatly the resulting decisions.

That decision might be to make foreign direct investments into a country to secure ownership, locational, and internalisation advantages. But government institutions may well have a part to play in the degree to which these advantages can be gained in the targeted country. But FDI does not exhaust the options. In fact there are six major approaches we looked at, though each with advantages and potential disadvantages. These are exporting, turnkey projects, licensing, franchising, joint ventures, wholly owned subsidiaries. We saw in chapter 4 how CEMEX rose to a global position through a series of acquisitions. But strategic alliances are another way to gain a strong foothold in a foreign market, though the risk of failure, according to the evidence, is high.

The important concluding point is that entry is usually part of a long journey and therefore the firm needs to plan an evolution from the optimal starting point. Of course it will make mistakes along the way, or even in its initial decision. But going abroad is invariably a risky affair, which gives added justification for being very aware of the advantages and disadvantage of different modes of entry discussed in this chapter.

In our final chapter, we look at the changing global context in which market entry, or market withdrawal decisions are going to be made in the 2020s.

References

Dunning, J. and Lunden, S. (2009), *Multinational Enterprises and the Global Economy*, Elgar, Cheltenham, UK

Ghemawat, P. (2018), *The New Global Road Map: Enduring Strategies For Turbulent Times*, Harvard Business Review Press, Boston, USA

Peng, M. and Meyer, K. (2019), *International Business*, Cengage Learning, London, UK

Tanev, S. (2012) 'Global From The Start: The characteristics of born global firms in the technology sector', *Technology Innovation Management Review*, March, pp. 5-8.

Willcocks, L. (2021), *Global Business Management*, SB Publishing, Stratford-upon-Avon, UK

"Foresight is not about predicting the future, it's about minimising surprise."

Karl Schroeder

"As the world becomes more connected, it also necessarily becomes more interdependent. This is the dark underbelly, the butterfly defect of globalisation, that, if left unmanaged, inevitably means that we will suffer escalating, increasingly dangerous systemic risks."

Ian Goldin and Robert Muggah, March 2020

Chapter 7

Global Business: Future Directions

7.1. Introduction

A business is shaped and constrained by its history and external context, but has a more active role in shaping its internal context, operational model, strategising and execution. Let's start with history and external context. We identified in Chapter 1 five major long term trends impacting on international business: changes in world output and trade patterns; increased foreign direct investment; the changing nature of the multinational enterprise; the changing world political order; and more recent moves towards de-globalisation and protectionism.

The 2020 pandemic and the ensuing economic crisis seriously disrupted these, emergent, complex patterns. To find a way forward, we first need to understand the point of departure—where the global economy was before the pandemic hit. This chapter reviews globalisation to 2020, then assesses how the ensuing health and economic crises disrupted prior discernable trends. We then look at future likely scenarios for the global economy, the aim being to establish the challenges, lessons and ways forward for international businesses.

7.2. Globalisation Trends Revisited

First, a further assessment of the major trends in the global economy over the last 35 years. We need to understand long-term trends as a basis for constructing future developments, and strategising and managing forward. So where did these trends get to by 2020?

The first long-term trend has been the vast expansion in world output and cross-border trading.

In 2018 world merchandise trade was US$19.67 trillion, and commercial services US$5.63 trillion, while world trade and Gross Domestic Product (GDP) grew 26 percent between 2008 and 2018. By the beginning of 2020 the value of world trade was 160 times larger than it was in 1960. By 2018, the USA accounted for 15.8 percent of world output, with China at 17.1 percent, and global leader, though the USA remained the largest economy overall. It is likely that India will become the third largest economy by 2030. China has been the worlds largest exporter since 2009, and in 2018 exported over US$2 trillion worth of goods and services. Throughout most of 2008–2020 so-called 'developing' countries equalled or outperformed developed economies in trade and results. Most forecasts suggest that today's 'developing' nations may account for more than 60 percent of world economic activity by 2025, with today's 'rich' nations declining from 55 percent in 2018 to 38 percent in 2025. Interestingly, while world trade increased 3.3 times between 2000 and 2020 the world economy increased only 2.6 times. Fundamentally, by 2020 we were producing more than ever before, but we also increased even more the rate at which we trade internationally what we produce. Thus the enormous rise in international business.

The second major long-term trend has been an increase in foreign direct investment (FDI).

The average yearly FDI outflow increased from US$14 billion in 1970 to US$1.45 trillion in 2016, when the global stock of FDI was about US$27 trillion. Note also the rising importance of developing nations as destinations for FDI. The directional flow of FDI has also become more complex. In the 1960s, US firms accounted for about two-thirds of worldwide FDI flows. Today, the United States accounts for less than one-fifth of worldwide FDI flows. Other 'developed' countries have followed a similar pattern. In contrast, the share of FDI accounted for by developing countries has risen. These trends reflect the internationalisation of company operations. By 2017 more than 80,000 companies had more than 800,000 affiliates in foreign markets, employing over 75 million people, making US$36 trillion in sales, and generating over 11 percent of global GDP. One interesting trend is that firms have been finding their home markets under increasing attack from foreign competitors. Multinationals originate from many more countries than ever before. By 2017, only 540 firms of the top 2000 global firms were US-based multinationals, a drop of some 236 firms in 15 years. China and other Asian countries increasingly have MNEs that compete directly with Western firms e.g. Alibaba, Ten Cent. This trend is expected to continue from 2021–2025.

The third trend in the years following the 2008/9 financial crisis is that multinationals have been doing less well.

In retrospect, multinationals had been overestimating the value of economies of scale, and, more recently, of arbitrage (see Chapter 4). Profits of the top biggest 700 MNEs dropped by 25 percent between 2014 and 2019. Meanwhile return on equity (ROE) fell from 18 percent in 2009 to 11 percent by 2019. ROE on foreign operations investments declined to 4–8 percent across the OECD. Emerging country MNEs fared no better—worldwide ROE was 8 percent. Half of the 700 largest MNEs saw ROE fall in 2016–2019, with 40 percent failing to make an ROE of 10 percent. The bright spot into 2021 has been technology companies. On many estimates, their importance will continue to rise over the next five years. More on this later.

Note also that companies were reporting lower ROE in foreign markets than domestic ones. As one example, between 2014 and 2019 US businesses gained 30 percent higher domestic returns than from foreign investments. By the end of 2019, firms with a domestic focus were winning market share, for example in India, Reliance *vs* Bharti Airtel. Governments and rules were becoming less supportive of multinationals. By the beginning of 2020, many sectors seemed to work best when based at national or regional level. Even before the major disruption arising from the coronavirus pandemic, multinationals needed to review strategies on the degree of globalisation of markets and production, and the sources of competitive advantage.

A fourth trend has been the continuously shifting political world order.

Many former communist nations in Europe and Asia had become more committed to forms of democratic politics and market economies, so creating new opportunities for international businesses. But there have been more recent signs of growing unrest and authoritarian tendencies in some countries, for example, Russia, Turkey, Poland. China and Latin America had also been moving toward greater market reforms. Over the years several Latin American countries have increased their attractiveness as markets for exports and as targets for FDI—or example Brazil, Chile and Mexico. Will this continue? Other parts of Latin America reflect a long history of economic mismanagement, with Venezuela, for example, running into serious problems in recent years. Bolivia and Ecuador have seen shifts to more state involvement, with FDI less welcome. For international businesses such newer developments change once again the risk profiles for those countries. Meanwhile, between 1983 and 2008 FDI in China increased from less than US$2 billion to US$90 billion annually. But China has moved to greater state control since 2012. From 2016 many other countries were taking a more protectionist, nationalistic stance, led by the USA.

A fifth recent trend has been towards de-globalisation.

Historically, of course, most companies have been regional rather than global. But during the 2010–2020 period there were indications of the long-term trend towards vertical and horizontal globalisation being reversed. Most recently, the global firm has most recently been in retreat. Some signs: by 2016 multinational cross border investment had fallen by 10–15 percent; Western firms' percentage of sales outside their home regions has shrunk, multinational profits have been falling, as has new investment relative to GDP. The pace of economic integration also slowed between 2015–2020. On 12 measures of global integration, eight signalled retreat. Some examples: supply chain capacity shrank; long term cross-border investment decreased to 1.3 percent GDP in 2018; trade volumes stayed stagnant and cross-border loans decreased. Meanwhile, gross capital flows moved from 7 percent of GDP in 2007 to 1.5 percent in 2018. However, cross-border migration (by people) and data flows have increased dramatically.

The summary from an international business perspective is that trade stopped getting cheaper, and straddling the world became less profitable. While services were growing in many economies, companies found them harder to export than products (only 7 percent of world GDP is service exports). Meanwhile 'emerging' economies were becoming more self reliant, economic activity became more regional, while protectionism, tariffs and counter-attacks against global intruders became more frequent. At the big picture level, the centre of gravity for international business has been shifting east and south, with 18 countries there recording five percent plus annual growth over the last 20 years. The role for high growth 'developing' economies has been expanding, as has the amount of South-South and China-South trade. Meanwhile, the pace of technological development has been accelerating, particularly with information and communication technologies and digitisation, one indicator being the dramatic increase in cross-border data flows in recent years. Technology may bring more opportunities to create value, while redefining work. But technological adoption has been uneven across countries, sectors and companies. There is a growing gulf between those who have embraced technological change and those that have not, which may place many companies, and even countries, at a growing disadvantage as the 2020s proceed.

Following on from this, the 2020 pandemic has been highly disruptive, and across 2020–2025, will create new winners and losers, and new globalisation and deglobalisation trends. Let us, then, look at the pressing questions: how have these trends been disrupted by the pandemic and economic crises; how far will the trends change once more, what will emerge, and what actions can businesses take in the new environment?

7.3. Coming to Terms with the Crisis

The five major trends were indeed highly disrupted by events in 2020. Expansion in world output and trade came to a grinding halt. FDI was put on pause, though many businesses anticipated opportunities in the event of an economic recovery. Multinationals continued to do less well, but some were more likely inheritors of the future than others. The political order continued to be dynamic and shifting, with the economic slump and health crisis creating bot political tensions and increased need to cooperate internationally. De-globalisation and protectionism played powerfully into these shifts as potential salves and ways forward in a dynamic, interconnected and uncertain world. Let us look at such developments in more detail.

By May 2020 The World Health Organisation (WHO) had recorded globally over two million cases of coronavirus, and 150,000 related deaths. New cases were coming in at around 85,000, and deaths 6,500, per day. This was likely a substantial underestimate due, for various reasons, to under-reporting. The impacts were unevenly distributed across 212 countries, but major economies, and so the global economy, were largely on semi-pause, and this was likely to continue for some time. Some suggested at this time that it could take most economies more than two years, i.e. until 2023, to recover. In numbers, the most disproportionately affected (in size order) were USA, Spain, Italy, Germany, UK, France, China, Iran and Turkey, but no country was left untouched due to the integratedness of the global economy.

The global economy takes a big hit.

According to the World Trade Organisation (trade forecast press conference, April 9, 2020), world merchandise trade was set to plummet by between 13 percent and 32 percent in 2020 due to the COVID-19 pandemic. On a relatively optimistic scenario, a sharp drop in trade would be followed by a recovery starting in the second half of 2020. A more pessimistic scenario would see a steeper initial decline and a more prolonged and incomplete recovery. A 2021 recovery in trade was expected, but depended on the duration of the outbreak and the effectiveness of the policy responses (see below). Nearly all regions would suffer double-digit declines in trade volumes in 2020, with exports from North America and Asia hit hardest. Trade would fall steeper in sectors with complex value chains, particularly electronics and automotive products. Merchandise trade volume had already fallen by 0.1 percent in 2019, weighed down by trade tensions and slowing economic growth. The dollar value of world merchandise exports in 2019 had fallen by 3 percent to US$18.89 trillion. The value of commercial services exports actually rose 2 percent to US$ 6.03 trillion in 2019. But services trade may be the component of world trade most directly affected by COVID-19 through the imposition of transport, social distancing and travel restrictions, and the closure of many retail, recreational, travel, tourist and hospitality establishments. Unlike goods, there are no inventories of services to be drawn down now and restocked at a later stage. Therefore, decline in services trade during the pandemic may be lost forever. Services are also interconnected, with air transport enabling an ecosystem of cultural, sporting and recreational activities. However, some services were benefiting from the crisis, most noticeably information technology services, as companies enabled employees to work from home and people socialise remotely.

In its April World Economic Outlook the International Monetary Fund (IMF) projected global growth in 2020 to fall to -3 percent. This represented a downgrade of 6.3 percentage points from January 2020, a major revision over a very short period. Advanced economies would be hardest hit, with negative growth at -6.1 percent. Emerging market and developing economies would have negative growth rates of -1.1 percent (-2.2 percent if China is excluded). But a note here: emerging market and developing economies faced additional challenges with unprecedented reversals in capital flows if global risk appetite declined, currency pressures, weaker health systems, and more limited fiscal space to provide support. Moreover, several economies entered the crisis in a vulnerable state already, with sluggish growth and high debt levels.

All this would make the 2020 pandemic crisis the worst recession since the Great Depression from 1929 to the late 1930s, and far worse than the global financial crisis, which experienced a -1 percent reduction in economic growth in 2009, though its impact stretched for a long period. For example, following the 2009 crisis merchandise exports never returned to their previous levels.

However, assuming the pandemic faded in the second half of 2020 and that policy actions around the world were effective in preventing widespread firm bankruptcies, extended job losses, and system-wide financial strains, the IMF projected global growth in 2021 to rebound to 5.8 percent. This recovery in 2021 would be only partial, as the level of economic activity would remain below the level the IMF had projected for 2021, before the virus hit. The cumulative loss to global GDP over 2020 and 2021 from the pandemic crisis could be around US$9 trillion.

The WTO and IMF projections were, of course, possible scenarios, the main assumption being a V shaped economic recovery from late 2020 through 2021, at different rates for different economies. But given the high uncertainty around the duration and intensity of the health crisis, the pandemic could lead to longer durations of containment, worsening financial conditions, and further breakdowns of global supply chains. In such cases, global GDP would fall even further. This would be more of a U-shaped recovery. The IMF suggested an additional 3 percent fall in 2020, while, if the pandemic continued into 2021, an additional 8 percent decline from the +5.5 percent growth projection. Most research groups at this time were not contemplating the most pessimistic scenario of an L-shaped depression, i.e. a dramatic fall, with no recovery for several years.

7.4. Business Context: Disruption and New Scenarios

The above is a compelling endorsement of using PESTEL analysis on a frequent basis in contemporary business environments (see Chapters 2 and 4). But it also suggests changes of emphasis are needed within the PESTEL framework. Clearly, *social factors* included accelerated moves to home and remote working, and potentially long terms shifting attitudes and preferences amongst consumers and workforces. On the *political, economic and legal* fronts, we saw, during 2020, massive government intervention in the conduct of business. This was contrary to globalisation's main direction of travel. Politically and legally, governments took on more command and control functions. Economically, governments moved to support faltering economies and businesses. Among the enormous relief programs to sustain companies and citizens during the lockdowns, the largest was the US stimulus valued at more than US$2 trillion. Meanwhile, the European Central Bank (ECB) announced EU€870 billion in quantitative easing, and, to forestall a credit crunch, also forbade eurozone banks from paying dividends to investors or buying back shares until late 2020. The European Parliament released EU€37 billion to support small and medium-size enterprises (SMEs) and the healthcare sector. By May 2020, the People's Bank of China had pumped the Chinese banks with more than 550 billion renminbi (around US$78 billion) in liquidity. The US Federal Reserve Board brought its policy rate near zero (0.00 to 0.25 percent) and announced $700 billion in quantitative easing.

But for international business, a pressing question arose for future environmental analyses: for how long, and how deeply would governmental command, control, and intervention persist? During 2020, all governments were building debt they would seek to repay, not least through taxation. Financial innovations that gave power to the state looked attractive enough to keep if they appeared to reduce systemic risk. Interventions to preserve firms, industries, jobs and worker incomes may well endure and become policy, not least to build national resilience in the face of any future crisis. State spending may become permanently higher. But how long could governments sustain such major interventions? And if everyone is a Keynseian in a crisis, what happens if crises are expected to be more frequent, and impactful?[1]

If government interventions made previous PESTEL analyses outdated, then global businesses now needed to factor in much more seriously than ever before *technological* factors. Technology proved not only very supportive in business terms during the crisis, but technology and hi-tech companies were probably going to be among the inheritors of the future, following the pandemic. Many businesses were likely to accelerate their digital transformation and adoption of what we call

---

[1] **Keynesian** economics, sometimes **Keynesianism**, named for the economist John Maynard **Keynes**) are various macroeconomic theories about how in the short run – and especially during recessions – economic output is strongly influenced by aggregate demand (total spending in the economy).

SMAC/BRAIDA[2] technologies in order to build resilience against future unpredictable risk, and also to recover economic performance by becoming more cost efficient, while driving revenues and competitiveness.

Even more surprising to many has been the new centrality of *environmental* factors. In particular, how one environmental factor—a pandemic—shaped the other five PESTEL factors so dramatically and pervasively. Of course, there had been warnings. Climate change correlates with a number of natural disasters this century. In 2019 alone there were 15 climate change related natural disasters, including wild fires, floods, rainstorms, cyclones and typhoons, costing over US$250 billion. The prognosis: such events will become more frequent. There have been pandemics, notably 1997 'bird flu', 2002/3 SARS and the H1H1 'swine flu' in 2009, to the point that Golding and Mariathasan, in their 2016 book, *The Butterfly Defect*, commented that the world had become so interdependent, another pandemic was long overdue. The interconnectedness can explain why a natural disaster such as the 2010 volcanic eruptions of Eyjafjallajökull in Iceland caused enormous disruption to air travel across western and northern Europe during April and May, affecting some 10 million travellers. Likewise, for human-made disasters, such as the 2011 Fukushima Daiichi nuclear plant disaster in Japan. Hopefully, these and the coronavirus experience will lead to a new business mindset about how interdependent the global economy is, and how, from now on, environmental risk needs high profile attention.

The 2020 pandemic and economic crises also highlighted for international businesses the criticality of scenario planning. This involves creating a series of more, or less, likely futures from which to derive actions points and business strategy. A brief lesson on scenario planning then … the secret here is to select powerful parameters, and map them against one another. Governments play a central role during and after pandemics, and public policy becomes a key environmental factor for businesses to consider. For 2020 it was useful to map out scenarios that took into account the spread of the virus, public health responses, the knock-on effects and economic policy interventions. One attempt is shown in Figure 7.1.

Within the more likely scenarios, we would choose four to focus on:

1. *Most optimistic*. There is rapid and effective control of virus spread, and no recurrence of the virus. Meanwhile, there is a strong policy response that prevents structural damage, and allows return to pre-crisis fundamentals and momentum. This is a V-shaped recovery.

---

[2] The acronym stands for **S**ocial media, **M**obile, **A**nalytics, **C**loud, **B**lockchain, **R**obotics, **A**utomation of knowledge work, **I**nternet of things, **D**igital fabrication and **A**ugmented reality. These are discussed in detail in Willcocks (2021), *Global Business Management*.

2. *Moderately optimistic.* There is an effective public health response but the virus recurs. Despite this, the economic policy intervention is effective and there is a strong global economy rebound. This would be somewhere between a V- and U-shaped recovery.

3. *Less optimistic.* The virus is effectively contained, but economic policy interventions only partially offset economic damage. A banking crisis is avoided, but recovery levels are slower. This would be a U-shaped recovery.

4. *Least optimistic.* The virus is effectively contained, then recurs. Meanwhile, economic policy interventions are only partially effective. This leads to a muted world recovery and slow long-term growth—a staggered U-shaped recovery.

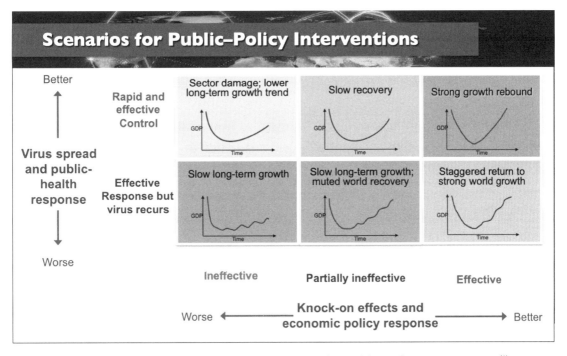

Figure 7.1 Global business context: scenarios for public policy interventions[3]

Note that one factor we have not taken into account is any broad failure in public health interventions. By April 2020 there was evidence that while some public health interventions were being more effective than others, for example in Taiwan, Germany, South Korea, Japan, China,

---

[3] Note that the McKinsey study generated nine scenarios by including the possibility of a broad failure in public health interventions. The McKinsey researchers saw this as very unlikely. By mid–2020 the evidence seemed to be that some interventions were more effective than others but there was, hopefully, going to be no broad failure.

193

there was (as yet) no broad failure simply because governments had no choice. By late–2020, however, the evidence was less convincing, with many spikes, often quite localised in developed economies. The possibility of failed health interventions had grown, as multiple countries accelerated the search for solutions in the form of management practices, treatments and vaccines.

A further factor not accounted for actually started to happen in mid-2020: the pandemic spread into countries/cities with crowded, poor neighbourhoods less well served by health care organisations (for example, India, Iran, Mexico). Given that some informed commentators positioned the pandemic as a likely disaster for developing nations (for example, Goldin, 2020), this is a serious limitation in our illustrative example. However, the model does develop scenarios assuming that the virus could recur. The key to scenario planning is not to discount all possibilities, but to focus primarily on those adjudged the most likely scenarios useful for which your business can develop action plans. Clearly the original McKinsey study was correct to develop the nine scenarios portrayed in Figure 7.2, but events quickly showed that, by August 2020 the three involving failed health interventions could not be so easily discounted. This illustrates why scenarios must be regularly revisited.

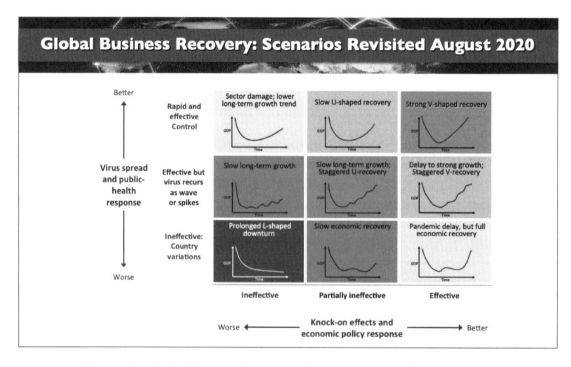

Figure 7.2: Global Business Recovery: Scenarios Revisited August 2020

Our conclusion with this example is that the scenario mapping exercise should not ignore the really worst-case scenarios. One 'worst-case' possibility was that in some countries government economic policies might actually be ineffective. And indeed by August 2020, projections were becoming less optimistic, and suggesting long-term disruption before recovering to 2019 trade levels. For example, the United Kingdom Treasury forecast a central scenario fall of 12.4 percent in gross domestic product (GDP) in 2020, with the UK only reaching the pre-virus GDP peak by the end of 2022. According to the Organisation for Economic Cooperation and Development (OECD), Germany's decline in national income (GDP) would be 6.6 percent in 2020, while Spain's GDP would fall by 11.1 percent, Italy's by 11.3 percent and France's by 11.4 percent. By this time, the OECD was seeing little evidence for a V-shaped recovery for the global economy, citing the long-lasting effects of the pandemic. Meanwhile as early as May 2020 The Economist was projecting the rise of the '90 percent economy', possibly lasting several years, with some countries and sectors more adversely affected than others.

A second 'worst-case' was the possibility that, in some countries or cities, there may well be a broad failure in public health interventions. And indeed, by August 2020, with no vaccine yet forthcoming, it was clear that some countries were not handling the pandemic at all well (e.g. USA, Brazil and UK) and this would be having even more adverse impacts on economic activity. This point is important because COVID-19 has some distinctive features that make scenario development particularly difficult. First, the virus is highly contagious. Second, symptoms take many days to be noticed. Third, it would take time to develop a vaccine or cure. This created considerable uncertainty over both length and depth of the contagion, but also in how public health and government agencies could respond. The point: one can generate several more worse case scenarios than Figure 7.1 accommodates—as shown in Figure 7.2. The likelihood of worst-case scenarios actually occurring can change quite dramatically in quite short periods of time. Welcome to the challenges of scenario planning!

What is the learning for an international business? The wise, pragmatic route is to proceed by taking the four likeliest scenarios, then building flexibility and resilience into future strategy and capabilities, sufficient to mitigate the risks if any scenario becomes real. But there are two other action pointers: do not rule out 'black swans'—that is, seemingly unlikely events that can have massive impact. Some describe the pandemic crisis as one such event, though, as we shall see, there were many warnings. Secondly, revisit the scenarios frequently. What the four, most likely, scenarios are can change quickly. We live in an accelerating world, not just of fast presents, but also of faster futures.

7.5. Global Business: Towards Systemic Risk

Commentators have suggested that the global economy, and just about everything else, will be irreversibly changed as a result of the coronavirus pandemic. There will be a before-coronavirus, and an after-coronavirus world. Ironically, with a few exceptions (for example, Goldin and Muggah, 2020), virtually no person or agency making such claims predicted the coronavirus pandemic itself. Nor is it clear if they are referring to how people think about the global economy or to changes in material circumstances, or perhaps both. One truth that has been made manifest is that businesses have been, slightly blindly, operating in an interconnected, integrated complex, dynamic world for some time, that these tendencies are accelerating, and are creating, for both the global and business environment, radical uncertainty and systemic risk.

Such tendencies were always inherent in, and in fact a defining feature, of the third wave of globalisation from the 1980s to the present. Globalisation brings risks, and these have become increasingly systemic. The obvious examples of likely impacts are the financial crisis that swept through South East Asia in the late 1990s; the financial crisis that started in the USA in 2008, and moved around the world; and the 2020 pandemic that impacted globally and interconnectedly on economies, affecting areas such as economic growth; social and personal lives; work; supply chains; and financial stability.

The pandemic crisis, then, is usefully taken as a metaphor for our general failure to entertain, let alone take actions to mitigate, global systemic risk. Coronavirus itself was a disaster foretold. As Goldin and Muggah (2020) suggest, infectious disease specialists had been raising the alarm about the accelerated pace of outbreaks for decades. Since 1980, more than ***12,000 documented outbreaks*** had infected and killed tens of millions of people around the world. One thing that must be different after the coronavirus experience is a change once and for all in our approach to assessing and mitigating global systemic risk, wherever it lies.

Globalisation and technological change have raced ahead of our institutional capacity, and how we shape, assess and respond to our changing human made and natural environments. By the beginning of the third decade of the 21st century, feeling overwhelmed by complexity and uncertainty, one major, understandable trend amongst governments, firms and individuals has been to turn towards localism and short-termism. It is unlikely to be a sustainable response.

7.6. Global Business: Navigating the Future

What emerges from the 2020 crisis, and how can businesses proceed? The pandemic and economic downturn saw trade, financial flows and travel contract, but a single trend towards deglobalisation was unlikely. In the longer term the globalisation trends would continue, while reflecting increasingly the growing role of Asia and China with their continued growth in incomes, and homing two thirds of the world's population. Speculating, we will see an acceleration of the trend towards reshoring production and services to move businesses closer to their final markets. This will be helped by the deployment of automation and digital technologies (see Willcocks, 2021). Capitalising on the pandemic experience, managers will also become more digital in order to build resilience in systems, and deal with cost reduction pressures, while responding to customers expecting fast delivery of more customised products and services. There will be a shakeout across business sectors and countries. This will show up weak business models, poor financial positions, and managements who failed to build resilience and adaptiveness into their competitive positioning and operations. Also during 2020 certain sectors were being hit more severely than others, notably travel, recreation, oil and gas, commercial aerospace, insurers, and (off-line) retail. Think American Airlines, event companies, the smaller oil companies, and Marks and Spencer (a British retailer). Thus damage was unevenly distributed. How much general damage, and the business propensity to recover, depended on the length and depth of the downturn. Just as a rising tide raises all boats, a receding (economic) tide can ground all too many. Government support for struggling businesses was strong everywhere, but could not be limitless.

Following the 2020 general drop in sales and profits, some firms will emerge even stronger; many firms, where they survive, will be weaker. In the past three recessions share prices of the top ten American firms in ten major sectors rose by an average of 6 percent, while those at the bottom fell by 44 percent. Some firms had the advantages of large size and strong financial position before 2020. Look at Apple with its US$207 billion cash mountain, and Unilever, still able to fund its suppliers during 2020. The Economist (2020) called such businesses 'top dogs'. Their analysis of over 800 European and American firms showed technology firms making up 48 of the top 100. Microsoft, Apple, Facebook and Alphabet operate with big cash buffers. High demand for their products surged further during 2020. Cisco Systems, Nvidia, and Adobe were also in this 'top dog' technology group. Another 24 were pharmaceutical and health-care firms with spare cash and a captive market of people needing drugs. Think Roche, Novo Nordisk and Johnson and Johnson.

There will also be winners and losers within sectors. As an indication, the technology sector saw Amazon add 100,000 workers to its US workforce, while Softbank was announcing US$41 billion in divestments to raise cash. In the energy sector BP, ExxonMobil and Royal Dutch Shell vastly outperformed smaller firms, and were better positioned to ride out the 2020 downturn in global oil prices. In cosmetics, L'Oreal has done better than its US rival, Coty. In plane manufacturing, Airbus had US$32 billion in liquid funds in March 2020, just as Boeing thought of seeking a US government bailout. These differing performances reflect previous good results and management, built-in financial and organisational adaptiveness and resilience, prescient long-term planning, all mixed in with happening to be in the right place, in the right industry, at the right time. As in previous recoveries, the 'winner' firms would be better placed to achieve, over time, greater market share and enduring advantage in their sectors. Better cash positions, higher profits, and lower cost of capital, put them in a stronger position than rivals to make further investments, pursue mergers and acquisitions, restructure the business, and change strategic direction.

Riding future trends

The problem and reality for all organisations is highly challenging: how to build a international business organisation for the new (ab)normal, that was likely to be increasingly in the hands of governments, developments in China and Asia, and the relatively few large corporations who emerged well from the health and economic crisis. There would be opportunities. Government and populations would need to increasingly address climate change, energy and water supply, and health care. In business terms, these all provided the source of not just potential crises, but also were potential growth markets for new products and services. Additionally, management could harness, rather than resist, six major future trends that accelerated during the pandemic period. What are these?

1. Digital technologies and automation. Global businesses have had a crash course in the value of moving to digitalisation. These technologies would be a central player in the new (ab)normal. Technology may bring more opportunities to create value, while redefining work. But technological adoption has been uneven across countries, sectors and companies. T here is a growing gulf between those who have embraced technological change and those that have not, which may place many companies, and even countries, at a growing disadvantage as the 2020s proceed.

2. Supply chain restructuring. The crisis highlighted the need for greater risk mitigation and resilience. This will speed moving a critical mass of production/service closer to home, rethinking processes and suppliers, bigger safety buffers in inventory, and even greater automation.

3. Repatriation and less cross border investment. This pushes further a pre-existing trend where better financial performance came from shrinking to regional or domestic markets.

4. Flexible labour models. The pandemic experience will push core-periphery models even further—minimising the number of (but privileging) core workers, while automating more work and increasing automated control over the part-time, temporary and contracted workforces

5. Resilience in the face of uncertainty over business environments and human-made

and natural disasters. While we expect this to be high on the agenda over 2021–2022, past experience indicates growing complacency if no further widespread crisis, of whatever sort, occurs for a few years.

6. Greater focus on South and East Asia. Countries here were likely to recover earlier, and contain two thirds of the world's population. Already rising to globalism, they will be in prime position to shape the new (ab)normal. Focus here will not just be on prospective markets and sourcing options. What can be learned from Asia is a key question for international businesses. This covers not just innovative uses of technology, but, for example, how retailing can be restructured, and how to mobilise resources fast and at scale. Marrying the learning and the opportunity with what is best for the business will be a key management task. Trade-offs will be necessary. For example, over-dependence on Chinese supply may be reduced by building resilience, and some repatriation of production.

7.7. Conclusion

Global business received a severe shock to the system in 2020–2021. It had received many economic shocks before. But few businesses saw this coming because they had not trained themselves to sufficiently factor environmental human-made and natural disasters into their long-term scanning and scenario planning. Several commentators, including Ian Goldin and Bill Gates, pointed out as early as 2015 that a pandemic was long overdue, and that the world was not ready. This crisis points to a new set of assumptions needed for managing what I have been calling the new (ab)normal. Interconnectedness has turned into a complex interdependence. This has created uncertainty and systemic risk. Systemic risk requires systemic thinking, to shape systemic responses.

We have seen how five major 2015–2020 global business trends have been shifted by the pandemic and subsequent crisis. Businesses came to terms with the disruptions in different ways. But many businesses did not. And many who would survive the crisis might not emerge in such good shape to compete with others who were building themselves more resilient business models even before the pandemic hit. The crisis produced six likely future trends that international business need to ride and seize opportunities from: technology deployment, resilience, restructured supply chains, less foreign investment, greater focus on home markets, but also a greater focus on events and markets in South and East Asia.

This book has provided an overview of how to conduct international business in an increasingly interconnected, dynamic, uncertain global environment. Taking the book as a whole, the management frameworks and principles will have lasting value, but they do need constant revisiting. There are no 'best practices' suitable for every organisation, whatever the circumstances. The book has taken a pragmatic, contingency approach. It has stressed the need to analyse comprehensively and frequently the global business and task environments, risk, and the relationships between factors. It has stressed the importance of strategic agility and fit with business environments. We have pointed to how the business operational model needs to be configured to support business direction and imperatives, both short term and long term. This is covered in detail in the companion volume, *Global Business Management* (2021).

This crisis points to the requirement for better forward planning, greater built-in resilience, and **the need for a new set of assumptions for managing what I have been calling the new (ab)normal**. Interconnectedness has turned into a complex interdependence. This has created uncertainty and systemic risk. **Systemic risk requires systemic thinking, to shape systemic responses**.

We enter this new (ab)normal with a great deal of knowledge and a better business education, but must leave ourselves open to ever newer learning. In international business, as in life, when learning stops, innovation and performance atrophy. As Albert Einstein once said: *"It is not that I'm so smart. But I stay with the questions much longer."* Take it from him—that's the way to get better answers.

References

Economist, The (2020), 'Best In Show', *The Economist* March 28th, pp63–64.

Goldin, I. (2020), 'Coronavirus is the biggest disaster for developing nations in our lifetime*', The Guardian*, April 21st.

Goldin, I. and Muggah, R. (2020), 'The world before this coronavirus and after cannot be the same', *The Conversation,* March 27th.

Goldin, I. and Mariathasan, M. (2016), *The Butterfly Defect: How globalisation creates systemic risk, and what to do about it, (*Princeton University Press, NJ and Oxford).

Hirt, M. Smit, S., Bradley, C., Uhlaner, R., Mysore, M., Atsmon, Y, and Northcote, N (2020), *Getting ahead of the next stage of the coronavirus crisis,* McKinsey website, April.

Willcocks, L. (2021), *Global Business Management*, (SB Publishing, Stratford-upon-Avon, UK).

The Author

Leslie P. Willcocks

Leslie has a global reputation for his work in robotic process automation; AI; cognitive automation and the future of work; digital innovation; outsourcing; global management strategy; organisational change; IT management; and managing digital business. He is professor emeritus at the London School of Economics and Political Science, and associate Fellow of Green Templeton College, Oxford.

Leslie is co-author of 67 books on the above subjects, and has published over 240 refereed papers in journals such as *Harvard Business Review*, *Sloan Management Review*, *California Management Review*, *MIS Quarterly*, and *Journal of Management Studies*. His work appears in major media outlets such as Forbes magazine and HBR Online. He keynotes regularly at international conferences, has delivered executive programmes globally for some 25 years, and has been retained as adviser and expert witness by major corporations and government institutions in the UK, USA, Europe and Australia.

Recent books:

- *Global Business Management* (2021), SB Publishing, UK

- *Global Business: Strategy in Context* (2021), SB Publishing, UK

- *Becoming Strategic with Robotic Process Automation* (2020), SB Publishing, UK

- *Global Outsourcing Discourse: Exploring Modes of IT Governance* (2019), Palgrave Macmillan UK

- *Robotic Process and Cognitive Automation: The Next Phase* (2018), SB Publishing, UK

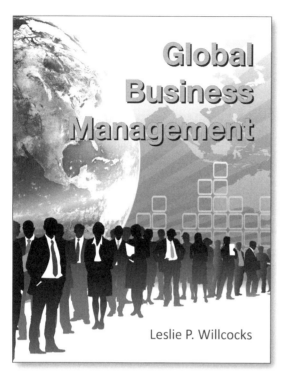

Leslie P. Willcocks

This book is a companion to *Global Business: Strategy in Context* and takes the learning further into managing the key, functional areas that underpin strategic positioning. It first focuses on the major challenges and ways of running marketing and R&D functions in an international business. The author then gives insights, through frameworks, studies and examples, into how businesses manage organisation structure and architecture; sourcing and the supply chain; information systems and emerging technologies; and human resources, in different parts of the world—globally, regionally and domestically. The book also reviews how an international business can manage exchange rates in the context of the international monetary system.

The book provides detailed understanding of challenges and practices in international project and change management, and concludes by establishing future, post–COVID-19, challenges, opportunities and directions for international businesses. Notable features of this title are …

- Based on up-to-date research studies.

- Reviews the post–COVID-19 shifting global context, changed business priorities and impacts on strategy.

- Covers the essential international business management functions.

- Includes extensive sections on international project and change management.

- Details how the 2020-2021 crises have accelerated the adoption of emerging technologies, and how global digital management can be executed.

- Focuses on the future. The book provides management principles for dealing with systemic risk and redesigning an international business for the new (ab)normal.

Global Business Management ISBN: 978-0-995682-09-2 Publication Date: January 2021
Publisher: SB Publishing, Stratford-upon-Avon, UK
Available from: www.sbpublishing.org

Robotic and Cognitive Automation

Despite the massive hype surrounding RPA, cognitive automation, artificial intelligence (AI), and blockchain, these emerging technologies are becoming more real, relevant and impactful every day.

Our objective, on this website, is to dispel myths and misinformation about risks and effective practices, through insightful, research-based commentary that is independent, objective, rigorous, ahead of the curve, and highly practical.

We are focusing on the bigger picture consequences of automation. This will lead us into interactive discussions on major issues as they arise, such as:

- ✿ **The Future of Work**
- ✿ **Technology and ethics**
- ✿ **Physical and psychological health**
- ✿ **Quality of work**
- ✿ **Risk mitigation**

- ✿ **Automation and the economy**
- ✿ **Automation and the environment**
- ✿ **Political and social challenges**
- ✿ **Emerging technologies**
- ✿ **Blockchain technology**

We will also be connecting up service automation and blockchain technologies with the broader digital transformation ongoing over the next ten years or more—especially in light of the 2020 Covid-19 pandemic. We will be running discerning and sceptical eyes and brains over emerging technologies in business and work contexts, to find out their capabilities, limitations, and likely diffusion—using our customary searching, evidence-based assessments.

There is a plethora of information available on the website, including free, downloadable reasearch papers; regular blogs; links to RPA & CA advisors and providers; and video interviews—where we anwser questions on robotic process and cognitive automation.

*"Whether you are an existing adopter of RPA & CA; thinking of moving in that direction; or just have a keen interest in where the trechnology is at right now, you can join us on the journey that is **Automation and The Future of Work"***

Professor Leslie Willcocks and **Professor Mary Lacity**